# Berlitz®

# Gree[ ]RY

phrase book & dict[ ]

OCT 2012

**Berlitz Publishing**
**New York   London   Singapore**

**Contacting the Editors**

Every effort has been made to provide accurate information in this publication, but changes are inevitable. The publisher cannot be responsible for any resulting loss, inconvenience or injury. We would appreciate it if readers would call our attention to any errors or outdated information. We also welcome your suggestions; if you come across a relevant expression not in our phrase book, please contact us at: **comments@berlitzpublishing.com**

All Rights Reserved
© 2007 Berlitz Publishing/APA Publications (UK) Ltd.
Berlitz Trademark Reg. U.S. Patent Office and other countries. Marca Registrada. Used under license from Berlitz Investment Corporation.

**Eleventh Printing:** March 2012
Printed in China

**Publishing Director:** Mina Patria
**Commissioning Editor:** Kate Drynan
**Editorial Assistant:** Sophie Cooper
**Translation:** updated by Wordbank
**Cover Design:** Beverley Speight
**Interior Design:** Beverley Speight
**Production Manager:** Raj Trivedi
**Picture Researcher:** Beverley Speight
**Cover Photo:** Main image and 'beads' image Britta Jaschinski/APA; 'traditional dress', 'ruins', 'sculpture' images Glyn Genin/APA; 'signs' Richard Nowitz/APA; 'currency' image Lucy Johnston/APA.

**Interior Photos:** iStockphoto 126, 138, 141, 150; Glyn Genin/APA 62, 67, 90, 100, 103, 134; Greg Gladman/APA 115; Britta Jaschinski/APA 1, 35, 45, 130; Lucy Johnston/APA 164; Richard Nowitz 12, 17, 20, 55, 56, 94, 96; Gregory Wrona/APA 76, 120, 85 Sylvaine Poitau/APA, 88 Rebecca Erol/APA.

# Contents

## Food & Drink

## People

## Leisure Time

## Special Requirements

## In an Emergency

## Dictionary

# Pronunciation

This section is designed to make you familiar with the sounds of Greek using our simplified phonetic transcription. You'll find the pronunciation of the Greek letters explained below, together with their 'imitated' equivalents. This system is used throughout the phrase book; simply read the pronunciation as if it were English, noting any special rules below.

Stress is important in Greek, as often the meaning of the word changes depending upon which syllable is stressed. In written Greek, stress is indicated by a small mark ( ´ ) on the syllable to be stressed. In the Greek phonetic transcription, stress is indicated with an underline.

Over the last 25 years, the Greek language has been greatly simplified, with the number of stress and breathing marks reduced; however, one may still encounter words written with the more elaborate stress marks, mainly in older Greek texts.

Please note that the question mark is indicated by the semi-colon (;) in Greek.

## Consonants

| Letter | Approximate Pronunciation | Symbol | Example | Pronunciation |
|--------|---------------------------|--------|---------|---------------|
| β | like v in voice | v | βάζο | _vah_•zoh |
| δ | voiced th, like th in then | TH | δεν | _THehn_ |
| ζ | like z in zoo | z | ζω | _zoh_ |
| θ | unvoiced th, like th in thing | th | θέλω | _theh_•loh |
| κ | like k in key | k | κότα | _koh_•tah |
| λ | like l in lemon | l | λεμόνι | leh•_moh_•nee |
| μ | like m in man | m | μαμά | mah•_mah_ |
| ν | like n in net | n | νέο | _neh_•oh |
| ξ | like x in fox | ks | ξένος | _kseh_•nohs |
| π | like p in pen | p | πένα | _peh_•nah |

| ρ | trilled like a Scottish r | r | ώρα | _oh_·rah |
| σ | like s in sit | s | σε | seh |
| ς* | like s in slim | s | ήλιος | _ee_·liohs |
| τ | like t in tea | t | τι | tee |
| φ | like f in fun | f | φως | fohs |
| x | like ch in Scottish loch | kh | χαρά | khah·_rah_ |
| ψ | like ps in tops | ps | ψάρι | _psah_·ree |
| γ | like g + h | gh | γάλα | _ghah_·lah |
| γγ, γκ | like g in go, but in some cases a more nasal ng as in sing | g | γκαρσόν | gahr·_sohn_ |
| μπ | like b in bath, but in some cases more like mp as in lamp | b | μπαρ | bahr |
| ντ | like d in do, but in some cases more like nd as in end | d | ντομάτα | doh·_mah_·tah |
| τζ | like j in jazz | j | τζατζίκι | jah·_jee_·kee |
| τσ | like ts in lets | ts | τσάντα | _tsahn_·dah |

* This character is used instead of σ, when the latter falls at the end of a word.

## Vowels

| Letter | Approximate Pronunciation | Symbol | Example | Pronunciation |
| α | like a in father | ah | μα | mah |
| ε | like e in ten | eh | θέλω | _theh_·loh |
| η, ι, υ | like ee in keen | ee | πίνω | _pee_·noh |
| ο, ω | like o in top | oh | πότε | _poh_·teh |
| αι | like e in ten | eh | μπαίνω | _beh_·noh |
| οι, ει, υι | like ee in keen | ee | πλοίο | _plee_·oh |

## Vowel Combinations

| Letters | Approximate Pronunciation | Symbol | Example | Pronunciation |
|---|---|---|---|---|
| **αυ** | 1) when followed by θ, κ, ξ, π, σ, τ, φ, χ, ψ, like af in after | **ahf** | **αυτός** | *ahf·tohs* |
| | 2) in all other cases, like av in avocado | **ahv** | **αύρα** | *ahv·rah* |
| **ευ** | 1) when followed by θ, κ, ξ, π, σ, τ, φ, χ, ψ, like ef in effect | **ehf** | **λευκός** | *lehf·kohs* |
| | 2) in all other cases, like ev in ever | **ehv** | **νεύρο** | *nehv·roh* |
| **ου** | like oo in zoo | **oo** | **ούζο** | *oo·zoh* |
| **για, γεια** | like yah in yard | **yah** | **για** | *yah* |
| **γε, γιε** | like ye in yet | **yeh** | **γερό** | *yeh·roh* |
| **ειο, γιο** | like yo in yogurt | **yoh** | **γιος** | *yohs* |
| **γι, γυ, γη** | like yea in yeast | **yee** | **γύρω** | *yee·roh* |
| **ια, οια** | like ia in piano | **iah** | **ποια** | *piah* |

Greek is a language with a long history. The language has
developed over the centuries into the modern Greek spoken today
by approximately 11 million people in Greece and Cyprus, as well as
Greek-speaking communities within other countries. It is a phonetic
language; the sound of each letter does not usually change with its
position. The characters may appear confusing at first; don't be put off by
this. With a bit of practice most people can read Greek in just a few hours.

# How to use this Book

Sometimes you see two alternatives separated by a slash. Choose the one that's right for your situation.

## ESSENTIAL

I'm here on vacation [holiday]/business.

**Είμαι εδώ για διακοπές/δουλειά.**
*ee·meheh·THoh yah THiah·koh·pehs/ THoo·liah*

I'm going to…
I'm staying at the…Hotel.

**Θα…** *thah…*
**Μένω στο…ξενοδοχείο.** *meh·noh stoh… kseh·noh·THoh·khee·oh*

## YOU MAY SEE…

Words you may see are shown in YOU MAY SEE boxes.

**ΝΑΥΑΓΟΣΩΣΤΙΚΗ ΛΕΜΒΟΣ**
*nah·vah·ghoh·sohs·tee· kee lehm·vohs*

life boats

**ΣΩΣΙΒΙΑ** *soh·see·vee·ah*

life jackets

Any of the words or phrases listed can be plugged into the sentence below.

## Train

Where is/are…?
the ticket office

**Πού είναι…;** *poo ee·neh…*
**το γραφείο εισιτηρίων**
*toh ghrah·fee·oh ee·see·tee·ree·ohn*

the information desk

**το γραφείο πληροφοριών**
*toh ghrah·fee·oh plee·roh·foh·ree·ohn*

the luggage lockers

**οι θυρίδες** *ee thee·ree·THehs*

Greek phrases appear in purple.

Read the simplified pronunciation as if it were English. For more on pronunciation, see page 7.

## Phone

Hello. This is...

**Εμπρός. Είμαι ο m /η f...**
ehm·<u>brohs</u> <u>ee</u>·meh oh /ee ...

I'd like to speak to...

**Θα ήθελα να μιλήσω με τον m /την f...** thah
<u>ee</u>·theh·lah nah mee·<u>lee</u>·soh meh tohn / teen ...

Extension...

**Εσωτερική γραμμή...**
eh·soh·teh·ree·<u>kee</u> ghrah·<u>mee</u>...

Speak louder/more slowly.

**Μιλείστε πιο δυνατά/πιο αργά.**
mee·<u>lees</u>·the pioh THee·nah·<u>tah</u>/ahr·<u>ghah</u>

Related phrases can be found by going to the page number indicated.

When different gender forms apply, the masculine form is followed by *m*; feminine by *f*; neuter by *n*

Athens is the only Greek city currently served by a **μετρό** (meh·troh), subway. Metro tickets can be purchased at ticket desks or machines located at each station. Validate your ticket by stamping it in a validation machine, found by the platform, before you get on.

Information boxes contain relevant country, culture and language tips.

Expressions you may hear are shown in You May Hear boxes.

## YOU MAY HEAR...

**Τα εισιτήριά σας, παρακαλώ.** tah
ee·see·<u>tee</u>·ree·<u>ah</u> sahs pah·rah·kah·<u>loh</u>

Tickets, please.

Color-coded side bars identify each section of the book.

# Survival

Κλειστό Γυμναστήριο
Indoor Hall
Tennis
Indoor Hall
Ανοιχτά Κολυμβητήρια

# Arrival & Departure

## ESSENTIAL

| | |
|---|---|
| I'm here on vacation [holiday]/business. | **Είμαι εδώ για διακοπές/δουλειά.** _ee•meh eh•THoh yah THiah•koh•pehs/THoo•liah_ |
| I'm going to… | **Θα…** _thah…_ |
| I'm staying at the…Hotel. | **Μένω στο…ξενοδοχείο.** _meh•noh stoh… kseh•noh•THoh•khee•oh_ |

## YOU MAY HEAR…

| | |
|---|---|
| **Το εισιτήριο/διαβατήριό σας, παρακαλώ.** _toh ee•see•tee•ree•oh/THee•ah•vah•tee•ree•oh sahs pah•rah•kah•loh_ | Your ticket/ passport, please. |
| **Ποιος είναι ο σκοπός του ταξιδιού σας;** _piohs ee•neh oh skoh•pohs too tah•ksee•THee•oo sahs_ | What's the purpose of your visit? |
| **Πού μένετε;** _poo meh•neh•teh_ | Where are you staying? |
| **Πόσο καιρό θα μείνετε;** _poh•soh keh•roh thah mee•neh•teh_ | How long are you staying? |
| **Με ποιον είστε εδώ;** _meh piohn ee•steh eh•THoh_ | Who are you with? |

## Border Control

| | |
|---|---|
| I'm just passing through. | **Απλώς περνώ από εδώ.** _ahp•lohs pehr•noh ah•poh eh•THoh_ |
| I would like to declare… | **Θα ήθελα να δηλώσω…** _thah ee•theh•lah nah THee•loh•soh…_ |
| I have nothing to declare. | **Δεν έχω να δηλώσω τίποτα.** _THehn eh•khoh nah THee•loh•soh tee•poh•tah_ |

## YOU MAY HEAR...

**Έχετε τίποτα να δηλώσετε;**
*eh•kheh•the tee•poh•tah nah THee•loh•seh•teh*

Do you have anything to declare?

**Πρέπει να πληρώσετε φόρο για αυτό.**
*preh•pee nah plee•roh•seh•teh foh•roh yah ahf•toh*

You must pay duty on this.

**Παρακαλώ ανοίξτε αυτή την τσάντα.**
*pah•rah•kah•loh ah•nee•ksteh ahf•tee teen tsah•ndah*

Please open this bag.

## YOU MAY SEE...

| | |
|---|---|
| **ΤΕΛΩΝΕΙΟ** *teh•loh•nee•oh* | customs |
| **ΑΦΟΡΟΛΟΓΗΤΑ ΕΙΔΗ** *ah•foh•roh•loh•yee•tah ee•THee* | duty-free goods |
| **ΕΙΔΗ ΓΙΑ ΔΗΛΩΣΗ** *ee•THee yah THee•loh•see* | goods to declare |
| **ΤΙΠΟΤΑ ΓΙΑ ΔΗΛΩΣΗ** *tee•poh•tah yah THee•loh•see* | nothing to declare |
| **ΕΛΕΓΧΟΣ ΔΙΑΒΑΤΗΡΙΩΝ** *eh•leh•ghohs THee•ah•vah•tee•ree•ohn* | passport control |
| **ΑΣΤΥΝΟΜΙΑ** *ah•stee•noh•mee•ah* | police |

# Money

## ESSENTIAL

| | |
|---|---|
| Where is...? | **Πού είναι...;** *poo ee·neh...* |
| the ATM | **το αυτόματο μηχάνημα ανάληψης** *toh ahf·toh·mee·khah·nee·mah ah·nah·lee·psees* |
| the bank | **η τράπεζα** *ee trah·peh·zah* |
| the currency exchange office | **γραφείο ανταλλαγής συναλλάγματος** *ghrah·fee·oh ahn·dah·lah·ghees see·nah·lahgh·mah·tohs* |
| What time does the bank open/close? | **Τι ώρα ανοίγει/κλείνει η τράπεζα;** *tee oh·rah ah·nee·ghee/klee·nee ee trah·peh·zah* |
| I'd like to change dollars/pounds into euros. | **Θα ήθελα να αλλάξω μερικά δολάρια/λίρες σε ευρώ.** *thah ee·theh·lah nah ah·lah·ksoh meh·ree·kah THoh·lah·ree·ah/meh·ree·kehs lee·rehs seh ehv·roh* |
| I want to cash some traveler's checks [cheques]. | **Θα ήθελα να εξαργυρώσω μερικές ταξιδιωτικές επιταγές.** *thah ee·theh·lah nah eh·ksahr·yee·roh·soh meh·ree·kehs tah·ksee·THee·oh·tee·kehs eh·pee·tah·yehs* |

## At the Bank

| | |
|---|---|
| Can I exchange foreign currency/get a cash advance here? | **Μπορώ να αλλάξω συνάλλαγμα εδώ;/να πάρω μετρητά προκαταβολικά εδώ;** *boh·roh nah ah·lah·ksoh see·nah·lahgh·mah eh·THoh/ nah pah·roh meh·tree·tah proh·kah·tah·voh·lee kah eh·THoh* |
| What's the exchange rate? | **Ποια είναι η τιμή συναλλάγματος;** *piah ee·neh ee tee·mee see·nah·lahgh·mah·tohs* |

| How much is the fee? | **Πόση προμήθεια χρεώνετε;** _poh·see proh·mee·thee·ah khreh·oh·neh·teh_ |
| I think there's a mistake. | **Νομίζω έγινε λάθος.** _noh·mee·zoh eh·ghee·neh lah·thohs_ |
| I've lost my traveler's checks. | **Έχασα τις ταξιδιωτικές επιταγές μου.** _eh·khah·sah tees tah·ksee·THee·oh·tee·kehseh·pee·ta·yehs moo_ |
| My card was lost. | **Χάθηκε η κάρτα μου.** _khah·thee·keh ee kahr·tah moo_ |
| My credit cards have been stolen. | **Μου έκλεψαν τις πιστωτικές μου κάρτες.** _Moo ehk·leh·psahn tees pees·toh·tee·kehs moo kahr·tehs_ |
| My card doesn't work. | **Η κάρτα μου δεν λειτουργεί.** _ee kahr·tah moo THehn lee·toor·ghee_ |
| The ATM ate my card. | **Το ATM κράτησε την κάρτα μου.** _toh ATM krah·tee·seh teen kahr·tah moo_ |

For Numbers, see page 156.

---

## YOU MAY SEE...

| | |
| --- | --- |
| **ΕΙΣΑΓΕΤΕ ΤΗΝ ΚΑΡΤΑ** _ee·sah·yeh·teh teen kahr·tah_ | insert card |
| **ΑΚΥΡΩΣΗ** _ah·kee·roh·see_ | cancel |
| **ΔΙΑΓΡΑΦΗ** _THee·ahgh·rah·fee_ | clear |
| **ΕΙΣΑΓΕΤΕ** _ee·sah·yeh·teh_ | enter |
| **PIN** _peen_ | PIN |
| **ΑΝΑΛΗΨΗ** _ah·nah·lee·psee_ | withdraw |
| **ΑΠΟ ΛΟΓΑΡΙΑΣΜΟ ΟΨΕΩΣ** _ah·poh loh·ghahr·yahz·moh oh·pseh·ohs_ | from checking [current] account |
| **ΑΠΟ ΛΟΓΑΡΙΑΣΜΟ ΤΑΜΙΕΥΤΗΡΙΟΥ** _ah·poh loh·ghahr·yahz·moh tah·mee·ehf·tee·ree·oo_ | from savings account |
| **ΑΠΟΔΕΙΞΗ** _ah·poh·THee·ksee_ | receipt |

All major foreign currencies, traveler's checks and Eurocheques are widely accepted at banks and currency exchange offices throughout Greece. In addition, ATMs can be found outside most main banks; these accept VISA, MasterCard, American Express, Eurocard and a variety of other international bank and credit cards.

Banks are generally open Monday through Friday from 7:30 a.m. or 8:00 a.m. to 2:30 p.m. (1:30 p.m. on Friday). Centrally located banks are also open on Saturday. Currency exchange offices usually stay open until late evening.

## YOU MAY SEE...

In 2002, the Greek drachma was replaced with the European Union currency, euro, € (**ευρώ** *ehv·<u>roh</u>*), which is divided into 100 cents (**λεπτό** *lehp·<u>toh</u>*).
Coins: 1, 2, 5, 10, 20, 50 **cents**; €1, 2
Notes: €5, 10, 20, 50, 100, 200, 500

# Getting Around

## ESSENTIAL

| | |
|---|---|
| How do I get to town? | **Πώς μπορώ να πάω στην πόλη;** pohs boh·_roh_ nah _pah_·oh steen _poh_·lee |
| Where's...? | **Πού είναι...;** poo _ee_·neh... |
| the airport | **το αεροδρόμιο** toh ah·eh·roh·_THroh_·mee·oh |
| the train [railway] station | **ο σταθμός των τρένων** oh stahth·_mohs_ ton _treh_·nohn |
| the bus station | **ο σταθμός των λεωφορείων** oh stahth·_mohs_ tohn leh·oh·foh·_ree_·ohn |
| the metro station | **ο σταθμός του μετρό** oh stahth·_mohs_ too meh·_troh_ |
| How far is it? | **Πόσο απέχει;** _poh_·soh ah·_peh_·khee |
| Where can I buy tickets? | **Από πού μπορώ να αγοράσω εισιτήρια;** ah·_poh_ poo boh·_roh_ nah ah·ghoh·_rah_·soh ee·see·_tee_·ree·ah |
| A one-way/ return-trip ticket. | **Ένα απλό εισιτήριο/εισιτήριο με επιστροφή** _eh_·nah ahp·_loh_ ee·see·_tee_·ree·oh/ee·see·_tee_·ree·oh meh eh·pees·troh·_fee_ |
| How much? | **Πόσο;** _poh_·soh |
| Is there a discount? | **Υπάρχει μειωμένο εισιτήριο;** ee·_pahr_·khee mee·oh·_meh_·noh ee·see·_tee_·ree·oh |
| Which...? | **Ποια...;** piah... |
| gate | **είσοδος** _ee_·soh·THohs |
| line | **γραμμή** ghrah·_mee_ |
| platform | **πλατφόρμα** plaht·_fohr_·mah |
| Where can I get a taxi? | **Πού μπορώ να βρω ταξί;** poo boh·_roh_ nah vroh tah·_ksee_ |
| Please take me to this address. | **Παρακαλώ πηγαίνετέ με σε αυτή τη διεύθυνση.** pah·rah·kah·_loh_ pee·_yeh_·neh·_the_ meh seh ahf·_tee_ tee THee·_ehf_·theen·see |

| Where can I rent a car? | **Πού μπορώ να νοικιάσω ένα αυτοκίνητο;** *poo boh-roh nah nee-kee-ah-soh eh-nah ahf-toh-kee-nee-toh* |
| Can I have a map? | **Μπορώ να έχω ένα χάρτη;** *boh-roh nah eh-khoh eh-nah khahr-tee* |

## Tickets

| When's...to Athens? | **Πότε αναχωρεί...για Αθήνα;** *poh-the ah-nah-khoh-ree...yah ah-thee-nah* |
| the (first) bus | **το (πρώτο) λεωφορείο** *toh (proh-toh) leh-oh-foh-ree-oh* |
| the (next) flight | **η (επόμενη) πτήση** *ee (eh-poh-meh-nee) ptee-see* |
| the (last) train | **το (τελευταίο) τρένο** *toh (teh-lehf-teh-oh) treh-noh* |
| Where can I buy tickets? | **Από πού μπορώ να αγοράσω εισιτήρια;** *ah-poh poo boh-roh nah ah-ghoh-rah-soh ee-see-tee-ree-ah* |
| One ticket./Two tickets. | **Ένα εισιτήριο./Δύο εισιτήρια.** *eh-nah ee-see-tee-ree-oh/THee-oh ee-see-tee-ree-ah* |
| For today/tomorrow. | **Για *σήμερα/αύριο.*** *yah see-meh-rah/ahv-ree-oh* |
| A first/economy class ticket. | **Ένα *πρώτης/οικονομικής θέσης* εισιτήριο.** *eh-nah proh-tees/ee-koh-noh-mee-kees theh-sees ee-see-tee-ree-oh* |
| A...ticket. | **Ένα εισιτήριο....** *eh-nah ee-see-tee-ree-oh* |
| one-way | **χωρίς επιστροφή** *khoh-rees eh-pee-stroh-fee* |
| return trip | **με επιστροφή** *meh eh-pee-stroh-fee* |
| business class | **για θέση business** *yah theh-see business* |
| How much? | **Πόσο;** *poh-soh* |
| Is there a discount for...? | **Υπάρχει μειωμένο εισιτήριο για...;** *ee-pahr-khee mee-oh-meh-noh ee-see-tee-ree-oh yah...* |
| children | **παιδιά** *peh-THyah* |
| students | **φοιτητές** *fee-tee-tehs* |

Αντaποκρίσεις
Transfer Flights

Παραλαβή Αποσ
Baggage Claim

Εξοδος

| | |
|---|---|
| senior citizens | **ηλικιωμένοι** *ee·lee·kee·oh·meh·nee* |
| tourists | **τουρίστες** *too·ree·stehs* |
| The express bus/ express train, please. | **Το λεωφορείο express/ τρένο express, παρακαλ** *toh leh·oh·foh·ree·oh express/ treh·noh express, pah·rah·kah·loh* |
| The local bus/train, please. | **Το τοπικό λεωφορείο/τρένο, παρακαλώ.** *toh toh·pee·koh leh·oh·foh·ree·oh/treh·noh, pah·rah·kah·lo* |
| I have an e-ticket. | **Έχω e-ticket.** *eh·khoh ee tee·keht* |
| Can I buy a ticket on the bus/train? | **Μπορώ να αγοράσω εισιτήριο στο λεωφορείο/ τρένο;** *boh·roh nah ah·ghoh·rah·soh ee·see·tee·ree·o stoh leh·oh·foh·ree·oh/treh·noh* |
| Do I have to stamp the ticket before boarding? | **Πρέπει να σφραγίσω το εισιτήριο πριν ανέβω;** *preh·pee nah sfrah·yee·soh toh ee·see·tee·ree·oh preen ah·neh·voh* |
| Can I return on the same ticket? | **Μπορώ να επιστρέψω με το ίδιο εισιτήριο;** *boh·roh nah eh·pee·streh·pso meh toh ee·THioh ee·see·tee·ree·oh* |
| I'd like to…my reservation. | **Θα ήθελα να…την κράτησή μου.** *Thah ee·theh·lah nah…teen krah·tee·see moo* |
| cancel | **ακυρώσω** *ah·kee·roh·soh* |
| change | **αλλάξω** *ah·lah·ksoh* |
| confirm | **επιβεβαιώσω** *eh·pee·veh·veh·oh·soh* |

# Plane

## Airport Transfer

How much is a taxi
to the airport?
**Πόσο κοστίζει το ταξί ως το αεροδρόμιο;** *poh·soh kohs· tee·zee toh tah·ksee ohs toh ah·eh·roh· THroh·mee·oh*

To...Airport, please.
**Στο...αεροδρόμιο, παρακαλώ.** *stoh...ah·eh·roh· THroh·mee·oh pah·rah·kah·loh*

My airline is...
**Πετάω με την εταιρία...** *peh·tah·oh meh teen eh·teh·ree·ah...*

My flight leaves at...
**Η πτήση μου φεύγει στις...** *ee ptee·see moo fehv·ghee stees...*

I'm in a rush.
**Βιάζομαι.** *vee·ah·zoh·meh*

Can you take an
alternate route?
**Μπορείτε να πάτε από άλλο δρόμο;** *boh·ree·teh nah pah·teh ah·poh ah·loh THroh·moh*

Can you drive
faster/slower?
**Μπορείτε να πάτε πιο γρήγορα/αργά;** *boh·ree·teh nah pah·teh pioh ghree·ghoh·rah/ahr·ghah*

## Checking In

Where is the
check-in desk
for flight...?
**Πού είναι το γραφείο παράδοσης αποσκευών για την πτήση...;** *poo ee·neh toh grah·fee·oh ah·rah·THoh·sees ah·poh·skeh·vohn yah teen tee·see...*

My name is...
**Λέγομαι...** *leh·ghoh·meh...*

## YOU MAY HEAR...

**Με ποια εταιρία πετάτε;** *meh piah eh·teh·ree·ah peh·tah·teh*  — What airline are you flying?

**Τοπική ή Διεθνή;** *toh·pee·kee ee THee·ehth·nee* — Domestic or International?

**Σε ποιον τερματικό σταθμό;** *seh piohn tehr·mah·tee·koh stahth·moh* — What terminal?

## YOU MAY SEE...

| | |
|---|---|
| **ΑΦΙΞΕΙΣ** *ah·fee·ksees* | arrivals |
| **ΑΝΑΧΩΡΗΣΕΙΣ** *ah·nah·khoh·ree·sees* | departures |
| **ΠΑΡΑΛΑΒΗ ΑΠΟΣΚΕΥΩΝ** *pah·rah·lah·vee ah·pohs·keh·vohn* | baggage claim |
| **Ασφάλεια** *ah·sfah·lee·ah* | security |
| **ΠΤΗΣΕΙΣ ΕΣΩΤΕΡΙΚΟΥ** *ptee·sees eh·soh·teh·ree·koo* | domestic flights |
| **ΠΤΗΣΕΙΣ ΕΞΩΤΕΡΙΚΟΥ** *ptee·sees eh·ksoh·teh·ree·koo* | international flights |
| **ΕΛΕΓΧΟΣ ΑΠΟΣΚΕΥΩΝ** *eh·legh·khos ah·pos·keh·vohn* | check-in |
| **E-TICKET CHECK-IN** *ee·tee·keht tsehk·een* | e-ticket check-in |
| **ΠΥΛΕΣ ΕΠΙΒΙΒΑΣΗΣ** *pee·lehs eh·pee·vee·vah·sees* | boarding gates |

| | |
|---|---|
| I'm going to... | **Πηγαίνω...** *pee·gheh·noh...* |
| I have... | **Έχω...** *eh·khoh* |
| one suitcase | **μία βαλίτσα** *mee·ah vah·lee·tsah* |
| two suitcases | **δύο βαλίτσες** *THee·oh vah·lee·tsehs* |
| one piece of hand luggage | **μία χειραποσκευή** *mee·ah khee·rah·poh·skehv·ee* |
| How much luggage is allowed? | **Πόσο είναι το επιτρεπόμενο βάρος;** *poh·soh ee·neh toh eh·pee·treh·poh·meh·noh vah·rohs* |
| Is that pounds or kilos? | **Είναι σε λίβρες ή σε κιλά;** *ee·neh seh lee·vrehs ee seh kee·lah* |
| Which terminal? | **Σε ποιο τέρμιναλ;** *seh pi·oh teh·rmee·nahl* |
| Which gate does | **Από ποια έξοδο φεύγει η πτήση...;** *ah·poh* |

| | |
|---|---|
| flight...leave from? | *piah eh·ksoh·THoh fehv·yee ee ptee·see...* |
| I'd like a window/ an aisle seat. | **Θα ήθελα μια θέση στο παράθυρο/ διάδρομο.** *thah ee·theh·lah mee·ah theh·see toh pah·rah·thee·roh/ THee·ah·THroh·moh* |
| When do we leave/ arrive? | **Πότε φεύγουμε/φθάνουμε;** *poh·the fehv·ghoo·meh/fthah·noo·meh* |
| Is flight...delayed? | **Υπάρχει καθυστέρηση στην πτήση...;** *e·pahr·khee kah·thee·steh·ree·see steen tee·see...* |
| How late will it be? | **Πόσο θα αργήσει;** *poh·soh thah ahr·ghee·see* |

23

## Luggage

| | |
|---|---|
| Where is/are...? | **Πού είναι...;** *poo ee·neh...* |
| the luggage carts [trolleys] | **τα καροτσάκια αποσκευών** *tah kah·roh·tsah·kee·ah ah·pohs·keh·vohn* |
| the luggage lockers | **οι θυρίδες** *ee thee·ree·THehs* |
| the luggage claim | **η φύλαξη αποσκευών** *ee fee·lah·ksee h·poh·skeh·vohn* |
| I've lost my luggage. | **Έχασα τις αποσκευές μου.** *eh·khah·sah tees ah·pohs·keh·vehs moo* |
| My luggage has been stolen. | **Μου έκλεψαν τις αποσκευές.** *Moo ehk·leh·psahn tees ah·pohs·keh·vehs* |
| My suitcase was damaged. | **Η βαλίτσα μου χάλασε στη μεταφορά** *ee vah·lee·tsah moo khah·lah·seh stee eh·tah·foh·rah* |

## Finding your Way

| | |
|---|---|
| Where is/are...? | **Πού είναι...;** *poo ee·neh...* |
| the currency exchange office | **το γραφείο ανταλλαγής συναλλάγματος** *toh ghrah·fee·oh ahn·dah·lah·ghees ee·nah·lahgh·mah·tohs* |
| the car hire | **το γραφείο ενοικιάσεως αυτοκινήτων** *toh ghrah·fee·oh eh·nee·kee·ah·seh·ohs ahf·toh·kee·nee·tohn* |
| the exit | **η έξοδος** *ee eh·ksoh·THohs* |
| the taxis | **τα ταξί** *tah tah·ksee* |

## YOU MAY HEAR...

**Ο επόμενος!** *oh eh·poh·meh·nohs*                    Next!

**Το εισιτήριο/διαβατήριο σας, παρακαλώ.**      Your ticket/
*toh ee·see·tee·ree·oh/THee·ah·vah·tee·ree·oh*    passport, please.
*sahs pah·rah·kah·loh*

**Πόσες αποσκευές έχετε;** *poh·sehs*             How much luggage
*ah·poh·skeh·vehs eh·kheh·teh*                   do you have?

**Έχετε υπέρβαρο.** *eh·kheh·teh ee·pehr·vah·roh*  You have excess
                                                baggage.

**Αυτό είναι πολύ βαρύ/μεγάλο για**              That's too heavy/
**αποσκευή χειρός.** *ahf·toh ee·neh poh·lee vah*  large for a carry-on
*·ree/meh·gha·loh yah ah·pohs·keh·vee khee·rohs*  [to carry on board].

**Φτιάξατε τις βαλίτσες σας μόνος σας**           Did you pack these
**m /μόνη σας f;** *ftee·ah·ksah·teh tees vah·*    bags yourself?
*lee·tses sahsmoh·nohs sahs/moh·nee sahs*

**Σας έδωσε κανείς να μεταφέρετε κάτι;** *sahs*   Did anyone give you
*eh·THoh·seh kah·nees nah meh·tah·feh·reh·the*    anything to carry?
*kah·tee*

**Αδειάστε τις τσέπες σας.**                      Empty your pockets.
*ah·THiah·steh tees tseh·pehs sahs*

**Βγάλτε τα παπούτσια σας.**                      Take off your shoes.
*vghahl·teh tah pah·poo·tsiah sahs*

**Τώρα αρχίζει η επιβίβαση για την πτήση...**     Now boarding flight...
*toh·rah ahr·khee·zee ee eh·pee·vee·vah·sec*
*yulı teen ptee·see...*

| Is there…into town? | **Υπάρχει…για την πόλη;** *ee-pahr-khee…yah teen poh-lee* |
| a bus | **λεωφορείο** *leh-oh-foh-ree-oh* |
| a train | **τρένο** *treh-noh* |
| a metro | **μετρό** *meh-troh* |

For Asking Directions, see page 34.

## Train

| How do I get to the (main) train station? | **Πώς πάνε στον (κεντρικό) σιδηροδρομικό σταθμό;** *pohs pah-neh stohn (kehn-dree-koh) see-THee-roh-THroh-mee-koh stahth-moh* |
| How far is it? | **Πόσο απέχει;** *poh-soh ah-peh-khee* |
| Where is/are…? | **Πού είναι…;** *poo ee-neh…* |
| the ticket office | **το γραφείο εισιτηρίων** *toh ghrah-fee-oh ee-see-tee-ree-ohn* |
| the information desk | **το γραφείο πληροφοριών** *toh ghrah-fee-oh plee-roh-foh-ree-ohn* |
| the luggage lockers | **οι θυρίδες** *ee thee-ree-THehs* |
| the platform | **η αποβάθρα** *ee ah-poh-vahth-rah* |
| Could I have a schedule [timetable]? | **Μπορώ να έχω ένα πρόγραμμα δρομολογίων;** *boh-roh nah eh-khoh eh-nah proh-ghrah-mah THroh-moh-loh-yee-ohn* |
| How long is the trip? | **Πόση ώρα διαρκεί το ταξίδι;** *poh-see oh-rah THee-ahr-kee toh tah-ksee-THee* |
| Is it a direct train? | **Είναι απευθείας τρένο;** *ee-neh ah-pehf-thee-ahs treh-noh* |
| Do I have to change trains? | **Χρειάζεται να αλλάξω τρένο;** *khree-ah-zeh-the nah ah-lah-ksoh treh-noh* |
| Is the train on time? | **Το τρένο είναι στην ώρα του;** *toh treh-noh ee-neh steen oh-rah too* |

## YOU MAY SEE...

| | |
|---|---|
| **ΠΡΟΣ ΑΠΟΒΑΘΡΕΣ** prohs ah·poh·_vahth_·rehs | to the platforms |
| **ΠΛΗΡΟΦΟΡΙΕΣ** plee·roh·foh·_ree_·ehs | information |
| **ΚΡΑΤΗΣΕΙΣ** krah·_tee_·sees | reservations |
| **ΑΙΘΟΥΣΑ ΑΝΑΜΟΝΗΣ** _eh_·thoo·sah ah·nah·moh·nees | waiting room |
| **ΑΦΙΞΕΙΣ** ah·_fee_·ksees | arrivals |
| **ΑΝΑΧΩΡΗΣΕΙΣ** ah·nah·khoh·_ree_·sees | departures |

## Departures

| | |
|---|---|
| When is the train to...? | **Πότε φεύγει το τρένο για...;** _poh_·teh _fehv_·ghee toh _treh_·noh yah... |
| Is this the right platform for...? | **Είναι αυτή η σωστή αποβάθρα για το τρένο για...;** _ee_·neh ahf·_tee_ ee sohs·_tee_ ah·poh·_vahth_·rah yah toh _treh_·noh yah... |
| Where is platform...? | **Πού είναι η αποβάθρα...;** poo _ee_·neh ee ah·poh·_vahth_·rah... |
| Where do I change for...? | **Πού αλλάζω για...;** poo ah·_lah_·zoh yah... |

For Tickets, see page 19.

## On Board

| | |
|---|---|
| Can I sit here/open the window? | **Μπορώ να καθίσω εδώ/ ανοίξω το παράθυρο;** boh·_roh_ nah kah·_thee_·soh eh·_THoh_/ ah·nee·_ksoh_ toh pah·rah·_thee_·roh |
| That's my seat. | **Νομίζω αυτή είναι η θέση μου.** noh·_mee_·zoh ahf·_tee_ _ee_·neh ee _theh_·see moo |
| Here's my reservation. | **Να η κράτησή μου.** nah ee _krah_·tee·_see_ moo |

The Greek train system is operated by OSE (**ΟΣΕ, Οργανισμός Σιδηροδρόμων Ελλάδος** *oh•seh, ohr•ghah•neez•mohs see•THee•roh•THroh•mohn eh•lah•THohs*). The network is quite limited and, though the journey is scenic, is usually quite slow. The I/C, Intercity (**Υπερταχεία** *ee•pehr•tah•khee•ah*), makes few stops, but is more expensive. Make sure you reserve a seat in advance. All trains have bars and a sleeping car for longer journeys.

## Bus

| | |
|---|---|
| Where's the bus station? | **Πού είναι ο σταθμός λεωφορείων;** *poo ee•neh oh stahth•mohs leh•oh•foh•ree•ohn* |
| How far is it? | **Πόσο απέχει;** *poh•soh ah•peh•khee* |
| How do I get to…? | **Πώς πάνε σε…;** *pohs pah•neh seh…* |
| Is this the bus to…? | **Είναι αυτό το λεωφορείο για…;** *ee•neh ahf•toh toh leh•oh•foh•ree•oh yah…* |
| Could you tell me when to get off? | **Μπορείτε να μου πείτε πού να κατέβω;** *boh•ree•teh nah moo pee•teh poo nah kah•teh•voh* |
| Do I have to change buses? | **Χρειάζεται να αλλάξω λεωφορείο;** *khree•ah•zeh•teh nah ah•lah•ksoh leh•oh•foh•ree•oh* |
| Stop here, please! | **Σταματείστε εδώ, παρακαλώ!** *stah•mah•tees•teh eh•THoh pah•rah•kah•loh* |

## YOU MAY SEE…

| | |
|---|---|
| **ΣΤΑΣΗ ΛΕΩΦΟΡΕΙΩΝ** *stah•see leh•oh•foh•ree•ohn* | bus stop |
| **ΕΙΣΟΔΟΣ/ΕΞΟΔΟΣ** *ee•soh•THohs/eh•ksoh•THohs* | enter/exit |
| **ΑΚΥΡΩΣΤΕ ΤΟ ΕΙΣΙΤΗΡΙΟ ΣΑΣ** *ah•kee•roh•steh toh ee•see• tee•ree•oh sahs* | validate your ticket |

## YOU MAY HEAR...

**Επιβιβαστείτε!** *eh·pee·vee·vahs·tee·teh* — All aboard!

**Τα εισιτήριά σας, παρακαλώ.** — Tickets, please
*tah ee·see·tee·ree·ah sahs pah·rah·kah·loh*

**Πρέπει να αλλάξετε σε...** — You have to change at...
*preh·pee nah ah·lah·kseh·teh seh...*

**Επόμενη στάση...** *eh·poh·meh·nee stah·see...* — Next stop...

### Metro

| | |
|---|---|
| Where's the nearest metro station? | **Πού είναι ο κοντινότερος σταθμός του μετρό;** *poo ee·neh oh koh·ndee·noh·teh·rohs stahth·mohs too meh·troh* |
| Could I have a map of the metro? | **Μπορώ να έχω ένα χάρτη του μετρό;** *boh·roh nah eh·khoh eh·nah khahr·tee too meh·troh* |
| Which line should I take for...? | **Ποια γραμμή πρέπει να πάρω για...;** *piah ghrah·mee preh·pee nah pah·roh yah...* |
| Which direction? | **Προς ποια κατεύθυνση;** *prohs piah kah·tehf·theen·see* |
| Where do I change for...? | **Πού αλλάζω για...;** *poo ah·lah·zoh yah...* |

Athens is the only Greek city currently served by a **μετρό** *(meh·troh)*, subway. Before boarding public transportation you need to buy a ticket at the special kiosks or automatic ticketing machines marked **ΕΙΣΙΤΗΡΙΑ** *(ee·see·tee·ree·ah)*. Validate your ticket in the machine, found by the platform, before you get on. In Athens, tickets are valid for 90 minutes and can be used for buses, metro, trolleybuses, trams and part of the suburban railway. Daily, weekly or monthly tickets and reduced fares are available.

It is likely that after your arrival in Athens, you will be heading straight for the port of Piraeus to catch a ferry. The harbor front is lined with ticket agents; ferry prices are fixed. Each agent tends to sell tickets for one company serving a particular route. A window display (usually in Greek and English) will tell you exactly what islands that ferry goes to. Sleeping on the deck is allowed, but make sure to take a sleeping bag and wear warm clothes, even in July!

Once on an island, you may decide to go on an island tour. Several converted fishing boats run daily trips. Note that throwing anything into the sea off a boat deck is an offense in Greece, and you will be fined if caught.

| | |
|---|---|
| Is this the right train for...? | **Είναι αυτό το σωστό τρένο για...;** *ee*·neh *ahf*·*toh* toh sohs·*toh* treh·noh yah... |
| How many stops to...? | **Πόσες στάσεις μέχρι...;** *poh*·sehs *stah*·sees *meh*·khree |
| Where are we? | **Πού είμαστε;** poo *ee*·mahs·the |

## Boat & Ferry

| | |
|---|---|
| When is the ferry to...? | **Πότε φεύγει το φέρρυ-μπωτ για...;** *poh*·the *fehv*·ghee toh *feh*·ree boht yah... |
| Can I take my car onboard? | **Μπορώ να επιβιβάσω το αυτοκίνητό μου;** boh·*roh* nah eh·pee·vee·*vah*·soh toh ahf·toh *kee*·nee·*toh* moo |
| What time is the next sailing? | **Πότε είναι ο επόμενος απόπλους;** *poh*·teh *ee*·nehoh eh·*poh*·meh·nohs ah·*poh*·ploos |
| Can I book a seat/cabin? | **Μπορώ να κλείσω θέση/καμπίνα;** boh·*roh* nah *klee*·soh theh·see/kah·bee·nah |
| How long is the crossing? | **Πόσο διαρκεί το πέρασμα;** *poh*·soh THee·ahr·*kee* toh peh·rah·smah |
| Where are the life jackets? | **Πού είναι τα σωσίβια;** poo *ee*·neh tah soh·*see*·vee·ah |

## YOU MAY SEE...

| | |
|---|---|
| **ΝΑΥΑΓΟΣΩΣΤΙΚΗ ΛΕΜΒΟΣ** *nah·vah·ghoh·sohs·tee·kee lehm·vohs* | life boats |
| **ΣΩΣΙΒΙΑ** *soh·see·vee·ah* | life jackets |

## Taxi

| | |
|---|---|
| Where can I get a taxi? | **Πού μπορώ να βρω ταξί;** *poo boh·roh nah vroh tah·ksee* |
| Can you send a taxi? | **Μπορείτε να στείλετε ταξί;** *boh·ree·teh nah stee·leh·te tah·ksee* |
| Do you have the number for a taxi? | **Έχετε το τηλέφωνο για ταξί;** *eh·kheh·teh toh tee·leh·foh·noh yah tah·ksee* |
| I'd like a taxi now/ for tomorrow at... | **Θα ήθελα ένα ταξί *τώρα/για αύριο στις...*** *thah ee·theh·lah eh·nah tah·ksee toh·rah/yah ahv·ree·oh stees...* |
| Pick me up at (place/time)... | **Ελάτε να με πάρετε *από/στις...*** *eh·lah·the nah meh pah·reh·teh ah·poh/stees...* |
| I'm going to... | **Πηγαίνω...** *pee·gheh·noh...* |
| this address | **σε αυτή τη διεύθυνση** *seh ahf·tee tee THee·ehf·theen·see* |
| the airport | **στο αεροδρόμιο** *stoh ah·eh·roh·THroh·mee·oh* |
| the train [railway] station | **στον σιδηροδρομικό σταθμό** *stohn see·THee·roh·THroh·mee·koh stahth·moh* |

---

In Athens, licensed taxis are yellow with a blue stripe. In all major cities, fares are fixed. For longer distances you should agree to a fare before the trip. Tipping is not compulsory, but it is common to round up the amount due.

| | |
|---|---|
| I'm late. | **Έχω αργήσει.** *eh·hoh ahr·ghee·see* |
| Can you drive faster/slower? | **Μπορείτε να πάτε πιο γρήγορα/αργά;** *boh·ree·teh nah pah·teh pioh gree·ghoh·rah/ahr·ghah* |
| Stop/Wait here. | **Σταματήστε/Περιμένετε εδώ.** *stah·mah·tee·steh/ peh·ree·meh·neh·teh eh·THoh* |
| How much? | **Πόσο;** *poh·soh* |
| You said it would cost...euros. | **Είπατε ότι θα κόστιζε...ευρώ.** *ee·pah·the oh·tee thah kohs·tee·zeh...ehv·roh* |
| Keep the change. | **Κρατείστε τα ρέστα.** *krah·tees·teh tah rehs·tah* |
| A receipt, please. | **Μια απόδειξη, παρακαλώ.** *miah ah·poh·THee·ksee pah·rah·kah·loh* |

## YOU MAY HEAR...

| | |
|---|---|
| **Πού μπορώ να;** *poo boh·roh nah* | Where to? |
| **Πού είναι η διεύθυνση;** *poo ee·neh ee THee·ehf·theen·see* | What's the address? |

## Bicycle & Motorbike

| | |
|---|---|
| I'd like to hire... | **Θα ήθελα να νοικιάσω...** *thah ee·theh·lah nah nee·kiah·soh...* |
| a bicycle | **ένα ποδήλατο** *eh·nah poh·THee·lah·toh* |
| a moped | **ένα μοτοποδήλατο** *eh·nah moh·toh·poh·THee·lah·toh* |
| a motorbike | **μία μοτοσικλέτα** *mee·ah moh·toh·see·kleh·tah* |
| How much per day/week? | **Πόσο κοστίζει την ημέρα/την εβδομάδα;** *poh·soh koh·stee·zee teen ee·meh·rah/tee ehv·THoh·mah·THah* |
| Can I have a helmet/lock? | **Μπορώ να έχω ένα κράνος/μία κλειδαριά;** *boh·roh nah eh·khoh eh·nah krah·nohs/mee·ah klee·THah·riah* |

## Car Hire

| Where can I hire a car? | **Πού μπορώ να νοικιάσω ένα αυτοκίνητο;** *poo boh‑roh nah nee‑kiah‑soh eh‑nah ahf‑toh‑kee‑nee‑toh* |
|---|---|
| I'd like to hire... | **Θα ήθελα να νοικιάσω ένα...** *thah ee‑theh‑lah nah nee‑kiah‑soh eh‑nah...* |

| a cheap/small car | **ένα φτηνό/μικρό αυτοκίνητο** *eh‑nah ftee‑noh/ mee‑kroh ahf‑toh‑kee‑nee‑toh* |
|---|---|
| a 2-/4-door car | **δίπορτο/τετράπορτο αυτοκίνητο** *ee‑poh‑rtoh/ teh‑trah‑poh‑rtoh ahf‑toh‑kee‑nee‑toh* |
| an automatic/ manual car | **αυτόματο αυτοκίνητο/ αυτοκίνητο με συμπλέκτη** *ahf‑toh‑mah‑toh ahf‑toh‑kee‑nee‑toh/ahf‑toh‑kee‑nee‑toh meh see‑bleh‑ktee* |
| a car with air-conditioning | **αυτοκίνητο με κλιματισμό** *ahf‑toh‑kee‑nee‑toh meh klee‑mah‑tee‑smoh* |

### YOU MAY HEAR...

**Έχετε διεθνή άδεια οδήγησης;** *eh‑kheh‑the THee‑ehth‑nee ah‑THee‑ah oh‑THee‑ghee‑sees* — Do you have an international driver's license?

**Μπορώ να δω το διαβατήριό σας, παρακαλώ;** *boh‑roh nah THoh toh THee‑ah‑vah‑tee‑ree‑oh sahs pah‑rah‑kah‑loh* — May I see your passport, please?

**Θέλετε ασφάλεια;** *theh‑leh‑teh ah‑sfah‑lee‑ah* — Do you want insurance?

**Υπάρχει μία προκαταβολή των...** *ee‑pahr‑khee miah proh‑kah‑tah‑voh‑lee tohn...* — There is a deposit of...

**Παρακαλώ υπογράψτε εδώ.** *pah‑rah‑kah‑loh ee‑poh‑ghrah‑psteh eh‑THoh* — Please sign here.

| a car seat | **παιδικό κάθισμα αυτοκινήτου** peh·THee·<u>koh</u> <u>kah</u>·thee·smah ahf·toh·kee·<u>nee</u>·too |
| How much…? | **Πόσο κάνει…;** <u>poh</u>·soh <u>kah</u>·nee… |
| per day/week | **την ημέρα/ενδομάδα** teen ee·<u>meh</u>·rah/ehv·THoh·<u>mah</u>·THah |
| per kilometer | **το χιλιόμετρο** toh khee·lee·<u>oh</u>·meht·roh |
| for unlimited mileage | **για απεριόριστη απόσταση** yah ah·peh·ree·<u>oh</u>·rees·tee ah·<u>poh</u>·stah·see |
| with insurance | **με ασφάλεια** meh ah·<u>sfah</u>·lee·ah |
| Are there any discounts? | **Υπάρχει έκπτωση;** ee·<u>pahr</u>·khee <u>ehk</u>·ptoh·see |

## Fuel Station

| Where's the next fuel station, please? | **Πού είναι το επόμενο βενζινάδικο, παρακαλώ;** poo <u>ee</u>· neh toh eh·<u>poh</u>·meh·noh vehn·zee·<u>nah</u>·THee·koh pah·rah·kah·<u>loh</u> |
| Fill it up, please. | **Γεμίστε το, παρακαλώ.** yeh·<u>mee</u>·steh toh pah·rah·kah·<u>loh</u> |
| …liters, please. | **…λίτρα βενζίνη, παρακαλώ.** …<u>lee</u>·trah vehn·<u>zee</u>· nee pah·rah·kah·<u>loh</u> |
| I'll pay in cash/by credit card. | **Θα πληρώσω τοις μετρητοίς/με πιστωτική κάρτα.** thah plee·<u>roh</u>·soh tees meh·tree·<u>tees</u>/meh pee·stoh·tee· kee <u>kah</u>·rtah |

### YOU MAY SEE…

| **ΑΠΛΗ** ah·<u>plee</u> | regular |
| **ΣΟΥΠΕΡ** soo·<u>pehr</u> | premium [super] |
| **ΝΤΗΖΕΛ** <u>dee</u>·zehl | diesel |

## Asking Directions

| | |
|---|---|
| Is this the right road to...? | **Είναι αυτός ο σωστός δρόμος για...;** _ee·neh ahf·tohs oh sohs·tohs THroh·mohs yah..._ |
| How far is it to...? | **Πόσο μακριά είναι για...;** _poh·soh mahk·ree·ah ee·neh yah..._ |
| Where's...? | **Πού είναι...;** _poo ee·neh..._ |
| ...Street | **η οδός...** _ee oh·THohs..._ |
| this address | **αυτή η διεύθυνση** _ahf·tee ee THee·ehf·theen·see_ |
| the highway [motorway] | **η εθνική οδός** _ee ehth·nee·kee oh·THohs_ |
| Can you show me on the map? | **Μπορείτε να μου δείξετε στο χάρτη;** _boh·ree·the nah moo THee·kseh·teh stoh khahr·tee_ |
| I'm lost. | **Έχω χαθεί.** _eh·hoh khah·thee_ |

## Parking

| | |
|---|---|
| Can I park here? | **Μπορώ να παρκάρω εδώ;** _boh·roh nah pahr·kah·roh eh·THoh_ |
| Is there a parking lot [car park] nearby? | **Υπάρχει χώρος στάθμευσης εδώ κοντά;** _ee·pahr·khee khoh·rohs stath·mehf·sees eh·THoh kohn·dah_ |
| Where's...? | **Πού είναι...;** _poo ee·neh_ |
| the parking garage | **το πάρκινγκ** _toh pah·rkee·ng_ |
| the parking meter | **το παρκόμετρο** _toh pah·rkoh·meh·troh_ |
| How much...? | **Πόσο κοστίζει...;** _poh·soh koh·stee·zee..._ |
| per hour | **την ώρα** _teen oh·rah_ |
| per day | **την ημέρα** _teen ee·meh·rah_ |
| overnight | **τη νύχτα** _tee neeh·khtah_ |

Parking in large cities, particularly Athens, can be a problem as spaces are limited. It is likely that you will need to park in an indoor or outdoor parking lot. Prices vary greatly, depending on your location.

**ΟΔΟΣ
ΓΟΥΛΙΕΛΜΥ ΔΑΙΡΠΦΕΛΔ
GOULIELMOS DERPFELD**

## YOU MAY HEAR...

| | |
|---|---|
| **ευθεία/ίσια** *ehf·thee·ah/ee·see·ah* | straight ahead |
| **στα αριστερά** *stah ah·rees·teh·rah* | on the left |
| **στα δεξιά** *stah THeh·ksee·ah* | on the right |
| **στη/μετά τη γωνία** *stee/meh·tah tee ghoh·nee·ah* | on/around the corner |
| **απέναντι** *ah·peh·nahn·dee* | opposite |
| **πίσω** *pee·soh* | behind |
| **δίπλα** *THee·plah* | next to |
| **μετά** *meh·tah* | after |
| **βόρεια/νότεια** *voh·ree·ah/noh·tee·ah* | north/south |
| **ανατολικά/δυτικά** *ah·nah·toh·lee·kah/THee·tee·kah* | east/west |
| **στο φανάρι** *stoh fah·nah·ree* | at the traffic light |
| **στη διασταύρωση** *stee THee·ah·stahv·roh·see* | at the intersection |

## YOU MAY SEE...

 **ΑΠΑΓΟΡΕΥΕΤΑΙ Η ΕΠΙ ΤΟΠΟΥ ΣΤΡΟΦΗ**     no u-turn
*ah·pah·ghoh·reh·veh·teh ee eh pee toh·poo stroh·fee*

 **ΥΠΟΧΡΕΩΤΙΚΗ ΠΑΡΑΧΩΡΗΣΗ ΠΡΟΤΕΡΑΙΟΤΗΤΑΣ**     yield
*ee·pohkh·reh·oh·tee·kee pah·rah·khoh·ree·see proh·teh·reh·oh·tee·tahs*

 **ΥΠΟΧΡΕΩΤΙΚΗ ΔΙΑΚΟΠΗ ΠΟΡΕΙΑΣ**     stop
*ee·pohkh·reh·oh·tee·kee THee·ah·koh·pee poh·ree·ahs*

 **ΠΕΡΙΟΧΗ ΑΠΑΓΟΡΕΥΣΗΣ ΣΤΑΘΜΕΥΣΗΣ**     no parking
*peh·ree·oh·khee ah·pah·ghoh·rehf·sees stahth·mehf·sees*

 **ΑΠΑΓΟΡΕΥΕΤΑΙ Η ΣΤΑΣΗ ΚΑΙ Η ΣΤΑΘΜΕΥΣΗ**     no stopping
*ah·pah·ghoh·reh·veh·teh ee stah·see keh ee stahth·mehf·see*

 **ΜΟΝΟΔΡΟΜΟΣ**     one way
*moh·noh·THroh·mohs*

## Breakdown & Repair

| | |
|---|---|
| My car broke down/won't start. | **Το αυτοκίνητό μου χάλασε/δεν παίρνει μπρος.** *toh ahf·toh·kee·nee·toh moo khah·lah·seh/THehn pehr·nee brohs* |
| Can you fix it today? | **Μπορείτε να το επισκευάσετε σήμερα;** *boh·ree·teh nah toh eh·pees·keh·vah·seh·the see·meh·rah* |

| | |
|---|---|
| When will it be ready? | **Πότε θα είναι έτοιμο;** _poh_•teh thah _ee_•neh _eh_•tee•moh |
| How much? | **Πόσο;** _poh_•soh |
| I have a puncture/ flat tyre (tire) | **Έχω σκασμένο λάστιχο** _eh_•khoh skah•_zmeh_•noh _lah_•stee•khoh |

## Accidents

| | |
|---|---|
| There's been an accident. | **Έγινε ένα ατύχημα.** _eh_•yee•neh _eh_•nah ah•_tee_•khee•mah |
| Call an ambulance/ the police. | **Καλέστε ένα ασθενοφόρο/την αστυνομία.** kah•_lehs_•teh _eh_•nah ahs•theh•noh•_foh_•roh/teen ahs•tee•noh•_mee_•ah |

# Places to Stay

## ESSENTIAL

| | |
|---|---|
| Can you recommend a hotel? | **Μπορείτε να μου συστήσετε ένα ξενοδοχείο;** boh•_ree_•teh nah moo sees•_tee_•seh•teh _eh_•nah kseh•noh•_THoh_•_khee_•oh |
| I have a reservation. | **Έχω κλείσει δωμάτιο.** _eh_•khoh _klee_•see _THoh_•_mah_•tee•oh |
| My name is... | **Λέγομαι...** _leh_•ghoh•meh... |
| Do you have a room...? | **Έχετε ελεύθερο δωμάτιο...;** _eh_•kheh•the _eh_•_lehf_•theh•roh _THoh_•_mah_•tee•oh... |
| for one/two | **μονόκλινο/δίκλινο** moh•_noh_•klee•noh/_THee_•klee•noh |
| with a bathroom | **με μπάνιο** meh _bah_•nioh |
| with air-conditioning | **με κλιματισμό** meh klee•mah•teez•_moh_ |
| For tonight. | **Γι' απόψε.** yah•_poh_•pseh |
| For two nights. | **Για δύο βράδια.** yah _THee_•oh vrah•_THee_•ah |
| For one week. | **Για μια εβδομάδα.** yah _mee_•ah ev•_THoh_•_mah_•THah |

| | |
|---|---|
| How much? | **Πόσο;** _poh_·soh |
| Do you have anything cheaper? | **Έχετε τίποτα φθηνότερο;** _eh_·kheh·the _tee_·poh·tah fthee·_noh_·teh·roh |
| When's check-out? | **Τι ώρα πρέπει να αδειάσουμε το δωμάτιο;** tee _oh_·rah _preh_·pee nah ah·_THee_·_ah_·soo·meh toh _THoh_·_mah_·tee·oh |
| Can I leave this in the safe? | **Μπορώ να αφήσω αυτό στη θυρίδα;** boh·_roh_ nah ah·_fee_·soh ahf·_toh_ stee thee·_ree_·THah |
| Could we leave our baggage here until…? | **Μπορούμε να αφήσουμε τα πράγματά μας εδώ ως τις…;** boh·_roo_·meh nah ah·_fee_·soo·meh tah _prahgh_·mah·_tah_ mahs eh·_THoh_ ohs tees… |
| Could I have the bill/a receipt? | **Μπορώ να έχω τον λογαριασμό/μιααπόδειξη;** boh·_roh_ nah _eh_·hoh tohn loh·ghahr·yahs·_moh_/miah ah·_poh_·THee·ksee |
| I'll pay in cash/by credit card. | **Θα πληρώσω τοις μετρητοίς/με πιστωτική κάρτα.** thah plee·_roh_·soh tees meht·ree·_tees_/meh pees·toh·tee·_kee_ _kahr_·tah |

## Somewhere to Stay

| | |
|---|---|
| Can you recommend a hotel? | **Μπορείτε να μου συστήσετε ένα ξενοδοχείο…;** boh·_ree_·teh nah moo sees·_tee_·seh·teh _eh_·nah kseh·noh·THoh·_khee_·oh… |
| Can you recommend…? | **Μπορείτε να προτείνετε…;** boh·_ree_·teh nah proh·_tee_·neh·teh |
| a hostel | **ένα ξενώνα** _eh_·nah kseh·_noh_·nah |
| a campsite | **ένα μέρος για κάμπινγκ;** _eh_·nah _meh_·rohs yah _kahm_·peeng |
| a bed and breakfast | **ένα δωμάτιο με πρωινό** _eh_·nah THoh·_mah_·tee·oh meh proh·ee·_noh_ |
| What is it near? | **Πού κοντά είναι;** poo kohn·_dah_ _ee_·neh |
| How do I get there? | **Πώς πάω εκεί;** pohs _pah_·oh eh·_kee_ |

# At the Hotel

| | |
|---|---|
| I have a reservation. | **Έχω κλείσει δωμάτιο.** *eh•hoh klee•see THoh•mah•tee•oh* |
| My name is… | **Λέγομαι…** *leh•ghoh•meh…* |
| Do you have a room…? | **Έχετε δωμάτιο…;** *eh•kheh•the THoh•mah•tee•oh…* |
| with a bathroom [toilet]/shower | **με μπάνιο/ντους** *meh bah•nioh/doo* |
| with air-conditioning | **με κλιματισμό** *meh klee•mah•teez•moh* |
| that's smoking/non-smoking | **για καπνιστές/μη καπνιστές** *yah kahp•nees•tehs/mee kahp•nees•tehs* |
| For tonight. | **Γι' απόψε.** *yah•poh•pseh* |
| For two nights. | **Για δύο βράδια.** *yah THee•oh vrah•THiah* |
| For one week. | **Για μία εβδομάδα.** *yah mee•ah ev•THoh•mah•THah* |
| Does the hotel have…? | **Έχει το ξενοδοχείο…;** *eh•khee toh kseh•noh•THoh•khee•oh…* |
| a computer | **υπολογιστή** *ee•poh•loh•ghees•tee* |
| an elevator [lift] | **ασανσέρ** *ah•sahn•sehr* |
| (wireless) internet service | **υπηρεσία (ασύρματου) internet** *ee•pee•reh•see•ah (ah•seer•mah•too) een•tehr•neht* |
| room service | **υπηρεσία δωματίου** *ee•pee•reh•see•ah THoh•mah•tee•oo* |
| a pool | **πισίνα** *pee•see•nah* |
| a gym | **γυμναστήριο** *gheem•nahs•tee•ree•oh* |

---

If you didn't reserve a place to stay before your trip, visit the local tourist information office for a list of places to stay. Booking ahead is recommended in the high season, from July to the end of August.

Greece offers a large variety of accommodation options:
**Ξενοδοχεία** (ksehn·oh·THoh·<u>khee</u>·ah), hotels; **Διαμερίσματα**
(THee·ah·meh·<u>reez</u>·mah·tah), furnished apartments; **Δωμάτια**
(THoh·<u>mah</u>·tee·ah) furnished rooms, with or without a private
bath; **Παραδοσιακά δωμάτια** (pah·rah·THoh·see·ah·<u>kah</u>
THoh·<u>mah</u>·tee·ah), apartments in traditional but renovated homes;
**Ξενώνας νεότητας** (kseh·<u>noh</u>·nahs neh·<u>oh</u>·tee·tahs), youth hostels;
**Κάμπιγκ** (<u>kahm</u>·peeng) campsites and more.

| | |
|---|---|
| I need... | **χρειάζομαι...** khree·<u>ah</u>·zoh·meh... |
| an extra bed | **άλλο ένα κρεβάτι** <u>ah</u>·loh eh·nah kreh·<u>vah</u>·tee |
| a cot | **ένα ράντζο** eh·nah <u>rahn</u>·joh |
| a crib | **ένα παιδικό κρεβάτι** eh·nah peh·THee·<u>koh</u> kreh·<u>vah</u>·tee |

## Price

| | |
|---|---|
| How much per night/week? | **Πόσο κάνει τη βραδιά/την εβδομάδα;** <u>poh</u>·soh <u>kah</u>·nee tee vrah·<u>iah</u>/teen ehv·oh·<u>mah</u>·ah |
| Does the price include breakfast/ sales tax [VAT]? | **Η τιμή συμπεριλαμβάνει πρωινό/ΦΠΑ;** ee tee·<u>mee</u> seem·beh·ree·lahm·<u>vah</u>·nee proh·ee·<u>noh</u>/fee·pee·<u>ah</u> |
| Are there any discounts? | **Έχει έκπτωση;** <u>eh</u>·khee <u>ehk</u>·ptoh·see |

## Preferences

| | |
|---|---|
| Can I see the room? | **Μπορώ να δω το δωμάτιο;** boh·<u>roh</u> nah doh toh THoh·<u>mah</u>·tee·oh |
| I'd like a...room. | **Θα ήθελα...δωμάτιο.** tha ee·theh·lah...THoh·<u>mah</u>·tee·oh |
| better | **καλύτερο** kah·<u>lee</u>·teh·roh |

| bigger | **μεγαλύτερο** *meh·ghah·lee·teh·roh* |
| cheaper | **πιο φθηνό** *pioh fthee·noh* |
| quieter | **πιο ήσυχο** *pioh ee·see·khoh* |
| I'll take it. | **Θα το πάρω.** *thah toh pah·roh* |
| No, I won't take it. | **Όχι, δεν θα το πάρω.** *oh·khee, THen thah toh pah·roh* |

## Questions

| Where's...? | **Πού είναι...;** *poo ee·neh...* |
| the bar | **το μπαρ** *toh bahr* |
| the bathroom | **το μπάνιο** *toh bah·nioh* |
| the elevator [lift] | **το ασανσέρ** *toh ah·sahn·sehr* |
| Can I have...? | **Μπορώ να έχω...;** *boh·roh nah eh·khoh...* |
| a blanket | **μια κουβέρτα** *miah koo·vehr·tah* |
| an iron | **ένα σίδερο** *eh·nah see·THeh·roh* |
| the room key/ | **το κλειδί δωματίου/την κάρτα** *toh klee·THee* |
| key card | *THoh·mah·tee·oo/teen kahr·tah* |
| a pillow | **ένα μαξιλάρι** *eh·nah mah·ksee·lah·ree* |
| soap | **σαπούνι** *sah·poo·nee* |
| toilet paper | **χαρτί υγείας** *khahr·tee ee·ghee·ahs* |
| a towel | **μια πετσέτα μπάνιου** *miah peh·tseh·tah bah·nee·oo* |

## YOU MAY HEAR...

**Το διαβατήριό σας/την πιστωτική σας κάρτα, παρακαλώ.** *toh ee·ah·vah·tee·ree·oh sahs/teen pees·toh·tee·kee sahs kahr·tah pah·rah·kah·loh* — Your passport/ credit card, please.

**Παρακαλώ συμπληρώστε αυτό το έντυπο.** *pah·rah·kah·loh seem·blee·rohs·teh ahf·toh toh ehn·dee·poh* — Please fill out this form.

**Υπογράψτε εδώ.** *ee·pohgh·rahp·steh eh·THoh* — Sign here.

| Can I use this adapter here? | **Μπορώ να χρησιμοποιήσω αυτόν τον προσαρμοστή εδώ;** *boh‑roh nah khree‑see‑moh‑pee‑ee‑soh ahf‑tohn tohn proh‑sahr‑mohs‑tee eh‑THoh* |
| How do I turn on the lights? | **Πώς ανάβουν τα φώτα;** *pohs ah‑nah‑voon tah foh‑tah* |
| Could you wake me at…? | **Μπορείτε να με ξυπνήσετε στις…;** *boh‑ree‑teh nah meh kseep‑nee‑seh‑teh stees…* |
| Could I have my things from the safe? | **Μπορώ να έχω τα πράγματά μου από τη θυρίδα;** *boh‑roh nah eh‑khoh tah prahgh‑mah‑tah moo ah‑poh tee thee‑ree‑THah* |
| Is there mail/ a message for me? | **Υπάρχει αλληλογραφία/κάποιο μήνυμα για μένα;** *ee‑pahr‑khee ah‑lee‑lohgh‑rah‑fee‑ah/kah‑pioh mee‑nee‑mah yah meh‑nah* |
| Do you have a laundry service? | **Έχετε υπηρεσία πλυντηρίων;** *eh‑kheh‑teh ee‑pee‑reh‑see‑ah plee‑dee‑ree‑ohn* |

## Problems

| There's a problem. | **Υπάρχει ένα πρόβλημα.** *ee‑pahr‑hee eh‑nah prohv‑lee‑mah* |
| I've lost my key/key card. | **Έχασα το κλειδί/την κάρτα μου.** *eh‑hah‑sah toh klee‑THee/teen kahr‑tah moo* |
| I've locked myself. out of my room | **Κλειδώθηκα έξω από το δωμάτιό μου.** *klee‑THoh‑thee‑kah eh‑ksoh ah‑poh toh THoh‑mah‑tee‑oh moo* |
| There's no hot water/toilet paper. | **Δεν υπάρχει ζεστό νερό/χαρτί υγείας.** *Then ee‑pahr‑khee zeh‑stoh neh‑roh/khahr‑tee ee‑yee‑ahs* |
| The room is dirty. | **Το δωμάτιο είναι βρώμικο.** *Toh THoh‑mah‑tee‑oh ee‑neh vroh‑mee‑koh* |
| There are bugs in. our room | **Υπάρχουν έντομα στο δωμάτιό μας.** *ee‑pahr‑hoon ehn‑doh‑mah stoh THoh‑mah‑tee‑oh mahs* |
| …is broken. | **…είναι σπασμένος m /σπασμένη f /σπασμένο n.** *…ee‑neh spahs‑mehn‑ohs/ spahs‑mehn‑ee/ spahs‑mehn‑oh* |

| | |
|---|---|
| Can you fix…? | **Μπορείτε να φτιάξετε…;** *boh·ree·teh nah ftiah·kseh·teh…* |
| the air conditioning | **τον κλιματισμό** *tohn klee·mah·teez·moh* |
| the fan | **τον ανεμιστήρα** *tohn ah·neh·mee·stee·rah* |
| the heating | **τη θέρμανση** *tee thehr·mahn·see* |
| the light | **το φως** *toh fohs* |
| the TV | **την τηλεόραση** *teen tee·leh·oh·rah·see* |
| the toilet | **την τουαλέτα** *teen too·ah·leh·tah* |
| I'd like to move to another room. | **Θα ήθελα να μεταφερθώ σε άλλο δωμάτιο.** *thah ee·theh·lah nah meh·tah·fehr·thoh she ah·loh THoh·mah·tee·oh* |

## YOU MAY SEE…

| | |
|---|---|
| **ΩΘΗΣΑΤΕ/ΕΛΞΑΤΕ** *oh·thee·sah·teh/ehl·ksah·teh* | push/pull |
| **ΜΠΑΝΙΟ/ΤΟΥΑΛΕΤΑ** *bah·nioh/too·ah·leh·tah* | bathroom/restroom [toilet] |
| **ΝΤΟΥΣ** *dooz* | shower |
| **ΑΣΑΝΣΕΡ** *ah·sahn·sehr* | elevator [lift] |
| **ΣΚΑΛΑ** *skah·lah* | stairs |
| **ΠΛΥΝΤΗΡΙΟ** *pleen·dee·ree·oh* | laundry |
| **ΜΗΝ ΕΝΟΧΛΕΙΤΕ** *meen eh·nohkh·lee·teh* | do not disturb |
| **ΠΥΡΟΣΤΕΓΗΣ ΘΥΡΑ** *pee·rohs·teh·ghees thee·rah* | fire door |
| **ΕΞΟΔΟΣ ΚΙΝΔΥΝΟΥ** *eh·ksoh·THohs keen·THee·noo* | emergency exit |
| **ΥΠΗΡΕΣΙΑ ΑΦΥΠΝΙΣΗΣ** *ee·pee·reh·see·ah ah·feep·nee·sees* | wake-up call |

Tipping depends largely on your class of hotel; the higher the class, the more generous the tip. As a guideline, a euro or two per service rendered is recommended in standard hotels.

## Checking out

| | |
|---|---|
| When's check-out? | **Τι ώρα πρέπει να αδειάσουμε το δωμάτιο;** *tee oh- rah preh-pee nah ah-THee-ah-soo-meh toh THoh-mah-tee-oh* |
| Could we leave our baggage here until…? | **Μπορούμε να αφήσουμε τα πράγματά μας εδώ ως τις…;** *boh-roo-meh nah ah-fee-soomeh tah prahgh-mah-tah mahs eh-THoh ohs tees…* |
| Can I have an itemized bill/ a receipt? | **Μπορώ να έχω έναν αναλυτικό λογαριασμό/ μια απόδειξη;** *boh-roh nah eh-khoh eh-nah nah-nah-lee-tee-koh loh-ghahr-yahz-moh/miah ah-poh-ee-ksee* |
| I think there's a mistake in this bill. | **Νομίζω ότι έγινε ένα λάθος στο λογαριασμό.** *noh-mee-zoh oh-tee eh-yee-neh eh-nah lah-thohs stoh loh-ghahr-yahz-moh* |
| I'll pay in cash/by credit card. | **Θα πληρώσω τοις μετρητοίς/με πιστωτική κάρτα.** *thah plee-roh-soh tees meht-ree-tees/meh pees-toh-tee-kee kahr-tah* |

## Renting

| | |
|---|---|
| I've reserved an apartment/ a room. | **Έχω κλείσει ένα διαμέρισμα/δωμάτιο.** *eh-hoh klee-see eh-nah ee-ah-meh-rees-mah/ oh-mah-tee-oh* |
| My name is… | **Λέγομαι…** *leh-ghoh-meh…* |
| Can I have the key/key card? | **Μπορώ να έχω το κλειδί/την κάρτα;** *boh-roh nah eh-hoh toh klee-THee/teen kahr-tah* |
| Are there…? | **Υπάρχουν…;** *ee-pahr-khoon…* |
| dishes | **πιάτα** *piah-tah* |

| | | |
|---|---|---|
| pillows | **μαξιλάρια** | mah·ksee·_lah_·ree·ah |
| sheets | **σεντόνια** | sehn·_doh_·niah |
| towels | **πετσέτες** | peh·_tseh_·tehs |
| kitchen utensils | **οικιακά σκεύη** | ee·kee·ah·_kah_ skeh·vee |
| When do I put out the bins/recycling? | **Πότε να βγάλω έξω τα σκουπίδια/ την ανακύκλωση;** | _poh_·teh nah _vghah_·loh eh·ksoh tah skoo·_pee_·THiah/ teen ah·nah·kee·kloh·see |
| ...has broken down. | **...χάλασε.** | ..._khah_·lah·seh |
| How does...work? | **Πώς λειτουργεί...;** | pohs lee·toor·_ghee_... |
| the air-conditioner | **το κλιματιστικό** | toh klee·mah·tees·tee·_koh_ |
| the dishwasher | **το πλυντήριο πιάτων** | toh plee·_ndee_·ree·oh _piah_·tohn |
| the freezer | **ο καταψύκτης** | oh kah·tah·_psee_·ktees |
| the heater | **ο θερμοσίφωνας** | oh thehr·moh·_see_·foh·nahs |
| the microwave | **ο φούρνος μικροκυμάτων** | oh _foor_·nohs meek·roh·kee·_mah_·tohn |
| the refrigerator | **το ψυγείο** | toh psee·_ghee_·oh |

---

In Greece the electricity supply is 220 V, with standard continental 2-pin or 3-pin plugs. A multi-adapter is recommended.

| the stove | **η κουζίνα** *ee koo-zee-nah* |
| the washing machine | **το πλυντήριο** *toh pleen-dee-ree-oh* |

## Domestic Items

| I need... | **Χρειάζομαι...** *khree-ah-zoh-meh...* |
| an adapter | **έναν προσαρμοστή** *eh-nahn proh-sahr-mohs-tee* |
| aluminum foil | **λίγο αλουμινόχαρτο** *lee-ghoh ah-loo-mee-noh-khahr-toh* |
| a bottle opener | **ένα τιρμπουσόν** *eh-nah teer-boo-sohn* |
| a broom | **μια σκούπα** *miah skoo-pah* |
| a can opener | **ένα ανοιχτήρι** *eh-nah ah-neeh-tee-ree* |
| cleaning supplies | **μερικά καθαριστικά** *meh-ree-kah kah-thah-rees-tee-kah* |
| a corkscrew | **ένα τιρμπουσόν** *eh-nah teer-boo-sohn* |
| detergent | **λίγο απορρυπαντικό** *lee-ghoh ah-poh-ree-pahn-dee-koh* |
| dishwashing liquid | **λίγο υγρό πιάτων** *lee-ghoh ee-ghroh piah-tohn* |
| bin bags | **μερικές σακκούλες σκουπιδιών** *meh-ree-kehs sah-koo-lehs skoo-pee-THee-ohn* |
| a light bulb | **μια λάμπα** *miah lah-mbah* |
| matches | **μερικά σπίρτα** *meh-ree-kah speer-tah* |
| a mop | **μια σφουγγαρίστρα** *miah sfoo-ghahr-ees-trah* |
| napkins | **χαρτοπετσέτες** *khah-rtoh-peh-tseh-tehs* |
| paper towels | **χαρτοπετσέτες** *khah-rtoh-peh-tseh-tehs* |
| plastic wrap [cling film] | **διαφανή μεμβράνη** *THee-ah-fah-nee mehm-vrah-nee* |
| a plunger | **μια βεντούζα** *miah vehn-doo-zah* |
| scissors | **ένα ψαλίδι** *eh-nah psah-lee-THee* |
| a vacuum cleaner | **μια ηλεκτρική σκούπα** *miah ee-lehk-tree-kee skoo-pah* |

## At the Hostel

| Do you have any places left for tonight? | **Έχετε θέση για απόψε;** *eh-kheh-teh theh-see yah ah-poh-pseh* |

| | |
|---|---|
| Can I have...? | **Μπορώ να έχω...;** *boh·roh nah eh·khoh...* |
| a single/ double room | **μονό/διπλό δωμάτιο** *moh·noh/THee·ploh THoh·mah· tee·oh* |
| a blanket | **μια κουβέρτα** *miah koo·vehr·tah* |
| a pillow | **ένα μαξιλάρι** *eh·nah mah·ksee·lah·ree* |
| sheets | **σεντόνια** *sehn·doh·niah* |
| a towel | **μια πετσέτα μπάνιου** *miah peh·tseh·tah bah·nioo* |
| Do you have lockers? | **Έχετε ντουλάπια;** *eh·kheh·teh doo·lah·piah* |
| What time are the doors locked? | **Τί ώρα κλειδώνετε;** *tee oh·rah klee·THoh·neh·the* |
| Do I need a membership card? | **Χρειάζομαι κάρτα μέλους;** *khree·ah·zoh·meh kahr· tah meh·loos* |
| Here's my international student card. | **Αυτή είναι η διεθνής φοιτητική μου κάρτα.** *ahf·tee ee·neh ee THee·eh·thnees fee·tee·tee·kee moo kahr·ta* |

## Going Camping

| | |
|---|---|
| Can I camp here? | **Μπορώ να κάνω κάμπινγκ εδώ;** *boh·roh nah kah· noh kahm·peeng·THoh* |
| Is there a campsite near here? | **Υπάρχει χώρος κάμπινγκ εδώ κοντά;** *ee·pahr·khee khoh·rohs kahm·peeng eh·THoh kohn·dah* |
| What is the charge per day/week? | **Ποιό είναι το κόστος για *την ημέρα/την εβδομάδα*;** *pioh ee·neh toh kohs·tohs yah teen ee·meh·rah/ehv· THoh·mah·THah* |

---

### YOU MAY SEE...

| | |
|---|---|
| **ΠΟΣΙΜΟ ΝΕΡΟ** *poh·see·moh neh·roh* | drinking water |
| **ΑΠΑΓΟΡΕΥΕΤΑΙ Η ΚΑΤΑΣΚΗΝΩΣΗ** *ahpah·ghoh·reh·vehteh ee kah·tahs·kee·nohsee* | no camping |
| **ΜΗΝ ΑΝΑΒΕΤΕ ΦΩΤΙΑ** *meen ah·nah·veh·teh foh·tee·ah* | no fires/barbecues |

| Are there...? | **Υπάρχουν...;** ee-*pahr*-hoon... |
| cooking facilities | **ηλεκτρική κουζίνα** ee-lehk-tree-*kee* koo-*zee*-nah |
| electrical outlets | **πρίζες** *pree*-zehs |
| laundry facilities | **πλυντήρια** pleen-*dee*-ree-ah |
| showers | **ντους** dooz |
| tents for hire | **σκηνές για ενοικίαση** skee-nehs yah eh-nee-*kee*-ah-se |
| Where can I empty the chemical toilet? | **Πού μπορώ να αδειάσω τη χημική τουαλέτα;** poo bohroh nah ah-THee-*ah*-soh tee khee-mee-kee too ah-*leh*-tah |

## Communications

### ESSENTIAL

| Where's an internet cafe? | **Πού υπάρχει internet cafe;** poo ee-*pahr*-khee een-tehr-neht kah-*feh* |
| Can I access the internet/check e-mail here? | **Μπορώ να μπω στο internet/να ελέγξω τα e-mail μου εδώ;** boh-*roh* nah boh stoh een-tehr-*neht*/nah eh-*lehng*-ksoh tah ee-meh-eel moo eh-*THoh* |
| How much per hour/half hour? | **Πόσο χρεώνεται η ώρα/μισή ώρα;** *poh*-soh hreh-*oh*-neh-teh ee *oh*-rah/mee-*see* oh-rah |
| How do I connect/log on? | **Πώς μπορώ να συνδεθώ/μπω;** pohs boh-*roh* nah seehn-THeh-*thoh*/ boh |
| I'd like a phone card. | **Θα ήθελα μια τηλεκάρτα.** thah *ee*-theh-lah miah tee-leh-*kahr*-tah |
| Can I have your phone number? | **Μπορώ να έχω τον αριθμό τηλεφώνου σας;** boh-*roh* nah *eh*-hoh tohn ah-reeth-*moh* tee-leh-*foh*-noo sahs |
| Here's my number /e-mail address. | **Ορίστε το τηλέφωνό μου/e-mail μου.** oh-*rees*-teh toh tee-*leh*-foh-*noh* moo/ee-*meh*-eel moo |
| Call me. | **Πάρτε με τηλέφωνο.** *pahr*-teh meh tee-*leh*-foh-noh |

| | |
|---|---|
| E-mail me. | **Στείλτε μου e-mail.** _steel_•teh moo ee•_meh_•eel |
| Hello. This is… | **Εμπρός. Είμαι…** ehm•_brohs_ ee•meh… |
| I'd like to speak to… | **Θα ήθελα να μιλήσω με…** thah ee•_theh_•lah nah mee•_lee_•soh meh… |
| Repeat that, please. | **Επαναλάβετέ το, παρακαλώ.** eh•pah•nah•lah•veh•_teh_ toh pah•rah•kah•_loh_ |
| I'll be in touch. | **Θα επικοινωνήσω μαζί σας.** thah eh•pee•kee•noh•_nee_•soh mah•_zee_ sahs |
| Bye. | **Αντίο.** ah•_dee_•oh |
| Where is the nearest/ main post office? | **Πού είναι το κοντινότερο/κεντρικό ταχυδρομείο;** poo ee•neh toh koh•ndee•_noh_•teh•roh/kehn•dree•_koh_ tah•khee•THroh•_mee_•oh |
| I'd like to send this to… | **Θα ήθελα να στείλω αυτό σε…** thah ee•theh•lah nah _stee_•loh ahf•_toh_ seh… |

## Online

| | |
|---|---|
| Where's an internet cafe? | **Πού υπάρχει ένα internet cafe;** poo ee•_pahr_•khee eh•nah een•tehr•_neht_ kah•_feh_ |
| Does it have wireless internet? | **Έχει ασύρματο internet;** _eh_•khee ah•_seer_•mah•toh een•tehr•_neht_ |
| What is the WiFi password? | **Ποιος είναι ο κωδικός πρόσβασης για το WiFi;** piohs ee•neh oh koh•THee•_kohs_ _proh_•svah•sees yah toh WiFi |
| Is the WiFi free? | **Το WiFi είναι δωρεάν;** toh WiFi ee•neh THo•reh•_ahn_ |
| Do you have bluetooth? | **Έχετε bluetooth;** _eh_•kheh•teh bluetooth |
| How do I turn the computer on/off? | **Πώς ανοίγει/κλείνει ο υπολογιστής;** pohs ah•_nee_•ghee/_klee_•nee oh ee•poh•loh•ghees•_tees_ |
| Can I…? | **Μπορώ…;** boh•_roh_… |
| access the internet here | **να έχω πρόσβαση στο internet από εδώ** nah _eh_•hoh _prohs_•vah•see stoh een•tehr•_neht_ ah•_poh_ eh•_THoh_ |

## YOU MAY SEE...

| | |
|---|---|
| **ΚΛΕΙΣΙΜΟ** _klee·see·moh_ | close |
| **ΔΙΑΓΡΑΦΗ** _THee·ahgh·rah·fee_ | delete |
| **EMAIL** _ee·meh·eel_ | e-mail |
| **ΕΞΟΔΟΣ** _eh·ksoh·THohs_ | exit |
| **ΒΟΗΘΕΙΑ** _voh·ee·thee·ah_ | help |
| **ΕΦΑΡΜΟΓΗ ΑΜΕΣΟΥ** | instant messenger |
| **ΜΗΝΥΜΑΤΟΣ** _eh·fahr·moh·yee ah·meh·soo mee·nee·mah·tohs_ | |
| **INTERNET** _een·tehr·neht_ | internet |
| **ΣΥΝΔΕΣΗ** _seen·theh·see_ | login |
| **ΝΕΟ (ΜΗΝΥΜΑ)** _neh·oh mee·nee·mah_ | new (message) |
| **ON/OFF** _ohn/ohf_ | on/off |
| **ΑΝΟΙΧΤΟ** _ah·neekh·toh_ | open |
| **ΕΚΤΥΠΩΣΗ** _ehk·tee·poh·see_ | print |
| **ΑΠΟΘΗΚΕΥΣΗ** _ah·poh·thee· kehf·see_ | save |
| **ΑΠΟΣΤΟΛΗ** _ah·pohs·toh·lee_ | send |
| **ΟΝΟΜΑ ΧΡΗΣΤΗ/** _oh·noh· mah khrees·tee_ | username/ password |
| **ΚΩΔΙΚΟΣ ΠΡΟΣΒΑΣΗΣ** _koh·THee·kohs prohs·vah·sees_ | |
| **ΑΣΥΡΜΑΤΟ INTERNET** _ah·seer·mah·toh een·tehr·neht_ | wireless internet |

| | | |
|---|---|---|
| check e-mail | **να ελέγξω τα e-mail μου** | _nah eh·leng·ksoh tah ee·meh·eel moo_ |
| print | **εκτυπώσω** _ehk·tee·poh·soh_ | |
| plug in/charge my laptop/iPhone/iPad /BlackBerry? | **να συνδέσω/φορτίσω το laptop/iPhone/iPad/ BlackBerry;** | _nah seen·THeh·soh toh laptop/iPhone/ iPad/BlackBerry_ |

| access Skype? | **να μπω στο Skype;** *nah boh stoh Skype* |
| How much per hour/half hour? | **Πόσο χρεώνεται η ώρα/μισή ώρα;** *poh·soh hreh·oh·neh·teh ee oh·rah/mee·see oh·rah* |
| How do I...? | **Πώς μπορώ να...;** *pohs boh·roh nah* |
| connect/ disconnect | **συνδεθώ/αποσυνδεθώ** *seen·theh·THoh/ah·poh· seen·theh·THoh* |
| log on/off | **συνδεθώ/αποσυνδεθώ** *seen·theh·THoh/ah·poh· seen·theh·THoh* |
| type this symbol | **πληκτρολογήσω αυτό το σύμβολο** *pleek·troh· loh·ghee·soh ahf·toh toh seem·voh·loh* |
| What's your e-mail? | **Ποιο είναι το e-mail σας;** *pioh ee·neh toh ee·meh·eel sahs* |
| My e-mail is... | **Το e-mail μου είναι...** *toh ee·meh·eel moo ee·neh...* |
| Do you have a scanner? | **Έχετε σαρωτή;** *eh·kheh·teh sah·roh·tee* |

## Social Media

| Are you on Facebook /Twitter? | **Είστε στο Facebook/Twitter;** *ee·steh stoh Facebook/Twitter* |
| What's your user name? | **Ποιο είναι το όνομα χρήστη;** *pioh ee·neh toh oh·noh· mah khree·stee* |
| I'll add you as a friend. | **Θα σε προσθέσω ως φίλο.** *thah seh proh·stheh·soh ohs fee·loh* |
| I'll follow you on Twitter. | **Θα σε ακολουθώ στο Twitter.** *thah seh ah·koh· loo·thoh stoh Twitter* |
| Are you following...? | **Ακολουθείς...;** *ah·koh·loo·thees* |
| I'll put the pictures on Facebook/Twitter. | **Θα βάλω τις φωτογραφίες στο Facebook/Twitter.** *thah vah·loh tees foh·toh·ghrah·fee·ehs sto Facebook/ Twitter* |
| I'll tag you in the pictures. | **Θα σε σημειώσω στις φωτογραφίες.** *thah seh see· mee·oh·soh stees foh·toh·ghrah·fee·ehs* |

## YOU MAY HEAR...

**Ποιος είστε;** *piohs ee·steh*
Who's calling?

**Περιμένετε, παρακαλώ.**
Hold on, please.
*peh·ree·meh·neh·the pah·rah·kah·loh*

**Θα σας συνδέσω.** *thah sahs seen·THeh·soh*
I'll put you through.

**Θέλετε να αφήσετε μήνυμα;** *theh·leh·teh nah*
Would you like to

*ah·fee·seh·teh mee·nee·mah*
leave a message?

**Ξανακαλέστε αργότερα/σε δέκα λεπτά.**
Call back later/in

*ksah·nah·kah·lehs·teh ahr·ghoh·teh·rah/she*
ten minutes.

*eh·kah lehp·tah*

**Να σας πάρει εκείνος/εκείνη;** *nah sahs*
Can he/she call you back?

*pah·ree eh·kee·nohs/eh·kee·nee*

**Ποιος είναι ο αριθμός σας;** *piohs ee·neh oh*
What's your number?

*ah·reeth·mohs sahs*

## Phone

| | | |
|---|---|---|
| A phone card/ prepaid phone, please. | **Μια τηλεκάρτα/χρονοκάρτα.** *miah tee·leh·kahr·tah/khroh·noh·kahr·tah* | |
| How much? | **Πόσο;** *poh·soh* | |
| Where's the pay phone? | **Πού είναι ένα καρτοτηλέφωνο;** *poo ee·neh toh kahr·toh·tee·leh·foh·noh* | |
| What's the area/ country code for...? | **Ποιος είναι ο κωδικός περιοχής/χώρας για...;** *piohs ee·neh oh koh·THee·kohs peh·ree·oh·khees/khoh·rahs yah...* | |
| What's the number for Information? | **Ποιος είναι ο αριθμός για Πληροφορίες;** *piohs ee·neh oh ah·reeth·mohs yah plee·roh·foh·ree·ehs* | |
| I'd like the number for... | **Θα ήθελα έναν αριθμό για...** *thah ee·theh·lah eh·nahn ah·reeth·moh yah...* | |

| | |
|---|---|
| I'd like to call collect [reverse the charges]. | **Θέλω να τηλεφωνήσω με αναστροφή χρέωσης.** *theh·loh nah tee·leh·foh·nee·soh meh ah·nah·stroh·fee khreh·oh·sees* |
| My phone doesn't. work here | **Το τηλέφωνό μου δεν λειτουργεί εδώ.** *toh tee·leh·foh·noh moo THehn lee·toor·ghee eh·THoh* |
| What network are you on? | **Σε ποιο δίκτυο είσαι;** *seh pioh THee·ktee·oh ee·seh* |
| Is it 3G? | **Είναι 3G;** *ee·neh 3G* |
| I have run out of credit/minutes. | **Δεν έχω μονάδες/λεπτά.** *THehn eh·khoh moh·nah·THehs/leh·ptah* |
| Can I buy some credit? | **Μπορώ να αγοράσω μονάδες;** *boh·roh nah ah·ghoh·rah·soh moh·nah·THehs* |
| Do you have a phone charger? | **Έχετε φορτιστή για τηλέφωνο;** *eh·kheh·teh foh·rtee·stee yah tee·leh·foh·noh* |
| Can I have your number? | **Μπορώ να έχω τον αριθμό τηλεφώνου σας;** *boh·roh nah eh·khoh tohn ah·reeth·moh tee·leh·foh·noo sahs* |
| Here's my number. | **Ορίστε ο αριθμός τηλεφώνου μου.** *oh·ree·steh oh ah·reeth·mohs tee·leh·foh·noo moo* |
| Please text me. | **Παρακαλώ, στείλτε μου μήνυμα.** *pah·rah·kah·loh steel·teh moo mee·nee·mah* |
| I'll call you. | **Θα σας πάρω τηλέφωνο.** *thah sahs pah·rohtee·leh·foh·noh* |

Throughout Greece, even in remote areas, there are plenty of public phones; these are mainly card operated. Phone cards can be purchased from **περίπτερα** *(peh·ree·pteh·rah)*, kiosks. You can also purchase a **κάρτα για κινητό** *(kah·rtah yiah kee·nee·toh)* prepaid card for your wireless phone from any of the conveniently located wireless phone stores.

## YOU MAY HEAR...

| | |
|---|---|
| **Παρακαλώ συμπληρώστε αυτήν την τελωνειακή δήλωση.** pah·rah·kah·<u>loh</u> seem·blee·<u>rohs</u>·teh ahf·<u>teen</u> teen teh·loh·nee·ah·<u>kee</u> <u>THee</u>·loh·see | Please fill out the customs declaration form. |
| **Ποια είναι η αξία;** piah <u>ee</u>·neh ee ah·<u>ksee</u>·ah | What's the value? |
| **Τι είναι μέσα;** tee <u>ee</u>·neh <u>meh</u>·sah | What's inside? |

## Telephone Etiquette

| | |
|---|---|
| Hello. This is... | **Εμπρός. Είμαι ο *m* /η *f* ...** ehm·<u>brohs</u> <u>ee</u>·meh oh/ee... |
| I'd like to speak to... | **Θα ήθελα να μιλήσω με τον *m* /την *f* ...** thah <u>ee</u>·theh·lah nah mee·<u>lee</u>·soh meh tohn/teen... |
| Extension... | **Εσωτερική γραμμή...** eh·soh·teh·ree·<u>kee</u> ghrah·<u>mee</u>... |
| Speak louder/more slowly. | **Μιλείστε πιο δυνατά/πιο αργά.** mee·<u>lees</u>·the pioh THee·nah·<u>tah</u>/ahr·<u>ghah</u> |
| Repeat that, please. | **Επαναλάβετέ το, παρακαλώ.** eh·pah·nah·<u>lah</u>·veh·<u>teh</u> toh pah·rah·kah·<u>loh</u> |
| I'll call back later. | **Θα έρθω σε επαφή μαζί σας αργότερα.** thah <u>ehr</u>·thoh seh eh·pah·<u>fee</u> mah·<u>zee</u> sahs ahr·<u>ghoh</u>·teh·rah |
| Bye. | **Αντίο.** ah·<u>dee</u>·oh |

## Fax

| | |
|---|---|
| Can I send/receive a fax here? | **Μπορώ να στείλω/λάβω φαξ από εδώ;** boh·<u>roh</u> nah <u>stee</u>·loh/<u>lah</u>·voh fahks ah·<u>poh</u> eh·<u>THoh</u> |
| What's the fax number? | **Ποιος είναι ο αριθμός φαξ;** piohs <u>ee</u>·neh oh ah·reeth·<u>mohs</u> fahks |
| Please fax this to... | **Παρακαλώ στείλτε αυτό το φαξ σε...** pah·rah·kah·<u>loh</u> <u>steel</u>·teh ahf·<u>toh</u> toh fahks seh... |

## Post

| | |
|---|---|
| Where's the post office/mailbox? | **Πού είναι το ταχυδρομείο/το γραμματοκιβώτιο;** *poo ee·neh toh tah·khee·roh·mee·oh/toh ghrah·mah·toh kee·voh·tee·oh* |
| A stamp for this postcard/letter. | **Ένα γραμματόσημο γι' αυτή την κάρτα/αυτό το γράμμα.** *eh·nah ghrah·mah·toh·see·moh yah ahf·teen teen kahr·tah/ahf·toh toh ghrah·mah* |
| How much? | **Πόσο;** *poh·soh* |
| I want to send. this package by airmail/express | **Θέλω να στείλω αυτό τοπακέτο αεροπορικώς/εξπρές.** *theh·lohnah stee·loh ahf·toh toh pah keh·toh· ah·eh·roh·poh·ree·kohs·ehks·prehs* |
| Can I have a receipt? | **Μπορώ να έχω μια απόδειξη;** *boh·roh nah eh·khoh miah ah·poh·THee·ksee* |

The post office is open from 8:00 a.m. to 8:00 p.m., except on Wednesday and Saturday when it closes at around 1:00 p.m. Main post offices are open Sunday morning. Mailboxes are yellow and bear the initials **ΕΛΤΑ** *(ehl·tah)*.

# Food & Drink

# Eating Out

## ESSENTIAL

| | |
|---|---|
| Can you recommend a good restaurant/bar? | **Μπορείτε να συστήσετε ένα καλό εστιατόριο/μπαρ;** boh·*ree*·teh nah sees·*tee*·seh·teh *eh*·nah kah·*loh* ehs·tee·ah·*toh*·ree·oh/bahr |
| Is there a traditional Greek/ an inexpensive restaurant near here? | **Υπάρχει κανένα ελληνικό/φθηνό εστιατόριο εδώ κοντά;** ee·*pahr*·khee kah·*neh*·nah eh·lee·nee·*koh*/fthee·*noh* ehs·tee·ah·*toh*·ree·oh eh·*THoh* kohn·*dah* |
| A table for..., please. | **Ένα τραπέζι για..., παρακαλώ.** *eh*·nah trah·*peh*·zee yah...pah·rah·kah·*loh* |
| Could we sit...? | **Μπορούμε να καθήσουμε...;** boh·*roo*·meh nah kah·*thee*·soo·meh... |
| here/there | **εδώ/εκεί** eh·*THoh*/eh·*kee* |
| outside | **έξω** *eh*·ksoh |
| in a non-smoking area | **σε έναν χώρο για μη καπνίζοντες** seh *eh*·nahnk hoh·roh yah mee kahp·*nee*·zohn·dehs |
| I'm waiting for someone. | **Περιμένω κάποιον.** peh·ree·*meh*·noh *kah*·piohn |
| Where are the toilets | **Πού είναι η τουαλέτα;** poo *ee*·neh ee too·ah·*leh*·tah |
| A menu, please. | **Έναν κατάλογο, παρακαλώ.** *eh*·nahn kah·*tah*·loh·ghoh pah·rah·kah·*loh* |
| What do you recommend? | **Τι προτείνετε;** tee proh·*tee*·neh·the |
| I'd like... | **Θα ήθελα...** thah *ee*·theh·lah... |
| Some more..., please. | **Λίγο ακόμη..., παρακαλώ.** *lee*·ghoh ah·*koh*·mee...pah·rah·kah·*loh* |
| Enjoy your meal! | **Καλή όρεξη!** kah·*lee* oh·*reh*·ksee |

| | |
|---|---|
| The check [bill], please. | **Τον λογαριασμό, παρακαλώ.** tohn loh•ghah•riahs•moh pah•rah•kah•loh |
| Is service included? | **Συμπεριλαμβάνεται και το φιλοδώρημα;** seem•beh•ree•lahm•vah•neh•teh keh toh fee•loh•THoh•ree•mah |
| Can I pay by credit card? | **Μπορώ να πληρώσω με πιστωτική κάρτα;** boh•roh nah plee•roh•soh meh pee•stoh•tee•kee kahr•tah |
| Can I have a receipt? | **Μπορώ να έχω απόδειξη;** boh•roh nah eh•khoh ah•poh•THee•ksee |
| Thank you. | **Ευχαριστώ.** ehf•hah•ree•stoh |

## Where to Eat

| | |
|---|---|
| Can you recommend...? | **Μπορείτε να συστήσετε...;** boh•ree•teh nah sees•tee•seh•teh... |
| a restaurant | **ένα εστιατόριο** eh•nah ehs•tee•ah•toh•ree•oh |
| a bar | **ένα μπαρ** eh•nah bahr |
| a cafe | **μια καφετέρια** miah kah•feh•teh•ree•ah |
| a fast-food place | **ένα φάστ φουντ** eh•nah fahst food |
| a cheap restaurant | **ένα φτηνό εστιατόριο** eh•nah ftee•noh eh•stee•ah•toh•ree•oh |
| an expensive restaurant | **ένα ακριβό εστιατόριο** eh•nah ah•kree•voh eh•stee•ah•toh•ree•oh |
| a restaurant with a good view | **ένα εστιατόριο με καλή θέα** eh•nah eh•stee•ah•toh•ree•oh meh kah•lee theh•ah |
| an authentic/a non-touristy restaurant | **ένα αυθεντικό/ όχι τουριστικό εστιατόριο** eh•nah ahf•theh•ntee•koh/oh•khee too•ree•stee•koh eh•stee•ah•toh•ree•oh |
| a souvlaki/gyros stand | **ένα σουβλατζίδικο** eh•nah soov•la•jee•THee•koh |

## YOU MAY HEAR...

| | |
|---|---|
| **Έχετε κάνει κράτηση;** *eh·kheh·teh kah·nee krah·tee·see* | Do you have a reservation? |
| **Πόσα άτομα;** *poh·sah ah·toh·mah* | How many? |
| **Καπνίζοντες ή μη καπνίζοντες;** *kah·pnee·zohn·dehs ee mee kah·pnee·zohn·dehs* | Smoking or non-smoking? |
| **Είσαστε έτοιμοι να παραγγείλετε;** *ee·sahs·teh eh·tee·mee nah pah·rah·gee·leh·teh* | Are you ready to order? |
| **Τι θα πάρετε;** *tee thah pah·reh·teh* | What would you like? |
| **Σας συστήνω...** *sahs sees·tee·noh...* | I recommend... |
| **Καλή όρεξη.** *kah·lee oh·reh·ksee* | Enjoy your meal. |

## Reservations & Preferences

| | |
|---|---|
| I'd like to reserve a table... | **Θα ήθελα να κλείσω ένα τραπέζι...** *thah ee·theh·lah nah klee·soh eh·nah trah·peh·zee...* |
|    for two | **για δύο** *yah THee·oh* |
|    for this evening | **γι' απόψε** *yah ah·poh·pseh* |
|    for tomorrow at... | **για αύριο στις...** *yah ahv·ree·oh stees...* |
| A table for two, please. | **Ένα τραπέζι για δύο, παρακαλώ.** *eh·nah trah·peh·zee yah THee·oh pah·rah·kah·loh* |
| We have a reservation. | **Έχουμε κλείσει τραπέζι.** *eh·khoo·meh klee·see trah·peh·zee* |
| My name is... | **Λέγομαι...** *leh·ghoh·meh...* |
| Can we sit...? | **Μπορούμε να καθίσουμε...;** *boh·roo·meh nah kah·thee·soo·meh* |
|    here/there | **εδώ/εκεί** *eh·THoh/eh·kee* |
|    outside | **έξω** *eh·ksoh* |
|    in a non-smoking area | **στους μη καπνίζοντες** *stoos mee kah·pnee·zoh·dehs* |
|    by the window | **δίπλα στο παράθυρο** *THee·plah stoh pah·rah·thee·roh* |

| | | |
|---|---|---|
| in the shade | **στη σκιά** | *stee skee·ah* |
| in the sun | **στον ήλιο** | *stohn ee·lioh* |
| Where is the restroom [toilet]? | **Πού είναι η τουαλέτα;** | *poo ee·neh ee too·ah·leh·tah* |

## How to Order

| | | |
|---|---|---|
| Waiter!/Waitress! | **Γκαρσόν!/Δεσποινίς!** | *gahr·sohn/THehs·pee·nees* |
| We're ready to order. | **Είμαστε έτοιμοι να παραγγείλουμε.** | *ee·mahs·teh eh·tee·mee nah pah·rah·gee·loo·meh* |
| May I see the wine list? | **Μπορώ να δω τον κατάλογο κρασιών;** | *boh·roh nah THoh tohn kah·tah·loh·ghoh krah·siohn* |
| I'd like… | **Θα ήθελα…** | *thah ee·theh·lah…* |
| a bottle of… | **ένα μπουκάλι…** | *eh·nah boo·kah·lee…* |
| carafe of… | **μια καράφα…** | *miah kah·rah·fah…* |
| glass of… | **ένα ποτήρι…** | *eh·nah poh·tee·ree…* |
| The menu, please. | **Τον κατάλογο, παρακαλώ.** | *tohn kah·tah·loh·ghoh pah·rah·kah·loh* |
| Do you have…? | **Έχετε…;** | *eh·kheh·teh…* |
| a menu in English | **έναν κατάλογο στα Αγγλικά** | *eh·nahn kah·tah·loh·ghoh stah ahng·lee·kah* |
| a fixed-price menu | **έναν κατάλογο με σταθερές τιμές** | *eh·nahnkah·tah·loh·ghoh meh stah·theh·rehs tee·mehs* |
| a children's menu | **παιδικό μενού** | *peh·THee·koh meh·noo* |
| What do you recommend? | **Τι προτείνετε;** | *tee proh·tee·neh·the* |
| What's this? | **Τι είναι αυτό;** | *tee ee·neh ahf·toh* |
| What's in it? | **Τι περιέχει;** | *tee peh·ree·eh·khee* |
| Is it spicy? | **Είναι πικάντικο;** | *ee·neh pee·kahn·dee·koh* |
| I'd like… | **Θα ήθελα…** | *thah ee·theh·lah…* |
| More…, please. | **Λίγο ακόμη…, παρακαλώ.** | *lee·ghoh ah·koh·mee… pah·rah·kah·loh* |

| With/Without... | **Με/Χωρίς...** meh/khoh·<u>rees</u>... |
| I can't have... | **Δεν πρέπει να φάω φαγητό που περιέχει...** THehn <u>preh</u>·pee nah <u>fah</u>·oh fah·yee·<u>toh</u> poo peh·ree·<u>eh</u>·khee... |
| rare | **με το αίμα του, σενιάν** meh toh <u>eh</u>·mah too seh·<u>nian</u> |
| medium | **μέτρια ψημένο** <u>meht</u>·ree·ah psee·<u>meh</u>·noh |
| well-done | **καλοψημένο** kah·loh·psee·<u>meh</u>·noh |
| It's to go [take away]. | **Είναι για το σπίτι.** <u>ee</u>·neh yah toh <u>spee</u>·tee |

## YOU MAY SEE...

| **ΚΟΥΒΕΡ** koo·<u>vehr</u> | cover charge |
| **ΣΤΑΘΕΡΗ ΤΙΜΗ** stah·theh·<u>ree</u> tee·<u>mee</u> | fixed-price |
| **ΚΑΤΑΛΟΓΟΣ** kah·<u>tah</u>·loh·ghohs | menu |
| **ΜΕΝΟΥ ΤΗΣ ΗΜΕΡΑΣ** meh·<u>noo</u> tees ee·<u>meh</u>·rahs | menu of the day |
| **Η ΕΞΥΠΗΡΕΤΗΣΗ (ΔΕΝ) ΠΕΡΙΛΑΜΒΑΝΕΤΑΙ** ee eh·ksee·pee <u>reh</u>·tee·see (THehn) peh·ree·lahm·<u>vahn</u>·eh·the | service (not) included |
| **ΠΙΑΤΑ ΤΗΣ ΗΜΕΡΑΣ** pee·<u>ah</u>·tah tees ee·<u>meh</u>·rahs | specials |

## Cooking Methods

| baked | **του φούρνου** too <u>foor</u>·noo |
| barbecued, grilled | **της σχάρας** tees <u>skhah</u>·rahs |
| boiled | **βραστό** vrah·<u>stoh</u> |
| braised | **κατσαρόλας** kah·tsah·<u>roh</u>·lahs |

| breaded | **πανέ** *pah·neh* |
| cooked in olive oil | **λαδερό** *lah·THeh·roh* |
| creamed | **με κρέμα γάλακτος** *meh kreh·mah ghah·lah·ktohs* |
| diced | **σε κύβους** *seh kee·voos* |
| filleted | **φιλέτο** *fee·leh·toh* |
| fried | **τηγανητό** *tee·ghah·nee·toh* |
| marinated | **μαρινάτο** *mah·ree·nah·toh* |
| poached | **ποσέ** *poh·seh* |
| roasted | **ψητό** *psee·toh* |
| sautéed | **σωτέ** *soh·teh* |
| smoked | **καπνιστό** *kah·pnee·stoh* |
| steamed | **στον ατμό** *stohn aht·moh* |
| stewed | **μαγειρευτό** *mah·yee·rehf·toh* |
| stewed in tomato sauce | **γιαχνί** *yahkh·nee* |
| stewed in wine | **κρασάτο** *krah·sah·toh* |
| stuffed | **γεμιστό** *yeh·mees·toh* |

## Dietary Requirements

| I'm… | **Είμαι…** *ee·meh…* |
| diabetic | **-διαβητικός** *m* **/διαβητική** *f THee·ah·vee·teek·ohs/ THee·ah·vee·tee·kee* |

| | |
|---|---|
| lactose intolerant | **έχω ευαισθησία στα γαλακτοκομικά** _eh_·khoh eh·vehs·thee·_see_·ah stah ghah·lahk·toh·koh·mee·_kah_ |
| vegetarian | **χορτοφάγος** khohr·toh·_fah_·ghohs |
| vegan | **χορτοφάγος** khoh·rtoh·_fah_·ghos |
| I'm allergic to… | **είμαι αλλεργικός** *m* **/αλλεργική** *f* **σε…** _ee_·meh ah·lehr·yeek·_ohs_/ah·lehr·yeek·_ee_ seh… |
| I can't eat… | **Δεν πρέπει να φάω φαγητό που περιέχει…** THehn _preh_·pee nah _fah_·oh fah·yee·_toh_ poo peh·ree·_eh_·khee… |
| dairy | **γαλακτοκομικά** ghah·lahk·toh·koh·mee·_kah_ |
| gluten | **γλουτένη** ghloo·_teh_·nee |
| nuts | **ξηρούς καρπούς** ksee·_roos_ kahr·_poos_ |
| pork | **χοιρινό** khee·ree·_noh_ |
| shellfish | **οστρακοειδή** ohs·trah·koh·ee·_THee_ |
| I can't eat… | **Δεν πρέπει να φάω φαγητό που περιέχει…** THehn _preh_·pee nah _fah_·oh fah·yee·_toh_ poo peh·ree·_eh_·khee… |
| spicy foods | **πικάντικα τρόφιμα** pee·_kahn_·dee·kah _troh_·fee·mah |
| wheat | **σιτάρι** see·_tah_·ree |
| Is it halal/kosher? | **Αυτό είναι χαλάλ/κόσερ;** ahf _toh_ _ee_·neh khah·_lahl_/_koh_·sehr |
| Do you have…? | **Έχετε…;** _eh_·kheh·teh |
| skimmed milk | **αποβουτυρωμένο γάλα** ah·poh·voo·tee·roh·_meh_·noh ghah·lah |
| whole milk | **πλήρες γάλα** _plee_·rehs ghah·lah |
| soya milk | **γάλα σόγιας** _ghah_·lah _soh_·yahs |

## Dining with Children

| | |
|---|---|
| Do you have a children's menu? | **Έχετε παιδικό μενού;** _eh_·kheh·teh peh·THee·_koh_ meh·_noo_ |
| Can we have a child's seat? | **Μπορούμε να έχουμε ένα παιδικό κάθισμα;** boh·_roo_·meh nah _eh_·khoo·meh _eh_·nah peh·THee·_koh_ kah·theez·mah |

| Where can I feed/ change the baby? | **Πού μπορώ να ταΐσω/αλλάξω το μωρό;** *poo boh-roh nah tah-ee-soh/ah-lah-ksoh toh moh-roh* |
| Can you warm this? | **Μπορείτε να το ζεστάνετε;** *boh-ree-teh nah toh zehs-tah-neh-teh* |

For Traveling with Children, see page 133.

## How to Complain

| How much longer will our food be? | **Πόση ώρα ακόμη θα κάνει το φαγητό;** *poh-see oh-rah ah-koh-mee thah kah-nee toh fah-yee-toh* |
| We can't wait any longer. | **Δεν μπορούμε να περιμένουμε άλλο.** *THehn boh-roo-meh nah peh-ree-meh-noo-meh ah-loh* |
| We're leaving. | **Φεύγουμε.** *fehv-ghoo-meh* |
| That's not what I ordered. | **Δεν παρήγγειλα αυτό.** *THehn pah-ree-ngee-lah ahf-toh* |
| I asked for... | **Ζήτησα...** *zee-tee-sah...* |
| I can't eat this. | **Δεν μπορώ να το φάω.** *THehn boh-roh nah toh fah-oh* |
| This is too... | **Αυτό είναι πολύ...** *ahf-toh ee-neh poh-lee...* |
| cold/hot | **κρύο/ζεστό** *kree-oh/zehs-toh* |
| salty/spicy | **αλμυρό/πικάντικο** *ahl-mee-roh/pee-kahn-dee-koh* |
| tough/bland | **σκληρό/ανάλατο** *sklee-roh/ahl-mee-roh* |
| This isn't clean/ fresh. | **Αυτό δεν είναι καθαρό/φρέσκο.** *ahf-toh THehn ee-neh kah-thah-roh/frehs-koh* |

## Paying

| The check [bill], please. | **Τον λογαριασμό, παρακαλώ.** *tohn loh-ghahr-yahs-moh pah-rah-kah-loh* |
| We'd like to pay separately. | **Θα πληρώσουμε ξεχωριστά.** *thah plee-roh-soo-meh kseh-khoh-rees-tah* |
| It's all together. | **Όλοι μαζί.** *oh-lee mah-zee* |
| Is service included? | **Συμπεριλαμβάνεται και το σέρβις;** *seem-beh-ree-lahm-vah-neh-teh keh toh sehr-vees* |
| What's this amount for? | **Τί είναι αυτό το ποσό;** *tee ee-neh ahf-toh toh poh-soh* |

In Greek restaurants the service charge is included in the price. However, it is still customary to leave a little extra if you are satisfied with the service.

| | | |
|---|---|---|
| I didn't have that. I had… | **Δεν πήρα αυτό. Πήρα…** | THehn pee·rah ahf·toh pee·rah… |
| Can I pay by credit card? | **Μπορώ να πληρώσω με αυτήν την πιστωτική κάρτα;** | boh·roh nah plee·roh·soh meh ahf·teen teen pees·toh·tee·kee kahr·tah |
| Can I have an itemized bill/a receipt? | **Μπορώ να έχω έναν αναλυτικό λογαριασμό/ μια αναλυτική απόδειξη;** | boh·roh nah eh·khoh eh·nahn ah·nah·lee·tee·koh loh·ghahr·yahs·moh/miah ah·nah·lee·tee·kee ah·poh·ee·ksee |
| That was a delicious meal. | **Ήταν ένα πολύ νόστιμο γεύμα.** | ee·tahn eh·nah poh·lee nohs·tee·moh yehv·mah |
| I've already paid | **Πλήρωσα ήδη** | plee·roh·sah ee·THee |

## Meals & Cooking

### Breakfast

| | | |
|---|---|---|
| bacon | **μπέϊκον** | beh·ee·kohn |
| bread | **ψωμί** | psoh·mee |
| butter | **βούτυρο** | voo·tee·roh |
| cereal (cold/hot) | **δημητριακά με (ζεστό/κρύο) γάλα** | THee·meet· ree·ah·kah meh (zehs·toh/kree·oh) ghah·lah |
| cheese | **τυρί** | tee·ree |
| coffee/tea | **καφέ/τσάι** | kah·feh/tsah·ee |
| cold cuts [charcuterie] | **αλλαντικά** | ah·lah·ndee·kah |

Greeks rarely eat breakfast (**πρωινό**/proh·ee·<u>noh</u>). They usually have a strong coffee with sugar (**βαρύ γλυκό**/vah·<u>ree</u> ghlee·<u>koh</u>) in the morning, followed by another one between 10:00 and 11:00 a.m., maybe with a pastry.

Lunch (**μεσημεριανό**/meh·see·meh·riah·<u>noh</u>) is the main meal, although because of the summer heat some Greeks eat lighter at lunchtime and have their main meal in the evening. It is usually eaten from 2:00 to 3:00 p.m., but most restaurants will serve it until 4:00 p.m. Dinner (**βραδυνό**/vrah·THee·<u>noh</u>) is often eaten late — normally at 9:00 or 10:00 p.m. It is not unusual to find restaurants serving food until midnight or later. Snacks can be bought at souvlaki stalls (**σουβλατζήδικα**/soov·lah·<u>jee</u>·THee·kah) or snack bars (**σνακ μπαρ**/ snahk bahr) until the early hours of the morning. You can also buy tasty snacks, such as cheese pie (**τυρόπιτα**/tee·<u>rhoh</u>·pee·tah), at bakeries, which are open from very early in the morning until the afternoon.

| scrambled eggs | **ομελέτα** oh·meh·<u>leh</u>·tah |
| juice | **χυμός** khee·<u>mohs</u> |
| granola [muesli] | **μούσλι** <u>moo</u>·slee |
| honey | **μέλι** <u>meh</u>·lee |
| muffin | **μάφιν** <u>mah</u>·feen |
| milk | **γάλα** <u>ghah</u>·lah |
| oatmeal | **κουάκερ** koo·<u>ah</u>·kehr |
| omelet | **ομελέτα** oh·meh·<u>leh</u>·tah |
| roll | **ψωμάκι** psoh·<u>mah</u>·kee |
| sausage | **λουκάνικο** loo·<u>kah</u>·nee·koh |
| toast | **ψωμί φρυγανιά** psoh·<u>mee</u> free·ghah·<u>niah</u> |
| yogurt (with honey) | **γιαούρτι (με μέλι)** yah·<u>oor</u>·tee (meh <u>meh</u>·lee) |

## Appetizers

| | | |
|---|---|---|
| cold meat | **κρύο κρέας** | _kree_•oh _kreh_•ahs |
| ...eggs | **αυγά...** | ahv•_ghah_... |
| soft-boiled | **μελάτα** | meh•_lah_•tah |
| hard-boiled | **σφικτά** | sfeekh•_tah_ |
| fried | **τηγανητά μάτια** | tee•ghah•nee•_tah_ _mah_•tiah |
| poached | **ποσέ** | poh•_seh_ |
| fish roe dip | **ταραμοσαλάτα** | tah•rah•moh•sah•_lah_•tah |
| fried baby squid | **καλαμαράκια** | kah•lah•mah•_rah_•kiah |
| fried meatballs | **κεφτεδάκια** | kef•teh•_THah_•kiah |
| fried whitebait | **μαρίδα τηγανητή** | mah•_ree_•THah tee•ghah•nee•_tee_ |
| herring (smoked) | **ρέγγα (καπνιστή)** | _rehn_•gah (kahp•nees•_tee_) |
| olive (stuffed) | **ελιά (γεμιστή)** | eh•_liah_ (yeh•mees•_tee_) |
| cheese omelet | **ομελέττα με τυρί** | oh•meh•_leh_•tah meh tee•_ree_ |
| ham omelet | **ομελέττα με ζαμπόν** | oh•meh•_leh_•tah meh zahm•_bohn_ |

**Μεζέδες** _(meh•zeh•dehs)_, appetizers, can be a meal alone. Greeks will often go out for a glass of **ούζο** _(oo•zoh)_, an anise-flavored liqueur, accompanied by appetizers.

| | |
|---|---|
| pâté | **πατέ** pah·_teh_ |
| spinach and feta in pastry dough | **σπανακόπιττα** spah·nah·_koh_·pee·tah |
| stuffed grape leaves | **ντολμαδάκι** dohl·mah·_THah_·kee |
| yogurt, garlic and cucumber dip | **τζατζίκι** jah·_jee_·kee |

A traditional and very tasty egg dish in Greece is **στραπατσάδα** (strah·pah·_tsah_·THah), scrambled eggs with fresh tomato, but sometimes with other ingredients depending on the region. Another traditional method of using egg is in **αυγολέμονο** (ahv·ghoh·_leh_·moh·noh): egg yolk and lemon are added to a sauce or soup. This sauce usually accompanies warm stuffed grape leaves and other vegetable dishes or stews.

## Soup

| | |
|---|---|
| bean soup with tomatoes and parsley | **φασολάδα** fah·soh·_lah_·THah |
| chicken soup | **κοτόσουπα** koh·_toh_·soo·pah |
| chickpea soup | **ρεβύθια σούπα** reh·_vee_·thiah _soo_·pah |
| cracked wheat soup | **τραχανάς** trah·khah·_nahs_ |
| fish soup thickened with egg and lemon | **ψαρόσουπα αυγολέμονο** psah·_roh_·soo·pah ahv·ghoh·_leh_·moh·noh |
| fish stew with tomatoes | **κακαβιά** kah·kahv·_yah_ |
| lentil soup | **φακές σούπα** fah·_kehs_ _soo_·pah |
| meat soup | **κρεατόσουπα** kreh·ah·_toh_·soo·pah |
| soup with rice, eggs | **σούπα αυγολέμονο** _soo_·pah ahv·ghoh·_leh_·moh·noh |

and lemon juice

| | | |
|---|---|---|
| tripe soup | **πατσάς** | *pah·tsahs* |
| tahini (sesame paste) soup | **ταχινόσουπα** | *tah·khee·noh·soo·pah* |
| tomato soup | **τοματόσουπα** | *toh·mah·toh·soo·pah* |
| vegetable soup | **χορτόσουπα** | *khohr·toh·soo·pah* |

## Fish & Seafood

| | | |
|---|---|---|
| anchovy | **αντσούγια** | *ahn·joo·yahs* |
| crab | **καβούρι** | *kah·voo·ree* |
| cuttlefish | **σουπιά** | *soo·piah* |
| eel | **χέλι** | *kheh·lee* |
| fresh cod | **μπακαλιάρος** | *bah·kah·liah·rohs* |
| grouper | **σφυρίδα** | *sfee·ree·THah* |
| mullet | **κέφαλος** | *keh·fah·lohs* |
| lobster | **αστακός** | *ahs·tah·kohs* |
| marinated mullet, sole or mackerel | **ψάρι μαρινάτο** | *psah·ree mah·ree·nah·toh* |
| mussels | **μύδι** | *mee·THee* |
| octopus | **χταπόδι** | *khtah·poh·THee* |
| oyster | **στρείδι** | *stree·THee* |
| red mullet | **μπαρμπούνι** | *bahr·boo·nee* |
| salted cod | **μπακαλιάρος παστός** | *bah·kah·liah·rohs pahs·tohs* |
| sardine | **σαρδέλα** | *sahr·THeh·lah* |
| shrimp [prawn] | **γαρίδα** | *ghah·ree·THah* |
| sole | **γλώσσα** | *ghloh·sah* |
| squid | **καλαμάρι** | *kah·lah·mah·ree* |
| swordfish | **ξιφίας** | *ksee·fee·ahs* |
| tuna | **τόννος** | *toh·nohs* |

## Meat & Poultry

| | | |
|---|---|---|
| beef | **βοδινό** | *voh·THee·noh* |
| beef or veal stewed with tomatoes and eggplant [aubergine] | **μελιτζανάτο** | *meh·lee·jah·nah·toh* |
| brains | **μυαλό** | *miah·loh* |
| Greek burger | **μπιφτέκι** | *beef·teh·kee* |
| chicken | **κοτόπουλο** | *koh·toh·poo·loh* |
| cutlet | **κοτολέτα** | *koh·toh·leh·tah* |
| duck | **πάπια** | *pah·piah* |
| fillet | **φιλέτο** | *fee·leh·toh* |
| goat | **κατσικάκι** | *kah·tsee·kah·kee* |
| goose | **χήνα** | *khee·nah* |
| ham | **ζαμπόν** | *zahm·bohn* |
| kidney | **νεφρό** | *neh·froh* |
| lamb | **αρνί** | *ahr·nee* |
| liver | **συκώτι** | *see·koh·tee* |
| layers of eggplant [aubergine], meat and white sauce | **μουσακάς** | *moo·sah·kahs* |
| meat with orzo pasta baked with tomatoes | **γιουβέτσι** | *yoo·veh·tsee* |
| pheasant | **φασιανός** | *fah·siah·nohs* |
| pork | **χοιρινό** | *khee·ree·noh* |
| rabbit | **κουνέλι** | *koo·neh·lee* |
| sausage | **λουκάνικο** | *loo·kah·nee·koh* |
| skewered pork or lamb, cooked over charcoal | **κοντοσούβλι** | *koh·ndoh·soov·lee dohs* |

| spiced lamb and potatoes baked in parchment or in filo pastry | **αρνάκι εξοχικό** ahr·_nah_·kee eh·ksoh·khee·_koh_ |
| turkey | **γαλοπούλα** ghah·loh·_poo_·lah |
| veal | **μοσχάρι** mohs·_khah_·ree |
| veal/pork steak | **μπριζόλα μοσχαρίσια/χοιρινή** bree·_zoh_·lah mohs·khah·_ree_·siah/khee·ree·_nee_ |

## Vegetables & Staples

| artichokes | **αγκινάρες** ahn·gkee·_nah_·rehs |
| asparagus | **σπαράγγια** spah·_rahn_·giah |
| bay leaf | **δαφνόφυλλο** THah·_fnoh_·fee·loh |
| basil | **βασιλικός** vah·see·lee·_kohs_ |
| bread | **ψωμί** psoh·_mee_ |
| broad beans | **κουκί** koo·_kee_ |
| butter bean | **φασόλι γίγαντας** fah·_soh_·lee _yee_·ghahn·dahs |
| cabbage | **λάχανο** _lah_·khah·noh |
| carrot | **καρότο** kah·_roh_·toh |
| cauliflower | **κουνουπίδι** koo·noo·_pee_·THee |
| celery | **σέλερι** _seh_·leh·ree |
| cinnamon | **κανέλλα** kah·_neh_·lah |
| cucumber | **αγγούρι** ahn·_goo_·ree |
| dill | **άνηθος** _ah_·nee·thohs |
| eggplant [aubergine] | **μελιτζάνα** meh·lee·_jah_·nah |
| garlic | **σκόρδο** _skohr_·THoh |
| green bean | **φασολάκι** fah·soh·_lah_·kee |
| green peppers | **πιπεριές πράσινες** pee·pehr·_yehs_ _prah_·see·nehs |
| leek | **πράσο** _prah_·soh |
| mastic | **μαστίχα** mahs·_tee_·khah |
| mint | **δυόσμος** THee·_ohz_·mohs |

| mushroom | **μανιτάρι** *mah-nee-tah-ree* |
| okra | **μπάμια** *bah-miah* |
| onion | **κρεμμύδι** *kreh-mee-Thee* |
| oregano | **ρίγανη** *ree-ghah-nee* |
| parsley | **μαϊντανός** *mah-ee-dah-nohs* |
| pasta | **ζυμαρικά** *zee-mah-ree-kah* |
| peas | **αρακάς** *ah-rah-kahs* |
| peppers | **πιπεριές** *pee-pehr-yehs* |
| potato | **πατάτα** *pah-tah-tah* |
| red cabbage | **κόκκινο λάχανο** *koh-kee-noh lah-khah-noh* |
| rosemary | **δεντρολίβανο** *THehn-droh-lee-vah-noh* |
| sage | **φασκόμηλο** *fahs-koh-mee-loh* |
| spinach | **σπανάκι** *spah-nah-kee* |
| sugar | **ζάχαρη** *zah-khah-ree* |
| thyme | **θυμάρι** *thee-mah-ree* |
| toast | **ψωμί φρυγανιά** *psoh-mee free-ghah-niah* |
| tomato | **ντομάτα** *ndoh-mah-tah* |
| unleavened bread | **λαγάνα** *lah-ghah-nah* |
| zucchini [courgette] | **κολοκυθάκι** *koh-loh-kee-thah-kee* |

## Fruit

| apple | **μήλο** *mee-loh* |
| apricot | **βερύκοκο** *veh-ree-koh-koh* |
| banana | **μπανάνα** *bah-nah-nah* |
| cherry | **κεράσι** *keh-rah-see* |
| date | **χουρμάς** *khoor-mahs* |
| fig | **σύκο** *see-koh* |
| grape | **σταφύλι** *stah-fee-lee* |
| grapefruit | **γκρέιπφρουτ** *greh-eep-froot* |
| lemon | **λεμόνι** *leh-moh-nee* |
| melon | **πεπόνι** *peh-poh-nee* |

| orange | **πορτοκάλι** *pohr·toh·kah·lee* |
| peach | **ροδάκινο** *roh·THah·kee·noh* |
| pear | **αχλάδι** *akh·lah·THee* |
| plum | **δαμάσκηνο** *THah·mahs·kee·noh* |
| pineapple | **ανανάς** *ah·nah·nahs* |
| tangerine | **μανταρίνι** *mahn·dah·ree·nee* |
| watermelon | **καρπούζι** *kahr·poo·zee* |

## Cheese

| feta cheese | **φέτα** *feh·tah* |
| Gruyere cheese | **γραβιέρα** *ghrah·vieh·rah* |
| Kaseri, yellow cheese | **κασέρι** *kah·seh·ree* |
| cottage cheese | **τυρί κότατζ** *tee·ree koh·tahtz* |

## Dessert

| apple pie | **μηλόπιτα** *mee·loh·pee·tah* |
| baklava, flaky pastry with nut filling | **μπακλαβάς** *bah·klah·vahs* |
| candy [sweets] | **καραμέλα** *kah·rah·meh·lah* |
| caramel custard | **κρέμα καραμελέ** *kreh·mah kah·rah·meh·leh* |
| filo pastry filled with almonds, orange juice and cinnamon | **κοπεγχάγη** *koh·pehn·khah·ghee* |
| flaky pastry filled with custard and steeped in syrup | **γαλακτομπούρεκο** *ghah·lah·ktoh·boo·reh·koh* |
| fruit salad | **φρουτοσαλάτα** *froo·toh·sah·lah·tah* |
| halva, sweet sesame seed paste | **χαλβάς** *khahl·vahs* |
| ice cream | **παγωτό** *pah·ghoh·toh* |
| rice pudding | **ρυζόγαλο** *ree·zoh·ghah·loh* |

| shredded pastry roll filled with nuts and steeped in syrup | **καταΐφι** kah·tah·<u>ee</u>·fee |
| Turkish delight | **λουκούμι** loo·<u>koo</u>·mee |
| walnut cake | **καρυδόπιτα** kah·ree·<u>THoh</u>·pee·tah |

## Sauces & Condiments

| salt | **Αλάτι** ah·<u>lah</u>·tee |
| pepper | **Πιπέρι** pee·<u>peh</u>·ree |
| mustard | **Μουστάρδα** moo·<u>stahr</u>·THah |
| ketchup | **Κέτσαπ** <u>keh</u>·tsahp |

## At the Market

| Where are the trolleys/baskets? | **Πού είναι τα καροτσάκια/καλάθια;** poo <u>ee</u>·neh tah kah·roh·<u>tsah</u>·kiah/kah·<u>lah</u>·thiah |
| Where is/are…? | **Πού είναι…;** poo <u>ee</u>·neh… |
| I'd like some of that/those. | **Θα ήθελα μερικά από αυτά/εκείνα.** thah <u>ee</u>·theh·lah meh·ree·<u>kah</u> ah·<u>poh</u> ahf·<u>tah</u>/eh·<u>kee</u>·nah |
| Can I taste it? | **Μπορώ να το δοκιμάσω;** boh·<u>roh</u> nah toh THoh·kee·<u>mah</u>·soh |
| I'd like… | **Θα ήθελα…** thah <u>ee</u>·theh·lah… |
| a kilo/half-kilo of… | **ένα/μισό κιλό…** <u>eh</u>·nah/mee·<u>soh</u> kee·<u>loh</u>… |
| a liter/half-liter of… | **ένα/μισό λίτρο…** <u>eh</u>·nah/mee·<u>soh</u> <u>leet</u>·roh… |

Measurements in Europe are metric — and that applies to the weight of food too. If you tend to think in pounds and ounces, it's worth brushing up on what the metric equivalent is before you go shopping for fruit and veg in markets and supermarkets. Five hundred grams, or half a kilo, is a common quantity to order, and that converts to just over a pound (17.65 ounces, to be precise).

## YOU MAY HEAR...

**Μπορώ να σας βοηθήσω;** *boh∙roh nah sahs*    Can I help you?
*voh∙ee∙thee∙soh*

**Τι θα πάρετε;** *tee thah pah∙reh∙teh*    What would you like?

**Τίποτε άλλο;** *tee∙poh∙teh ah∙loh*    Anything else?

**Αυτά είναι...ευρώ.** *ahf∙tah ee∙neh...ehv∙roh*    That's...euros.

| | |
|---|---|
| a piece of... | **ένα κομμάτι...** *eh∙nah koh∙mah∙tee...* |
| a slice of... | **μια φέτα...** *miah feh∙tah...* |
| More/Less. | **Περισσότερο/Λιγότερο.** *peh∙ree∙soh∙teh∙roh/ lee∙ghoh∙teh∙roh* |
| How much? | **Πόσο;** *poh∙soh* |
| Where do I pay? | **Πού πληρώνω;** *poo plee∙roh∙noh* |
| A bag, please. | **Μια σακούλα, παρακαλώ.** *miah sah∙koo∙lah pah∙ rah∙kah∙loh* |
| I'm being helped. | **Εξυπηρετούμαι.** *eh∙ksee∙pee∙reh∙too∙meh* |

For Conversion Tables, see page 162.

For Meals & Cooking, see page 65.

Large-scale supermarkets can be found on the outskirts of most towns; smaller supermarkets are located near city centers. There are several large chains, including: **ΑΒ Βασιλόπουλος** *(ahl∙fah vee∙tah vah∙see∙loh∙poo∙lohs)*, **Dia** *(dee∙ah)*, **Champion** *(chahm∙pee∙ohn)*, **ΣΚΛΑΒΕΝΙΤΗΣ** *(sklah∙veh∙nee∙tees)* and **Spar** *(spahr)*.

## YOU MAY SEE...

| | |
|---|---|
| **ΑΝΑΛΩΣΗ ΚΑΤΑ ΠΡΟΤΙΜΗΣΗ ΠΡΙΝ ΑΠΟ...** *ah·nah·loh·see kah·tah proh·tee·mee·see preen ah·poh* | best before... |
| **ΘΕΡΜΙΔΕΣ** *thehr·mee·THehs* | calories |
| **ΧΩΡΙΣ ΛΙΠΑΡΑ** *khoh·rees lee·pah·rah* | fat free |
| **ΔΙΑΤΗΡΕΙΤΑΙ ΣΤΟ ΨΥΓΕΙΟ** *THee·ah·tee·ree·teh stoh psee·yee·oh* | keep refrigerated |
| **ΜΠΟΡΕΙ ΝΑ ΠΕΡΙΕΧΕΙ ΙΧΝΗ ΑΠΟ...** *boh·ree nah peh·ree·eh·khee eekh·nee ah·poh...* | may contain traces of... |
| **για φούρνο μικροκυμάτων** *yah foo·rnoh mee·kroh·kee·mah·tohn* | microwaveable |
| **πώληση μέχρι...** *poh·lee·see meh·khree* | sell by... |
| **κατάλληλο για χορτοφάγους** *kah·tah·lee·loh yah khoh·rtoh·fah·ghoos* | suitable for vegetarians |

## In the Kitchen

| | | |
|---|---|---|
| bottle opener | **τιρμπουσόν** | teer·mboo·_sohn_ |
| bowls | **τα μπωλ** | tah bohl |
| can opener | **ανοιχτήρι** | ah·neekh·_tee_·ree |
| corkscrew | **τιρμπουσόν** | teer·boo·_sohn_ |
| cups | **τα φλυτζάνια** | tah flee·_jah_·niah |
| forks | **τα πηρούνια** | tah pee·_roo_·niah |
| frying pan | **τηγάνι** | tee·_ghah_·nee |
| glasses | **τα ποτήρια** | tah poh·_teer_·yah |
| knives | **τα μαχαίρια** | tah mah·_khehr_·yah |
| measuring cup/ spoon | **μεζούρα φλυτζάνι/κουτάλι** | meh·_zoo_·rah flee·_jah_·nee/koo·_tah_·lee |
| napkin | **χαρτοπετσέτα** | khahr·toh·peh·_tseh_·tah |
| plates | **τα πιάτα** | tah _piah_·tah |
| pot | **κανάτα** | kah·_nah_·tah |
| saucepan | **κατσαρόλα** | kah·tsah·_roh_·lah |
| spatula | **σπάτουλα** | _spah_·too·lah |
| spoons | **κουτάλια** | koo·_tah_·liah |

# Drinks

## ESSENTIAL

| | |
|---|---|
| May I see the wine list/drinks menu? | **Μπορώ να δω τον κατάλογο με τα κρασιά/ποτά;** *boh-roh nah THoh tohn kah-tah-loh-ghoh meh tah krah-siah/poh-tah* |
| What do you recommend? | **Τι συστήνετε;** *tee see-stee-neh-the* |
| I'd like a bottle/glass of red/white wine. | **Θα ήθελα ένα μπουκάλι/ποτήρι κόκκινο/λευκό κρασί.** *thah ee-theh-lah eh-nah boo-kah-lee/poh-tee-ree koh-kee-noh/lehf-koh krah-see* |
| The house wine, please. | **Το κρασί του καταστήματος, παρακαλώ.** *toh krah-see too kah-tah-stee-mah-tohs pah-rah-kah-loh* |
| Another bottle/glass, please. | **Άλλο ένα μπουκάλι/ποτήρι, παρακαλώ.** *ah-loh eh-nah boo-kah-lee/poh-tee-ree pah-rah-kah-loh* |
| I'd like a local beer. | **Θα ήθελα μια τοπική μπύρα.** *thah ee-theh-lah miah toh-pee-kee bee-rah* |
| Let me buy you a drink. | **Να σασκεράσω ένα ποτό.** *nah sahs keh-rah-soh eh-nah poh-toh* |
| Cheers! | **Στην υγειά σας!** *steen ee-ghiah sahs* |
| A coffee/tea, please. | **Έναν καφέ/Ένα τσάι, παρακαλώ.** *eh-nahn kah-feh/eh-nah tsah-ee pah-rah-kah-loh* |
| Black. | **Σκέτος.** *skeh-tohs* |
| With... | **Με...** *meh...* |
| milk | **γάλα** *ghah-lah* |
| sugar | **ζάχαρη** *zah-khah-ree* |
| artificial sweetener | **ζαχαρίνη** *zah-khah-ree-nee* |
| ..., please. | **..., παρακαλώ.** *...pah-rah-kah-loh* |
| A juice | **Ένα χυμό** *eh-nah khee-moh* |
| A soda | **Μία σόδα** *mee-ah soh-THah* |

| A sparkling water | **Ενα ανθρακούχο νερό** _eh_·nah ahn·thrah·_koo_·khoh neh·_roh_ |
| A still water | **Ενα νερό χωρίς ανθρακικό** _eh_·nah neh·_roh_ khoh·_rees_ ahn·thrah·kee·_koh_ |
| Is the tap water safe to drink? | **Είναι το νερό βρύσης πόσιμο;** _ee_·neh toh neh·_roh_ _vree_· sees _poh_·see·moh |

## Non-alcoholic Drinks

| . . . coffee | **έναν καφέ. . .** _eh_·nahn kah·_feh_. . . |
| instant | **ένα Νεσκαφέ** _eh_·nah nehs·kah·_feh_ |
| Greek | **ελληνικό** eh·lee·nee·_koh_ |
| with cream/milk | **με κρέμα/γάλα** meh _kreh_·mah/_ghah_·lah |
| . . . juice | **χυμός. . .** khee·_mohs_. . . |
| apple | **μήλο** _mee_·loh |
| grapefruit | **γκρέιπφρουτ** _greh_·eep·froot |
| orange | **πορτοκάλι** poh·rtoh·_kah_·lee |
| iced tea | **παγωμένο τσάι** pah·ghoh·_meh_·noh tsah·ee |
| tea with milk/lemon | **τσάι με γάλα/λεμόνι** _tsah_·ee meh _ghah_·lah/ leh·_moh_·nee |
| mineral water | **μεταλλικό νερό** meh·tah·lee·_koh_ neh·_roh_ |
| hot chocolate | **ζεστή σοκολάτα** zeh·_stee_ soh·koh·_lah_·tah |

The most popular drinks in the summer are **φραπέ** (frah·_peh_), iced instant coffee shaken to produce a thick coffee froth, with or without milk and sugar, and **φρέντο** (_frehd_·doh), iced espresso with or without milk, found at most coffee shops and bars. Freshly squeezed juices are also widely consumed. Tap water is drinkable almost everywhere, but if you prefer you can get **εμφιαλωμένο νερό** (ehm·fee·ah·loh·_meh_·noh neh·_roh_), bottled water.

## YOU MAY HEAR...

**Θέλετε κάτι να πιείτε;** _theh·leh·teh kah·tee_   Can I get you a drink?
_nah pee·ee·teh_

**Με γάλα/ζάχαρη;** _meh ghah·lah/zah·khah·ree_   With milk/sugar?

**Νερό ανθρακούχο/χωρίς ανθρακικό;**   Sparkling/Still
_neh·roh ahn·thrah·koo·khoh/khoh·rees_   water?
_ahn·thrah·kee·koh_

## Aperitifs, Cocktails & Liqueurs

| | | |
|---|---|---|
| Greek brandy | **Μεταξά** _meh·tah·ksah_ | |
| kumquat liqueur (Corfu) | **κουμ-κουάτ** _koom·koo·aht_ | |
| straight [neat] | **σκέτο** _skeh·toh_ | |
| on the rocks | **με πάγο** _meh pah·ghoh_ | |
| ouzo | **ούζο** _oo·zoh_ | |

## Beer

| | |
|---|---|
| beer | **μπύρα** _bee·rah_ |
| bottled | **εμφιαλωμένη** _ehm·fee·ah·loh·meh·nee_ |
| draft | **βαρελίσια** _vah·reh·lee·siah_ |
| light/dark | **ξανθή/μαύρη** _ksahn·thee/mahv·ree_ |
| local/imported | **τοπικό/εισαγόμενο** _toh·pee·koh/ee·sah·ghoh·meh·noh_ |

## Wine

| | |
|---|---|
| blush [rosé] | **ροζέ** _roh·zeh_ |
| chilled | **παγωμένο** _pah·ghoh·meh·noh_ |
| dry | **ξηρό** _ksee·roh_ |
| red | **μπουκάλι κόκκινο** _boo·kah·lee koh·kee·noh_ |
| sweet | **γλυκό** _ghlee·koh_ |

A typical Greek wine that takes some getting used to is **ρετσίνα** (reh·_tsee_·nah), a white wine containing pine resin.

Wine is usually produced and consumed locally — a restaurant owner will often bring you a carafe of his or her very own wine if you ask for **κρασί βαρελίσιο** (krah·_see_ vah·reh·_lee_·sioh), the house wine.

| white | **λευκό** _lehf_·koh |
| wine | **κρασί** krah·_see_ |

## On the Menu

| anchovy | **αντσούγια** ahn·_joo_·yah |
| apple | **μήλο** _mee_·loh |
| apple pie | **μηλόπιτα** mee·_loh_·pee·tah |
| apricot | **βερίκοκο** veh·_ree_·koh·koh |
| artichoke | **αγκινάρα** ahn·gkee·_nah_·rah |
| artificial sweetener | **ζαχαρίνη** zah·khah·_ree_·nee |
| asparagus | **σπαράγγι** spah·_rahn_·gee |
| bacon | **μπέικον** _beh_·ee·kohn |
| baklava, flaky pastry with nut filling | **μπακλαβάς** bah·klah·_vahs_ |
| banana | **μπανάνα** bah·_nah_·nah |
| basil | **βασιλικός** vah·see·lee·_kohs_ |
| bay leaf | **δαφνόφυλλο** THah·_fnoh_·fee·loh |
| bean soup with tomatoes and parsley | **φασολάδα** fah·soh·_lah_·THah |

| beef | **βοδινό** voh·THee·<u>noh</u> |
| beef or veal stewed with tomatoes and eggplant [aubergine] | **μελιτζανάτο** meh·lee·jah·<u>nah</u>·toh |
| beer | **μπίρα** <u>bee</u>·rah |
| brains | **μυαλό** miah·<u>loh</u> |
| bread | **ψωμί** psoh·<u>mee</u> |
| bread roll | **ψωμάκι** psoh·<u>mah</u>·kee |
| broad bean | **κουκί** koo·<u>kee</u> |
| butter | **βούτυρο** <u>voo</u>·tee·roh |
| butter bean | **φασόλι γίγαντας** fah·<u>soh</u>·lee <u>yee</u>·ghahn·dahs |
| cabbage | **λάχανο** <u>lah</u>·khah·noh |
| candy [sweets] | **καραμέλα** kah·rah·<u>meh</u>·lah |
| caramel custard | **κρέμα καραμελέ** <u>kreh</u>·mah kah·rah·meh·<u>leh</u> |
| carrot | **καρότο** kah·<u>roh</u>·toh |
| cauliflower | **κουνουπίδι** koo·noo·<u>pee</u>·THee |
| celery | **σέλερι** <u>seh</u>·leh·ree |
| cereal (cold/hot) | **δημητριακά με (ζεστό/κρύο) γάλα** THee·meet·ree·ah·<u>kah</u> meh (zehs·<u>toh</u>/<u>kree</u>·oh) ghah·lah |
| cheese | **τυρί** tee·<u>ree</u> |
| cheese omelet | **ομελέττα με τυρί** oh·meh·<u>leh</u>·tah meh tee·<u>ree</u> |
| cherry | **κεράσι** keh·<u>rah</u>·see |
| chicken | **κοτόπουλο** koh·<u>toh</u>·poo·loh |
| chicken soup | **κοτόσουπα** koh·<u>toh</u>·soo·pah |
| chickpea soup | **ρεβύθια σούπα** reh·<u>vee</u>·thiah <u>soo</u>·pah |
| chilled | **παγωμένο** pah·ghoh·<u>meh</u>·noh |
| cinnamon | **κανέλλα** kah·<u>neh</u>·lah |
| club soda | **σόδα** <u>soh</u>·THah |
| coffee | **καφέ** kah·<u>fehs</u> |
| cold cuts [charcuterie] | **αλλαντικά** ah·lah·ndee·<u>kah</u> |
| cold meat | **κρύο κρέας** <u>kree</u>·oh <u>kreh</u>·ahs |

| | | |
|---|---|---|
| cottage cheese | **τυρί κότατζ** | tee·ree koh·tahtz |
| crab | **καβούρι** | kah·voo·ree |
| cracked wheat soup | **τραχανάς** | trah·khah·nahs |
| cream | **κρέμα** | kreh·mah |
| cucumber | **αγγούρι** | ahn·goo·ree |
| cutlet | **κοτολέτα** | koh·toh·leh·tah |
| cuttlefish | **σουπιά** | soo·piah |
| date | **χουρμάς** | khoor·mahs |
| dill | **άνηθος** | ah·nee·thohs |
| draft | **βαρελίσια** | vah·reh·lee·siah |
| duck | **πάπια** | pah·piah |
| eel | **χέλι** | kheh·lee |
| egg | **αυγό** | ahv·ghoh |
| eggplant [aubergine] | **μελιτζάνα** | meh·lee·jah·nah |
| fig | **σύκο** | see·koh |
| fillet | **φιλέτο** | fee·leh·toh |
| filo pastry filled with almonds, orange juice and cinnamon | **κοπεγχάγη** | koh·pehn·khah·ghee |
| filo pastry filled with custard and steeped in syrup | **γαλακτομπούρεκο** | ghah·lah·ktoh·boo·reh·koh |
| fish | **ψάρι** | psah·ree |
| fish soup thickened with egg and lemon | **ψαρόσουπα αυγολέμονο** | psah·roh·soo·pah ahv·ghoh·leh·moh·noh |
| fish stew with tomatoes | **κακαβιά** | kah·kahv·yah |
| fresh cod | **μπακαλιάρος** | bah·kah·liah·rohs |
| fried baby squid | **καλαμαράκια** | kah·lah·mah·rah·kiah |
| fried meatballs | **κεφτεδάκια** | kef·teh·THah·kiah |
| fried whitebait | **μαρίδα τηγανητή** | mah·ree·THah tee·ghah·nee·tee |

| | |
|---|---|
| fruit | **φρούτο** _froo_·toh |
| fruit juice | **χυμός φρούτων** khee·_mohs_ _froo_·tohn |
| fruit salad | **φρουτοσαλάτα** froo·toh·sah·_lah_·tah |
| garlic | **σκόρδο** _skohr_·THoh |
| goat | **κατσικάκι** kah·tsee·_kah_·kee |
| goose | **χήνα** _khee_·nah |
| granola [muesli] | **μούσλι** _moos_·lee |
| grape | **σταφύλι** stah·_fee_·lee |
| grapefruit | **γκρέιπφρουτ** greh·eep·froot |
| Greek brandy | **Μεταξά** meh·tah·_ksah_ |
| green bean | **φασολάκι** fah·soh·_lah_·kee |
| green peppers | **πιπεριές πράσινες** pee·pehr·_yehs_ _prah_·see·nehs |
| grouper | **σφυρίδα** sfee·_ree_·THah |
| halva, sweet sesame seed paste | **χαλβάς** khahl·_vahs_ |
| ham | **ζαμπόν** zahm·_bohn_ |
| ham omelet | **ομελέττα με ζαμπόν** oh·meh·_leh_·tah meh zahm·_bohr_. |
| herring (smoked) | **ρέγγα (καπνιστή)** _rehn_·gah (kahp·nees·_tee_) |
| honey | **μέλι** _meh_·lee |
| ice cream | **παγωτό** pah·ghoh·_toh_ |
| iced tea | **παγωμένο τσάι** pah·ghoh·_meh_·noh tsah·ee |
| instant coffee | **Νεσκαφέ** nehs·kah·_feh_ |
| juice | **χυμός** khee·_mohs_ |
| kidney | **νεφρό** neh·_froh_ |
| kumquat liqueur (Corfu) | **κουμ-κουάτ** koom·koo·_aht_ |
| lamb | **αρνί** ahr·_nee_ |
| layers of eggplant [aubergine], meat and white sauce | **μουσακάς** moo·sah·_kahs_ |
| leek | **πράσο** _prah_·soh |

| lemon | **λεμόνι** *leh·moh·nee* |
| lentil soup | **φακές σούπα** *fah·kehs soo·pah* |
| liqueur | **λικέρ** *lee·kehr* |
| liver | **συκώτι** *see·koh·tee* |
| lobster | **αστακός** *ahs·tah·kohs* |
| mackerel | **σκουμπρί** *skoo·mbree* |
| marinated mullet, sole or mackerel | **ψάρι μαρινάτο** *psah·ree mah·ree·nah·toh* |
| mastic | **μαστίχα** *mahs·tee·khah* |
| mayonnaise | **μαγιονέζα** *mah·yoh·neh·zah* |
| meat | **κρέας** *kreh·ahs* |
| meat soup | **κρεατόσουπα** *kreh·ah·toh·soo·pah* |
| meat with orzo pasta baked with tomatoes | **γιουβέτσι** *yoo·veh·tsee* |
| melon | **πεπόνι** *peh·poh·nee* |
| milk | **γάλα** *ghah·lah* |
| mint | **δυόσμος** *THee·ohz·mohs* |
| muffin | **μάφιν** *mah·feen* |
| mullet | **κέφαλος** *keh·fah·lohs* |
| mushroom | **μανιτάρι** *mah·nee·tah·ree* |
| mussels | **μύδι** *mee·THee* |

| nuts | **ξηροί καρποί** ksee-_ree_ kah-_rpee_ |
| oatmeal | **κουάκερ** koo-_ah_-kehr |
| octopus | **χταπόδι** khtah-_poh_-THee |
| okra | **μπάμια** _bah_-miah |
| olive (stuffed) | **ελιά (γεμιστή)** eh-_liah_ (yeh-mees-_tee_) |
| olive oil | **ελαιόλαδο** eh-leh-_oh_-lah-THoh |
| omelet | **ομελέτα** oh-meh-_leh_-tah |
| on the rocks | **με πάγο** meh _pah_-ghoh |
| onion | **κρεμμύδι** kreh-_mee_-THee |
| orange | **πορτοκάλι** poh-rtoh-_kah_-lee |
| oregano | **ρίγανη** _ree_-ghah-nee |
| ouzo | **ούζο** _oo_-zoh |
| oyster | **στρείδι** _stree_-THee |
| parsley | **μαϊντανός** mah-ee-dah-_nohs_ |
| pasta | **ζυμαρικά** zee-mah-ree-_kah_ |
| paté | **πατέ** pah-_teh_ |
| peach | **ροδάκινο** roh-_THah_-kee-noh |
| pear | **αχλάδι** akh-_lah_-THee |
| peas | **αρακάς** ah-rah-_kahs_ |
| pheasant | **φασιανός** fah-siah-_nohs_ |
| pineapple | **ανανάς** ah-nah-_nahs_ |
| plum | **δαμάσκηνο** THah-_mahs_-kee-noh |
| poached | **ποσέ** poh-_seh_ |
| pork | **χοιρινό** khee-ree-_noh_ |
| porksteak | **μπριζόλα χοιρινή** bree-_zoh_-lah khee-ree-_nee_ |
| potato | **πατάτα** pah-_tah_-tah |
| rabbit | **κουνέλι** koo-_neh_-lee |
| red cabbage | **κόκκινο λάχανο** _koh_-kee-noh _lah_-khah-noh |
| red mullet | **μπαρμπούνι** bahr-_boo_-nee |
| red wine | **κόκκινο κρασί** _koh_-kee-noh _krah_-see |
| rice | **ρύζι** _ree_-zee |

| | | |
|---|---|---|
| rice pudding | **ρυζόγαλο** | *ree·zoh·ghah·loh* |
| roast | **ψητό** | *psee·toh* |
| roll | **ψωμάκι** | *psoh·mah·kee* |
| rosemary | **δεντρολίβανο** | *THehn·droh·lee·vah·noh* |
| sage | **φασκόμηλο** | *fahs·koh·mee·loh* |
| salad | **σαλάτα** | *sah·lah·tah* |
| salted cod | **μπακαλιάρος παστός** | *bah·kah·liah·rohs pahs·tohs* |
| sardine | **σαρδέλα** | *sahr·THeh·lah* |
| sauce | **σάλτσα** | *sah·ltsah* |
| sausage | **λουκάνικο** | *loo·kah·nee·koh* |
| scrambled eggs | **ομελέτα** | *oh·meh·leh·tah* |
| shellfish | **όστρακα** | *oh·strah·kah* |
| shredded pastry roll filled with nuts and steeped in syrup | **καταΐφι** | *kah·tah·ee·fee* |
| shrimp [prawn] | **γαρίδα** | *ghah·ree·THah* |
| skewered pork or lamb cooked over charcoal | **κοντοσούβλι** | *koh·ndoh·soov·lee* |
| snack | **σνακ** | *snahk* |
| soda | **αναψυκτικό** | *ah·nah·psee·ktee·koh* |
| soft-boiled eggs | **μελάτα αυγά** | *meh·lah·tah ahv·gah* |
| sole (fish) | **γλώσσα** | *ghloh·sah* |
| soup | **σούπα** | *soo·pah* |
| soup with rice, eggs and lemon juice | **σούπα αυγολέμονο** | *soo·pah ahv·ghoh·leh·moh·noh* |
| spiced lamb and potatoes baked in parchment or in filo pastry | **αρνάκι εξοχικό** | *ahr·nah·kee eh·ksoh·khee·koh* |
| spices | **μπαχαρικά** | *bah·khah·ree·kah* |

| | | |
|---|---|---|
| spinach | **σπανάκι** | spah·_nah_·kee |
| spinach and feta in pastry dough | **σπανακόπιττα** | spah·nah·_koh_·pee·tah |
| stuffed grape leaves | **ντολμαδάκι** | dohl·mah·_THah_·kee |
| squid | **καλαμάρι** | kah·lah·_mah_·ree |
| steak | **μπριζόλα** | bree·_zoh_·lah |
| sugar | **ζάχαρη** | _zah_·khah·ree |
| swordfish | **ξιφίας** | ksee·_fee_·ahs |
| syrup | **σιρόπι** | see·_roh_·pee |
| tahini (sesame paste) soup | **ταχινόσουπα** | tah·khee·_noh_·soo·pah |
| tangerine | **μανταρίνι** | mahn·dah·_ree_·nee |
| taramosalata, fish roe dip | **ταραμοσαλάτα** | tah·rah·moh·sah·_lah_·tah |
| tea | **τσάι** | _tsah_·ee |
| thyme | **θυμάρι** | thee·_mah_·ree |
| toast | **ψωμί φρυγανιά** | psoh·_mee_ free·ghah·_niah_ |
| tomato | **ντομάτα** | ndoh·_mah_·tah |
| tomato soup | **τοματόσουπα** | toh·mah·_toh_·soo·pah |
| tongue (meat) | **γλώσσα** | _ghloh_·sah |
| tonic water | **τόνικ** | _toh_·neek |

| | | |
|---|---|---|
| tripe soup | **πατσάς** | *pah·tsahs* |
| tuna | **τόννος** | *toh·nohs* |
| turkey | **γαλοπούλα** | *ghah·loh·poo·lah* |
| Turkish delight | **λουκούμι** | *loo·koo·mee* |
| unleavened bread | **λαγάνα** | *lah·ghah·nah* |
| veal | **μοσχάρι** | *mohs·khah·ree* |
| veal steak | **μπριζόλα μοσχαρίσια** | *bree·zoh·lah mohs·khah·ree·siah* |
| vegetable | **λαχανικό** | *lah·khah·nee·koh* |
| vegetable soup | **χορτόσουπα** | *khohr·toh·soo·pah* |
| walnut cake | **καρυδόπιτα** | *kah·ree·THoh·pee·tah* |
| water | **νερό** | *neh·roh* |
| watermelon | **καρπούζι** | *kahr·poo·zee* |
| wheat | **σιτάρι** | *see·tah·ree* |
| wine | **κρασί** | *krah·see* |
| yogurt (with honey) | **γιαούρτι (με μέλι)** | *yah·oor·tee (meh meh·lee)* |
| yogurt, garlic and cucumber dip | **τζατζίκι** | *jah·jee·kee* |
| zucchini [courgette] | **κολοκυθάκι** | *koh·loh·kee·thah·kee* |

# People

# ESSENTIAL

| | |
|---|---|
| Hello. | **Χαίρετε.** *kheh•reh•teh* |
| How are you? | **Πώς είστε;** *pohs ee•steh* |
| Fine, thanks. And you? | **Καλά, ευχαριστώ. Εσείς;** *kah•lah ehf•khah•ree•stoh eh•sees* |
| Excuse me! | **Συγγνώμη!** *seegh•noh•mee* |
| Do you speak English? | **Μιλάτε Αγγλικά;** *mee•lah•the ahng•lee•kah* |
| What's your name? | **Πώς λέγεστε;** *pohs leh•yeh•steh* |
| My name is... | **Λέγομαι...** *leh•ghoh•meh...* |
| Nice to meet you. | **Χαίρω πολύ.** *kheh•roh poh•lee* |
| Where are you from? | **Από πού είστε;** *ah•poh poo ee•steh* |
| I'm from the U.S./U.K. | **Είμαι από τις Ηνωμένες Πολιτείες/το Ηνωμένο Βασίλειο.** *ee•meh ah•poh tees ee•noh•meh•nehs poh•lee•tee•ehs/toh ee•noh•meh•noh vah•see•lee•oh* |
| What do you do? | **Τι δουλειά κάνετε;** *tee THoo•liah kah•neh•teh* |
| I work for... | **Δουλεύω για...** *THoo•leh•voh yah...* |
| I'm a student. | **Είμαι φοιτητής m /φοιτήτρια f.** *ee•meh fee•tee•tees/ fee•tee•tree•ah* |
| I'm retired. | **Είμαι συνταξιούχος.** *ee•meh seen•dah•ksee•oo•khohs* |
| Do you like...? | **Σου αρέσει...;** *soo ah•reh•see...* |
| Goodbye. | **Γεια σας.** *yah sahs* |
| See you later. | **Τα λέμε αργότερα.** *tah leh•meh ahr•ghoh•teh•rah* |

In Greek, Mrs. is **κυρία** (kee•_ree_•ah), Mr. is **κύριος** (kee•_ree_•ohs) and Miss is **δεσποινίς** (THehs•pee•_nees_).
Greek has a formal and an informal form of 'you': **γεια σας** (yah sahs) and **γεια σου** (yah soo), respectively. The informal is used between friends or when addressing children. Use the formal **γεια σας** unless prompted to do otherwise.

## Language Difficulties

| | |
|---|---|
| Do you speak English? | **Μιλάτε Αγγλικά;** mee•_lah_•teh ahng•lee•_kah_ |
| Does anyone here speak English? | **Μιλάει κανείς εδώ Αγγλικά;** mee•_lah_•ee kah•_nees_ eh•_THoh_ ahng•lee•_kah_ |
| I don't speak Greek. | **Δεν μιλώ Ελληνικά.** THehn mee•_loh_ eh•lee•nee•_kah_ |
| Could you speak more slowly? | **Μπορείτε να μιλάτε πιο αργά;** boh•_ree_•the nah mee•_lah_•teh pioh ahr•_ghah_ |
| Could you repeat that? | **Μπορείτε να το επαναλάβετε;** boh•_ree_•the nah toh eh•pah•nah•_lah_•veh•teh |
| Excuse me! | **Συγγνώμη!** seegh•_noh_•mee |
| What was that? | **Τι είπατε;** tee _ee_•pah•teh |
| Can you spell it? | **Μπορείς να το συλλαβίσεις;** boh•_rees_ nah toh see•lah•_vee_•sees |
| Can you write it down, please? | **Μου το γράφετε παρακαλώ;** moo toh _ghrah_•feh•teh pah•rah•kah•_loh_ |
| Can you translate this for me? | **Μπορείτε να μου μεταφράσετε αυτό;** boh•_ree_•teh nah moo meh•tahf•_rah_•seh•teh ahf•_toh_ |
| What does this/that mean? | **Τι σημαίνει αυτό/εκείνο;** tee see•_meh_•nee ahf•_toh_/eh•_kee_•noh |
| I (don't) understand | **(Δεν) Καταλαβαίνω.** (THehn) kah•tah•lah•_veh_•noh |
| Do you understand? | **Καταλαβαίνετε;** kah•tah•lah•_veh_•neh•teh |

## YOU MAY HEAR...

**Μιλώ (μόνο) λίγα Αγγλικά.**
*mee·loh (moh·noh) lee·ghah ahng·lee·kah*

**Δεν μιλώ Αγγλικά.**
*THehn mee·loh ahng·lee·kah*

I speak (only) a little English.

I don't speak English.

## Making Friends

| | |
|---|---|
| Hello. | **Χαίρετε.** *kheh·reh·teh* |
| Good morning. | **Καλημέρα.** *kah·lee·meh·rah* |
| Good afternoon/ evening. | **Καλησπέρα.** *kah·lee·speh·rah* |
| Good night. | **Καληνύχτα.** *kah·lee·neekh·tah* |
| My name is... | **Λέγομαι...** *leh·ghoh·meh...* |
| What's your name? | **Πώς λέγεστε;** *pohs leh·yehs·teh* |
| I'd like to introduce you to... | **Θα ήθελα να σας συστήσω τον** *m* **/την** *f* **...** *thah ee·theh·lah nah sahs sees·tee·soh tohn/teen...* |
| Pleased to meet you. | **Χαίρω πολύ.** *kheh·roh poh·lee* |
| How are you? | **Πώς είστε;** *pohs ees·teh* |
| Fine, thanks. | **Καλά, ευχαριστώ.** *kah·lah ehf·khah·rees·toh* |
| And you? | **Εσείς;** *eh·sees* |

Greeks shake hands when they meet for the first time and on subsequent meetings. With close friends, it is customary to exchange kisses on both cheeks when meeting and parting. It is polite to address people you meet for the first time by their surname until prompted to use their first name.

## Travel Talk

| | | |
|---|---|---|
| I'm here... | **Είμαι εδώ...** | _ee·meh eh·THoh..._ |
| on business | **για δουλειά** | _yah THoo·lee·ah_ |
| vacation [holiday] | **για διακοπές** | _yah THiah·koh·pehs_ |
| studying | **για σπουδές** | _yah spoo·THehs_ |
| I'm staying here for... | **Μένω εδώ για...** | _meh·noh eh·THoh yah..._ |
| I've been here... | **Είμαι εδώ...** | _ee·meh eh·THoh..._ |
| a day | **μια ημέρα** | _miah meh·rah_ |
| a week | **μια εβδομάδα** | _miah ehv·THoh·mah·THah_ |
| a month | **ένα μήνα** | _eh·nah mee·nah_ |
| Where are you from? | **Από πού είστε;** | _ah·poh poo ee·steh_ |
| I'm from... | **Είμαι από...** | _ee·meh ah·poh..._ |

For Numbers, see page 156.

## Personal

| | | |
|---|---|---|
| Who are you with? | **Με ποιον/ποιαν είστε;** | _meh piohn/piahn ee·steh_ |
| I'm on my own. | **Είμαι μόνος _m_/μόνη _f_ μου.** | _ee·meh moh·nohs/ moh·nee moo_ |
| I'm with... | **Είμαι με...** | _ee·meh meh..._ |
| my husband/wife | **τον σύζυγο/την σύζυγό μου** | _tohn see·zee·ghoh/teen see·zee·ghoh moo_ |

| my boyfriend/ girlfriend | **τον φίλο/την κοπέλα μου** tohn fee·loh/teen koh·peh·lah moo |
| a friend | **ένα φίλο** m **/μια φίλη** f eh·nah fee·loh/miah fee·lee |
| a colleague | **έναν συνάδελφο** eh·nahn see·nah·THehl·foh |
| When's your birthday? | **Πότε είναι τα γενέθλιά σου;** poh·teh ee·neh tah gheh·nehth·lee·ah soo |
| How old are you? | **Πόσο χρονών είσαι;** poh·soh khroh·nohn ee·seh |
| I'm... | **Είμαι...** ee·meh... |
| Are you married? | **Είστε παντρεμένος;** ee·steh pah·dreh·meh·nohs |
| I'm... | **Είμαι...** ee·meh... |
| single | **ελεύθερος** m **/ελεύθερη** f eh·lehf·theh·rohs/ eh·lehf·theh·ree |
| in a relationship | **δεσμευμένος** m **/δεσμευμένη** f THehs·mehv·meh·nohs/THehs·mehv·meh·nee |
| engaged | **αρραβωνιασμένος** ah·rah·voh·niah·zmeh·nohs |
| married | **παντρεμένος** m **/παντρεμένη** f pahn·dreh·meh·nohs m /pahn·dreh·meh·nee f |
| divorced | **διαζευγμένος** m **/διαζευγμένη** f THee·ah·zehv·ghmeh·nohs/THee·ah·zehv·ghmeh·ee |
| separated | **σε διάσταση** seh THee·ah·stah·see |
| I'm widowed. | **Είμαι χήρος** m **/χήρα** f . ee·meh khee·rohs/khee·rah |
| Do you have children/ grandchildren? | **Έχετε παιδιά/εγγόνια;** eh·kheh·the peh·THyah/ eh·goh·niah |

For Numbers, see page 156.

## Work & School

| What do you do? | **Τι δουλειά κάνετε;** tee THoo·liah kah·neh·teh |
| What are you studying? | **Τι σπουδάζετε;** tee spoo·THah·zeh·teh |
| I'm studying... | **Σπουδάζω...** spoo·THah·zoh... |
| I... | **Εγώ...** Eh·ghoh |

| | | |
|---|---|---|
| work full-/part-time | **δουλεύω με πλήρη/μερική απασχόληση** | THoo-*lehv*-oh meh *plee*-ree/meh-ree-*kee* ah-pah-*skhoh*-lee-see |
| am unemployed | **δεν δουλεύω** | THehn THoo-*lehv*-oh |
| work at home | **δουλεύω στο σπίτι** | THoo-*lehv*-oh stoh *spee*-tee |
| Who do you work for...? | **Για ποιον δουλεύετε...;** | yah piohn THoo-*leh*-veh-teh.. |
| I work for... | **Δουλεύω για...** | THoo-*leh*-voh yah... |
| Here's my business card. | **Ορίστε η κάρτα μου.** | oh-*ree*-steh ee *kahr*-tah moo |

## Weather

| | | |
|---|---|---|
| What's the weather forecast for tomorrow? | **Τι λέει η πρόβλεψη του καιρού για αύριο;** | tee *leh*-ee ee *proh*-vleh-psee too keh-*roo* yah *ah*-vree-oh |
| What beautiful/ terrible weather! | **Τι ωραίος/απαίσιος καιρός!** | tee oh-*reh*-ohs/ ah-*peh*-see-ohs keh-*rohs* |
| It's cool/warm. | **Έχει δροσιά/ζέστη.** | *eh*-khee roh-*siah*/*zeh*-stee |
| It's cold/hot. | **Κάνει κρύο/ζέστη.** | *kah*-nee *kree*-oh/*zeh*-stee |
| It's rainy/sunny. | **Ο καιρός είναι βροχερός/ηλιόλουστος.** | oh keh-*rohs* ee-neh vroh-kheh-*rohs*/ee-*lioh*-loo-stohs |
| It's snowy/icy. | **Έχει παγωνιά.** | *eh*-khee pah-ghoh-*niah* |
| Do I need a jacket/ an umbrella? | **Να πάρω ζακέτα/ομπρέλα;** | nah *pah*-roh zah-*keh*-tah/ ohm-*breh*-lah |

## ESSENTIAL

| | |
|---|---|
| Would you like to go out for a drink/dinner? | **Θέλετε να βγούμε για ποτό/φαγητό;** theh·leh·teh nah vghoo·meh yah poh·toh/fah·yee·toh |
| What are your plans for tonight/tomorrow? | **Ποια είναι τα σχέδιά σας για απόψε/αύριο;** piah ee·neh tah skheh·THee·ah sahs yah ah·poh·pseh/ahv·ree·oh |
| Can I have your number? | **Μπορώ να έχω τον αριθμό τηλεφώνου σας;** boh·roh nah eh·khoh tohn ah·reeth·moh tee·leh·foh·noo sahs |
| May we join you? | **Να έρθουμε μαζί σας;** nah ehr·thoo·meh mah·zee sahs |
| Let me buy you a drink. | **Να σε κεράσω ένα ποτό.** nah seh keh·rah·soh eh·nah poh·toh |
| I like you. | **Μου αρέσεις.** moo ah·reh·sees |
| I love you. | **Σ' αγαπώ.** sah·ghah·poh |

## The Dating Game

| | |
|---|---|
| Would you like to go out for coffee? | **Θα θέλατε να βγούμε για καφέ;** thah theh·lah·teh nah vghoo·meh yah kah·feh |
| Would you like to go out for a drink/to dinner? | **Θέλεις να βγεις για ποτό/φαγητό;** theh·lees nah vghees yah poh·toh/fah·ghee·toh |
| What are your plans for…? | **Ποια είναι τα σχέδιά σας για…;** piah ee·neh tah skheh·THee·ah sahs yah… |
| tonight | **απόψε** ah·poh·pseh |
| tomorrow | **αύριο** ahv·ree·oh |

| this weekend | **αυτό το Σαββατοκύριακο** ahf·<u>toh</u> toh sah·vah·toh·<u>kee</u>·riah·koh |
| Where would you like to go? | **Πού θα θέλατε να πάμε;** poo thah <u>theh</u>·lah·the nah <u>pah</u>·meh |
| I'd like to go to… | **Θα ήθελα να πάω…** thah <u>ee</u>·theh·lah nah <u>pah</u>·oh.. |
| Do you like…? | **Σου αρέσει…;** soo ah·<u>reh</u>·see… |
| Can I have your number/e-mail? | **Μου δίνετε το τηλέφωνο/e-mail σας;** moo <u>THee</u>·neh·teh toh tee·<u>leh</u>·foh·noh/ee·<u>meh</u>·eel sahs |
| Are you on Facebook/Twitter? | **Είσαι στο Facebook/Twitter;** ee·seh stoh Facebook/ Twitter |
| Can I join you? | **Να έρθω κι εγώ στην παρέα σας;** nah <u>ehr</u>·thoh kee eh·<u>ghoh</u> steen pah·<u>reh</u>·ah sahs |
| You look great! | **Είστε πολύ όμορφος** *m* **/όμορφη** *f* **!** <u>ee</u>·steh poh·<u>lee</u> oh·mohr·fohs/<u>oh</u>·mohr·fee |
| Shall we go somewhere quieter? | **Πάμε κάπου πιο ήσυχα;** <u>pah</u>·meh <u>kah</u>·poo pioh <u>ee</u>·see·khah |

For Communications, see page 48.

## Accepting & Rejecting

| Thank you. I'd love to. | **Ευχαριστώ. Θα το ήθελα πολύ.** ehf·khah·rees·<u>toh</u> thah toh <u>ee</u>·theh·lah poh·<u>lee</u> |
| Where should we meet? | **Πού θα συναντηθούμε;** poo thah see·nahn·dee·<u>t hoo</u>·meh |
| I'll meet you at the bar/your hotel. | **Θα σε συναντήσω στο μπαρ/στο ξενοδοχείο σου.** thah seh see·nahn·<u>dee</u>·soh stoh bahr/stoh kseh·noh·THoh·<u>khee</u>·oh soo |
| I'll come by at… | **Θα περάσω στις…** thah peh·<u>rah</u>·soh stees… |
| Thank you, but I'm busy. | **Σας ευχαριστώ, αλλά είμαι πολύ απασχολημένος** *m* **/απασχολημένη** *f* **.** sahs ehf·khah·rees·<u>toh</u> ah·<u>lah</u> ee·meh poh·<u>lee</u> ah·pahs·khoh·lee·<u>meh</u>·nohs/ah·pahs·khoh·lee·<u>meh</u>·nee |

| | |
|---|---|
| I'm not interested. | **Δεν ενδιαφέρομαι.** THehn ehn·THee·ah·_feh_·roh·meh |
| Leave me alone, please! | **Σας παρακαλώ, αφήστε με ήσυχο m / ήσυχη f !** sahs pah·rah·kah·_loh_ ah·_fees_·the meh ee·see·khoh/_ee_·see·khee |
| Stop bothering me! | **Σταματείστε να με ενοχλείτε!** stah·mah·tee·_tee_·steh nah meh eh·noh·_khlee_·the |

## Getting Intimate

| | |
|---|---|
| Can I hug/kiss you? | **Μπορώ να σε αγκαλιάσω/φιλήσω;** boh·_roh_ nah seh ahn·gah·_liah_·soh/fee·_lee_·soh |
| Yes. | **Ναι.** neh |
| No. | **Όχι.** _oh_·khee |
| Stop! | **Σταμάτα!** stah·_mah_·tah |
| I love you. | **Σ' αγαπώ.** sah·ghah·_poh_ |

## Sexual Preferences

| | |
|---|---|
| Are you gay? | **Είσαι γκέι;** _ee_·seh _geh_·ee |
| I'm… | **Είμαι…** _ee_·meh… |
| heterosexual | **ετεροφυλόφιλος m /ετεροφυλόφιλη f** eh·teh·roh·fee·_loh_·fee·lohs/eh·teh·roh·fee·_loh_·fee·lee |
| homosexual | **ομοφυλόφιλος m /ομοφυλόφιλη f** oh·moh·fee·_loh_·fee·lohs/oh·moh·fee·_loh_·fee·lee |
| bisexual | **αμφιφυλόφιλος m /αμφιφυλόφιλη f** ahm·fee·fee·_loh_·fee·lohs/ahm·fee·fee·_loh_·fee·lee |
| Do you like men/women? | **Σου αρέσουν οι άνδρες/γυναίκες;** soo ah·_reh_·soon ee _ahn_·THrehs/ghee·_neh_·kehs |

For Grammar, see page 151.

# Leisure Time

# Sightseeing

## ESSENTIAL

| | |
|---|---|
| Where's the tourist information office? | **Πού είναι το γραφείο τουρισμού;** *poo ee·neh toh ghrah·fee·oh too·reez·moo* |
| What are the main points of interest? | **Ποια είναι τα κυριότερα αξιοθέατα;** *piah ee·neh tah kee·ree·oh·teh·rah ah·ksee·oh·theh·ah·tah* |
| Do you have tours in English? | **Γίνονται ξεναγήσεις στα αγγλικά;** *ghee·nohn·deh kseh·nah·ghee·sees stah ahng·lee·kah* |
| Could I have a map/guide? | **Μπορώ να έχω έναν χάρτη/οδηγό;** *boh·roh nah eh·khoh eh·nahn khahr·tee/oh·THee·ghoh* |

## Tourist Information

| | |
|---|---|
| Do you have any information on...? | **Έχετε πληροφορίες για...;** *eh·kheh·the plee·roh·foh·ree·ehs yah...* |
| Can you recommend...? | **Μπορείτε να συστήσετε έναν/μία/ένα...;** *boh·ree·teh nah sees·tee·seh·teh eh·nahn/mee·ah/eh·nah...* |
| a bus tour | **περιήγηση με λεωφορείο** *peh·ree·ee·ghee·see meh leh·oh·foh·ree·oh* |
| a boat trip | **μια εκδρομή με βάρκα** *mee·ah ehk·THroh·mee meh vahr·kah* |
| an excursion | **μια εκδρομή** *mee·ah ehk·THroh·mee* |
| a sightseeing tour | **μια ξενάγηση στα αξιοθέατα** *mee·ah kseh·nah·yee·see stah ah·ksee·oh·theh·ah·tah* |

## On Tour

| | |
|---|---|
| I'd like to go on the tour to... | **Θα ήθελα να πάω στην ξενάγηση στο...** *thah ee·theh·lah nah pah·oh steen kseh·nah·yee·see stoh...* |

The official, government-run tourist information offices are known as **EOT** *(eh·oht)*, **Ελληνικός Οργανισμός Τουρισμού** *(eh·lee·nee·kohs ohr·ghah·nees·mohs too·rees·moo)*, in Greece and **ΚΟΤ** *(koht)*, **Κυπριακός Οργανισμός Τουρισμού** *(keep·ree·ah·kohs ohr·ghah·nees·mohs too·rees·moo)* in Cyprus. They can be found in most tourist resorts and major towns.

| | |
|---|---|
| When's the next tour? | **Πότε είναι η επόμενη περιήγηση;** *poh·teh ee·neh ee eh·poh·meh·nee peh·ree·ee·ghee·see* |
| Are there tours in English? | **Γίνονται ξεναγήσεις στα αγγλικά;** *ghee·nohn·deh kseh·nah·yee·sees stah ahng·lee·kah* |
| What time do we leave/return? | **Τι ώρα αναχωρούμε/επιστρέφουμε;** *tee oh·rah ah·nah·khoh·roo·meh/eh·pees·treh·foo·meh* |
| We'd like to have a look at the... | **Θα θέλαμε να ρίξουμε μια ματιά...** *thah theh·lah·meh nah ree·ksoo·meh miah mah·tiah...* |
| Can we stop here...? | **Μπορούμε να σταματήσουμε εδώ...;** *boh·roo·meh nah stah·mah·tee·soo·meh eh·THoh...* |
| to take photographs | **για να βγάλουμε φωτογραφίες** *yah nah vghah·loo·meh foh·toh·ghrah·fee·ehs* |
| to buy souvenirs | **για να αγοράσουμε σουβενίρ** *yah nah ah·ghoh·rah·soo·meh soo·veh·neer* |
| to use the restroom [toilet] | **για τουαλέτα** *yah too·ah·leh·tah* |
| Is there access for the disabled? | **Υπάρχει πρόσβαση για άτομα με ειδικές ανάγκες;** *ee·pahr·khee prohz·vah·see yah ah·toh·mah meh ee·THee·kehs ah·nahn·gehs* |

For Tickets, see page 19.

## Seeing the Sights

| | | |
|---|---|---|
| Where is…? | **Πού είναι…;** | _poo <u>ee</u>•neh…_ |
| the battleground | **το πεδίο μάχης** | _toh peh•<u>THee</u>•oh <u>mah</u>•khees_ |
| the botanical garden | **ο βοτανικός κήπος** | _oh voh•tah•nee•<u>kohs</u> <u>kee</u>•pohs_ |
| the castle | **το κάστρο** | _toh <u>kahs</u>•troh_ |
| Where is…? | **Πού είναι…;** | _poo <u>ee</u>•neh…_ |
| the downtown area | **το κέντρο της πόλης** | _toh <u>kehn</u>•droh tees <u>poh</u>•lees_ |
| the fountain | **το συντριβάνι** | _toh seen•dree•<u>vah</u>•nee_ |
| the library | **η βιβλιοθήκη** | _ee veev•lee•oh•<u>thee</u>•kee_ |
| the market | **η αγορά** | _ee ah•ghoh•<u>rah</u>_ |
| the museum | **το μουσείο** | _toh moo•<u>see</u>•oh_ |
| the old town | **η παλιά πόλη** | _ee pah•<u>liah</u> <u>poh</u>•lee_ |
| the opera house | **το μέγαρο μουσικής** | _toh <u>meh</u>•ghah•roh moo•see•<u>kees</u>_ |
| the palace | **τα ανάκτορα** | _tah ah•<u>nahk</u>•toh•rah_ |
| the park | **το πάρκο** | _toh <u>pahr</u>•koh_ |
| the ruins | **τα αρχαία** | _tah ahr•<u>kheh</u>•ah_ |
| the shopping area | **η εμπορική περιοχή** | _ee ehm•boh•ree•<u>kee</u> peh•ree•oh•<u>khee</u>_ |
| the town hall | **το Δημαρχείο** | _toh <u>THee</u>•mahr•<u>khee</u>•oh_ |

| Can you show me on the map? | **Μπορείτε να μου δείξετε στο χάρτη;** |
| | *boh·ree·teh nah moo THee·kseh·teh stoh khahr·tee* |
| It's... | **Είναι...** *ee·neh...* |
| amazing | **καταπληκτικό** *kah·tah·plee·ktee·koh* |
| beautiful | **όμορφο** *oh·mohr·foh* |
| boring | **βαρετός** *vah·reh·toh* |
| interesting | **ενδιαφέρον** *ehn·THee·ah·feh·rohn* |
| magnificent | **μεγαλοπρεπές** *meh·ghah·lohp·reh·pehs* |
| romantic | **ρομαντικό** *roh·mahn·dee·koh* |
| strange | **παράξενο** *pah·rah·kseh·noh* |
| terrible | **απαίσιο** *ah·peh·see·oh* |
| ugly | **άσχημο** *ahs·khee·moh* |
| I (don't) like it. | **(Δεν) Μου αρέσει.** *(THen) moo ah·reh·see* |

For Asking Directions, see page 34.

## Religious Sites

| Where is...? | **Πού είναι...;** *poo ee·neh...* |
| the cathedral | **ο καθεδρικός** *oh kah·theh·THree·kohs* |
| the Catholic/ Protestant church | **η καθολική/ προτεσταντική εκκλησία** *ee kah·thoh· lee·kee/proh·teh·stahn·dee·kee ehk·lee·see·ah* |
| the mosque | **το τζαμί** *toh jah·mee* |
| the shrine | **ο ιερός χώρος** *oh ee·eh·rohs khoh·rohs* |
| the synagogue | **η συναγωγή** *ee see·nah·ghoh·yee* |
| the temple | **ο ναός** *oh nah·ohs* |
| What time is mass/ the service? | **Τι ώρα είναι η λειτουργία;** *tee oh·rah ee·neh ee lee·toor·yee·ah* |

## ESSENTIAL

| | |
|---|---|
| Where is the market/mall? | **Πού είναι η αγορά/το εμπορικό κέντρο;** *poo ee•neh ee ah•ghoh•rah/toh ehm•boh•ree•koh kehn•droh* |
| I'm just looking. | **Απλώς κοιτάω.** *ahp•lohs kee•tah•oh* |
| Can you help me? | **Μπορείτε να με βοηθήσετε;** *boh•ree•teh nah meh voh•ee•thee•seh•teh* |
| I'm being helped. | **Με εξυπηρετούν.** *meh eh•ksee•pee•reh•toon* |
| How much? | **Πόσο;** *poh•soh* |
| This/That one, thanks. | **Αυτό/Εκείνο, παρακαλώ.** *ahf•toh/eh•kee•noh pah•rah•kah•loh* |
| That's all, thanks. | **Τίποτε άλλο, ευχαριστώ.** *tee•poh•teh ah•loh ehf•khah•rees•toh* |
| Where do I pay? | **Πού πληρώνω;** *poo plee•roh•noh* |
| I'll pay in cash/by credit card. | **Θα πληρώσω τοις μετρητοίς/με πιστωτική κάρτα.** *thah plee•roh•soh tees meht•ree•tees/meh pees•toh• tee•kee kahr•tah* |
| A receipt, please. | **Μια απόδειξη, παρακαλώ.** *miah ah•poh•THee•ksee pah•rah•kah•loh* |

Shopping can be a great pleasure in Greece. Apart from the standard department stores, you can wander through flea markets and seek out the small handicraft stores that line the narrow alleys of most islands and old towns.

## At the Shops

| | |
|---|---|
| Where is...? | **Πού είναι...;** *poo ee•neh...* |
| the antiques store | **το κατάστημα με αντίκες** *toh kah•tahs•tee•mah meh ahn•tee•kehs* |
| the bakery | **το αρτοποιείο** *toh ahr•toh•pee•ee•oh* |
| the bank | **η τράπεζα ee** *trah•peh•zah* |
| the bookstore | **το βιβλιοπωλείο** *toh veev•lee•oh•poh•lee•oh* |
| the clothing store | **το κατάστημα ρούχων** *toh kah•tahs•tee•mah roo•khohn* |
| the delicatessen | **τα τυριά-αλλαντικά** *tah teer•yah ah•lahn•dee•kah* |
| the department store | **το πολυκατάστημα** *toh poh•lee•kah•tahs•tee•mah* |
| the gift shop | **το κατάστημα σουβενίρ** *toh kah•tah•stee•mah soo•veh•neer* |
| the health food store | **το κατάστημα με υγιεινές τροφές** *toh kah•tahs•tee•mah meh ee•yee•ee•nehs troh•fehs* |
| the jeweler | **το κοσμηματοπωλείο** *toh kohz•mee•mah•toh•poh•lee•oh* |
| the liquor store [off-licence] | **η κάβα** *ee kah•vah* |
| the market | **η αγορά** *ee ah•ghoh•rah* |
| the music store | **το κατάστημα μουσικής** *toh kah•tah•stee•mah moo•see•kees* |
| the pastry store | **το ζαχαροπλαστείο** *toh zah•khah•rohp•lahs•tee•oh* |
| Where is...? | **Πού είναι...;** *poo ee•neh...* |
| the pharmacy | **το φαρμακείο** *toh fahr•mah•kee•oh* |
| the produce [grocery] store | **το παντοπωλείο** *toh pahn•doh•poh•lee•oh* |
| the shoe store | **το κατάστημα υποδημάτων** *toh kah•tahs•tee•mah ee•poh•THee•mah•tohn* |
| the shopping mall | **το εμπορικό κέντρο** *toh ehm•boh•ree•koh kehn•droh* |

| the souvenir store | **το κατάστημα σουβενίρ** *toh kah-tahs-tee-mah soo-veh-neer* |
| the supermarket | **το σουπερμάρκετ** *toh soo-pehr mahr-keht* |
| the tobacconist | **το καπνοπωλείο** *toh kahp-noh-poh-lee-oh* |
| the toy store | **το κατάστημα παιχνιδιών** *toh kah-tahs-tee-mah pehkh-neeTH-yohn* |

## Ask an Assistant

| When do you open/close? | **Τι ώρα ανοίγετε/κλείνετε;** *tee oh-rah ah-nee-gheh-teh/klee-neh-teh* |
| Where is...? | **Πού είναι...;** *poo ee-neh...* |
| the cashier | **το ταμείο** *toh tah-mee-oh* |
| the escalator | **οι κυλιόμενες σκάλες** *ee kee-lee-oh-meh-nehs skah-lehs* |
| the elevator [lift] | **το ασανσέρ** *toh ah-sahn-sehr* |
| the fitting room | **το δοκιμαστήριο** *toh THoh-kee-mahs-tee-ree-oh* |
| the store directory | **ο οδηγός καταστήματος** *oh oh-THee-ghohs kah-tahs-tee-mah-tohs* |
| Can you help me? | **Μπορείτε να με βοηθήσετε;** *boh-ree-teh nah meh voh-ee-thee-seh-teh* |
| I'm just looking. | **Απλώς κοιτάω.** *ahp-lohs kee-tah-oh* |
| I'm being helped. | **Εξυπηρετούμαι.** *eh-ksee-pee-reh-too-meh* |
| Do you have any...? | **Έχετε καθόλου...;** *eh-kheh-teh kah-thoh-loo...* |
| Could you show me...? | **Μπορείτε να μου δείξετε...;** *boh-ree-teh nah moo THee-kseh-teh...* |
| Can you ship/wrap it? | **Μπορείτε να το στείλετε/τυλίξετε;** *boh-ree-teh nah toh stee-leh-teh/tee-lee-kseh-teh* |
| How much? | **Πόσο;** *poh-soh* |
| That's all, thanks. | **Τίποτε άλλο, ευχαριστώ.** *tee-poh-teh ah-loh ehf-khahr-ees-toh* |

## YOU MAY HEAR...

**Μπορώ να σας βοηθήσω;** *boh·roh* | Can I help you?
*nah sahs voh·ee·thee·soh*

**Μισό λεπτό.** *mee·soh lehp·toh* | Just a moment.

**Τί θα θέλατε;** *tee thah thel·lah·teh* | What would you like?

**Τίποτε άλλο;** *tee·poh·teh ah·loh* | Anything else?

## YOU MAY SEE...

| | |
|---|---|
| **ανοιχτό/κλειστό** | open/closed |
| *ah·nee·khtoh/klee·stoh* | |
| **κλειστό για το μεσημέρι** | closed for lunch |
| *klee·stoh yah toh meh·see·meh·ree* | |
| **δοκιμαστήριο** | fitting room |
| *THoh·kee·mah·stee·ree·oh* | |
| **ταμείο** *tah·mee·oh* | cashier |
| **μόνο μετρητά** | cash only |
| *moh·noh meh·tree·tah* | |
| **δεκτές πιστωτικές κάρτες** | credit cards accepted |
| *THeh·ktehs pee·stoh·tee·kehs kahr·tehs* | |
| **εργάσιμες ώρες** | business hours |
| *ehr·ghah·see·mehs oh·rehs* | |
| **έξοδος** *eh·ksoh·THohs* | exit |

## Personal Preferences

| I want something... | **Θέλω κάτι...** *theh·loh kah·tee...* |
|---|---|
| cheap | **φτηνό** *ftee·noh* |
| expensive | **ακριβό** *ahk·ree·voh* |
| larger | **μεγαλύτερο** *meh·ghah·lee·teh·roh* |

| smaller | **μικρότερο** *meek·roh·teh·roh* |
|---|---|
| from this region | **από αυτό το μέρος** *ah·poh ahf·toh toh meh·rohs* |
| Around…euros. | **Γύρω στα…ευρώ.** *yee·roh stah…ehv·roh* |
| Is it real? | **Είναι αληθινό;** *ee·neh ah·lee·thee·noh* |
| Could you show me this/that? | **Μπορείτε να μου δείξετε αυτό/εκείνο;** *boh·ree·teh nah moo THee·kseh·teh ahf·toh/eh·kee·noh* |
| That's not quite what I want. | **Δεν είναι ακριβώς αυτό που θέλω.** *THehn ee·neh ahk·ree·vohs ahf·toh poo theh·loh* |
| I don't like it. | **Δεν μου αρέσει.** *THehn moo ah·reh·see* |
| That's too expensive. | **Είναι πολύ ακριβό.** *ee·neh poh·lee ahk·ree·voh* |
| I'd like to think about it. | **Θα ήθελα να το σκεφτώ.** *thah ee·theh·lah nah toh skehf·toh* |
| I'll take it. | **Θα το πάρω.** *thah toh pah·roh* |

109

## Paying & Bargaining

| How much? | **Πόσο;** *poh·soh* |
|---|---|
| I'll pay… | **Θα πληρώσω…** *thah plee·roh·soh…* |
| by cash | **τοις μετρητοίς** *tees meht·ree·tees* |
| by credit card | **με πιστωτική κάρτα** *meh pees·toh·tee·kee kahr·tah* |
| by traveler's check | **με ταξιδιωτική επιταγή** *meh tah·ksee·THyo·tee·kee eh·pee·tah·yee* |
| A receipt, please. | **Μια απόδειξη, παρακαλώ.** *miah ah·poh·THee·ksee pah·rah·kah·loh* |
| That's too much. | **Είναι πολλά.** *ee·neh poh·lah* |
| I'll give you… | **Θα σας δώσω…** *thah sahs THoh·soh…* |
| I only have…euros. | **Έχω μόνο…ευρώ.** *eh·khoh moh·noh…ehv·roh* |
| Is that your best price? | **Αυτή είναι η καλύτερη τιμή σας;** *ahf·tee ee·neh ee kah·lee·teh·ree tee·mee sahs* |
| Can you give me a discount? | **Μπορείτε να μου κάνετε έκπτωση;** *boh·ree·teh nah moo kah·neh·teh ehkp·toh·see* |

For Numbers, see page 156.

## YOU MAY HEAR...

**Πώς θα πληρώσετε;** *pohs thah plee·roh·seh·teh*

How are you paying?

**Η πιστωτική σας κάρτα απορρίφθηκε.** *ee pee· stoh·tee·kee sahs kahr·tah ah·poh·ree·fthee·keh*

Your credit card has been declined.

**Ταυτότητα, παρακαλώ.** *tahf·toh·tee· tah, pah·rah·kah·loh*

ID, please.

**Δεν δεχόμαστε πιστωτικές κάρτες.** *THehn THe· khoh·mah·steh pee·stoh·tee·kehs kahr·tehs*

We don't accept credit cards.

**Μόνο μετρητά, παρακαλώ.** *moh·noh meht·ree·tah pah·rah·kah·loh*

Cash only, please.

**Εχετε ψιλά;** *eh·kheh·teh psee·lah*

Do you have any smaller change?

### Making a Complaint

| I'd like... | **Θα ήθελα...** *thah ee·theh·lah...* |
| --- | --- |
| to exchange this | **να αλλάξω αυτό** *nah ah·lah·ksoh ahf·toh* |
| to return this | **να επιστρέψω αυτό** *nah eh·pees·treh·psoh ahf·toh* |
| a refund | **επιστροφή των χρημάτων μου** *eh·pees·troh·fee tohn khree·mah·tohn moo* |
| to see the manager | **να δω τον διευθυντή** *nah THoh tohn THee·ehf·theen·dee* |

### Services

| Can you recommend...? | **Μπορείτε να συστήσετε...;** *boh·ree·teh nah sees·tee·seh·teh...* |
| --- | --- |
| a barber | **έναν κουρέα** *eh·nahn koo·reh·ah* |
| a dry cleaner | **ένα καθαριστήριο** *eh·nah kah·thah·rees·tee·ree·oh* |

| a hairdresser | **ένα κομμωτήριο** _eh·nah koh·moh·tee·ree·oh_ |
| a laundromat [launderette] | **πλυντήριο ρούχων** _plee·dee·ree·oh roo·khohn_ |
| a nail salon | **ένα σαλόνι νυχιών** _eh·nah sah·loh·nee nee·khiohn_ |
| a spa | **ένα σπα** _eh·nah spah_ |
| a travel agency | **ένα ταξιδιωτικό γραφείο** _n eh·nah tah·ksee·THee·oh·tee·koh ghrah·fee·oh_ |
| Can you...this? | **Μπορείτε να...αυτό;** _boh·ree·teh nah...ahf·toh_ |
| alter | **μεταποιήσετε** _meh·tah·pee·ee·seh·teh_ |
| clean | **καθαρίσετε** _kah·thah·ree·seh·teh_ |
| mend | **επιδιορθώσετε** _eh·pee·THee·ohr·thoh·seh·teh_ |
| press | **σιδερώσετε** _see·THeh·roh·seh·teh_ |
| When will it/they be ready? | **Πότε θα είναι έτοιμο/έτοιμα;** _poh·teh thah ee·neh eh·tee·moh/eh·tee·mah_ |

## Hair & Beauty

| I'd like... | **Θα ήθελα...** _thah ee·theh·lah..._ |
| an appointment for today/ tomorrow | **να κλείσω ένα ραντεβού για σήμερα/αύριο** _nah klee·soh eh·nah rahn·deh·voo yah see·meh·rah/ahv·ree·oh_ |
| some colour/ highlights | **βαφή/ανταύγειες** _vah·fee/ah·dahv·yehs_ |
| my hair styled/ blow-dried | **ένα χτένισμα/στέγνωμα με πιστολάκι** _eh·nah khteh·nee·smah/steh·ghnoh·mah meh pee·stoh·lah·kee_ |
| a haircut | **ένα κούρεμα** _eh·nah koo·reh·mah_ |
| I'd like... | **Θα ήθελα...** _thah ee·theh·lah..._ |
| an eyebrow/ bikini wax | **χαλάουα στα φρύδια/στο μπικίνι** _khah·lah·oo·ah stah free·yah/stoh bee·kee·nee_ |
| a facial | **έναν καθαρισμό προσώπου** _eh·nahn kah·thah·reez·moh proh·soh·poo_ |

You will find spas and wellness centers, particularly at luxury hotels, in every major city and on most islands in Greece. You can visit these spas for a full day or for one treatment, without being a guest at the hotel. You will usually have to make an appointment in advance. Tipping is customary, particularly in hair salons, where customers may choose to tip the assistants or trainees.

| | | |
|---|---|---|
| a manicure/ pedicure | **ένα μανικιούρ/πεντικιούρ** *eh·nahmah·nee·kee·oor, pehn·dee·kee·oor* | |
| a (sports) massage | **ένα (αθλητικό) μασάζ** *eh·nah (ahth·lee·tee·koh) mah·sahz* | |
| A trim, please. | **Κόψιμο, παρακαλώ** *koh·psee·moh, pah·rah·kah·loh* | |
| Don't cut it too short. | **Μην τα κόψετε πολύ κοντά.** *meen tah koh·pseh·teh poh·lee kohn·dah* | |
| Shorter here. | **Πιο κοντά εδώ.** *pioh kohn·dah eh·THoh* | |
| Do you do…? | **Κάνετε…;** *kah·neh·teh…* | |
| acupuncture | **βελονισμό** *veh·loh·neez·moh* | |
| aromatherapy | **αρωματοθεραπεία** *ah·roh·mah·toh·theh·rah·pee·ah* | |
| oxygen treatment | **οξυγονοθεραπεία** *oh·ksee·ghoh·noh·theh·rah·pee·ah* | |
| Is there a sauna? | **Υπάρχει σάουνα;** *ee·pahr·kee sah·oo·nah* | |

## Antiques

| | |
|---|---|
| How old is this? | **Πόσο παλιό είναι αυτό;** *poh·soh pah·lioh ee·neh ahf·toh* |
| Do you have anything from the…period? | **Έχετε τίποτα από την…περίοδο;** *eh·kheh·teh tee·poh·tah ah·poh teen….peh·ree·oh·THoh* |
| Do I have to fill out any forms? | **Πρέπει να συμπληρώσω έντυπα;** *preh·pee nah see·blee·roh·soh eh·ndee·pah* |

| Will I have problems with customs? | **Θα έχω προβλήματα με το τελωνείο;** *thah eh·khoh prohv·lee·mah·tah meh toh teh·loh·nee·oh* |
| Is there a certificate of authenticity? | **Υπάρχει πιστοποιητικό γνησιότητας;** *ee·pahr·khee pees·toh·pee·ee·tee·koh ghnee·see·oh·tee·tahs* |
| Can you ship/wrap it? | **Μπορείτε να το στείλετε/τυλίξετε;** *boh·ree·teh nah toh stee·leh·teh/tee·lee·kseh·teh* |

## Clothing

| I'd like... | **Θα ήθελα...** *thah ee·theh·lah...* |
| Can I try this on? | **Μπορώ να το δοκιμάσω;** *boh·roh nah toh THoh·kee·mah·soh* |
| It doesn't fit. | **Δεν μου κάνει.** *THehn moo kah·nee* |
| It's too... | **Είναι πολύ...** *ee·neh poh·lee...* |
| big | **μεγάλο** *meh·ghah·loh* |
| small | **μικρό** *meek·roh* |
| short | **κοντό** *kon·doh* |
| long | **μακρύ** *mak·ree* |
| tight | **στενό** *steh·noh* |
| loose | **φαρδύ** *fahr·THee* |
| Do you have this in size...? | **Το έχετε στο μέγεθος...;** *toh eh·kheh·teh stoh meh·yeh·thohs...* |
| Do you have this in a bigger/smaller size? | **Το έχετε σε μεγαλύτερο/μικρότερο μέγεθος;** *kheh·teh seh meh·ghah·lee·teh·roh/meek·roh·teh·roh meh·gheh·thohs* |

### YOU MAY SEE...

| **ΑΝΔΡΙΚΑ** *ahn·THree·kah* | men's clothing |
| **ΓΥΝΑΙΚΕΙΑ** *yee·neh·kee·ah* | women's clothing |
| **ΠΑΙΔΙΚΑ** *peh·THee·kah* | children's clothing |

> **YOU MAY HEAR...**
>
> **Σας πηγαίνει.** *sahs pee·gheh·nee*
> **Πώς σας είναι;** *pohs sahs·ee·neh*
> **Δεν έχουμε το μέγεθός σας.** *THen eh· khoo·meh toh meh·gheh·thohs sahs*
>
> That looks great on you.
> How does it fit?
> We don't have
> your size.

## Colors

| | |
|---|---|
| I'm looking for something in... | **Ψάχνω κάτι σε...** *psahkh·noh kah·tee seh...* |
| beige | **μπεζ** *behz* |
| black | **μαύρο** *mahv·roh* |
| blue | **μπλε** *bleh* |
| brown | **καφέ** *kah·feh* |
| green | **πράσινο** *prah·see·noh* |
| gray | **γκρι** *gree* |
| orange | **πορτοκαλί** *pohr·toh·kah·lee* |
| pink | **ροζ** *rohz* |
| purple | **μωβ** *mohv* |
| red | **κόκκινο** *koh·kee·noh* |
| white | **άσπρο** *ahs·proh* |
| yellow | **κίτρινο** *keet·ree·noh* |

## Clothes & Accessories

| | |
|---|---|
| a backpack | **το σακκίδιο** *toh sah·kee·THee·oh* |
| a belt | **η ζώνη** *ee zoh·nee* |
| a bikini | **το μπικίνι** *toh bee·kee·nee* |
| a blouse | **η μπλούζα** *ee bloo·zah* |
| a bra | **το σουτιέν** *toh soo·tiehn* |
| briefs [underpants] (women's) | **το κυλοτάκι** *toh kee·loh·tah·kee* |

| | | |
|---|---|---|
| briefs [underpants] (men's and women's) | **το σλιπ** | toh sleep |
| a coat | **το παλτό** | toh pahl·_toh_ |
| a dress | **το φόρεμα** | toh _foh_·reh·mah |
| a hat | **το καπέλλο** | toh kah·_peh_·loh |
| a jacket | **το σακάκι** | toh sah·_kah_·kee |
| jeans | **το μπλου-τζην** | toh bloo·_jeen_ |
| pajamas | **πιτζάμες** | pee·_tzah_·mehs |
| pants [trousers] | **το παντελόνι** | toh pahn·deh·_loh_·nee |
| pantyhose [tights] | **το καλσόν** | toh kahl·_sohn_ |
| a purse [handbag] | **η τσάντα** | ee _tsahn_·dah |
| a raincoat | **το αδιάβροχο** | toh ah·_THee_·ahv·roh·khoh sah·_kah_·kee |
| a scarf | **το κασκώλ** | toh kahs·_kohl_ |
| a shirt | **το πουκάμισο** | toh poo·_kah_·mee·soh |
| shorts | **το σόρτς** | toh sohrts |
| a skirt | **η φούστα** | ee _foos_·tah |
| socks | **οι κάλτσες** | ee _kahl_·tsehs |
| a suit (men's/ women's) | **το κουστούμι/ταγιέρ** | toh koos·_too_·mee/ tah·_yehr_ |
| sunglasses | **τα γυαλιά ηλίου** | tah yah·_liah_ ee·_lee_·oo |
| a sweater | **το πουλόβερ** | toh poo·_loh_·vehr |

| a sweatshirt | **το φούτερ** toh foo·ter |
| swimming trunks/<br>a swimsuit | **το μαγιό** toh mah·yoh |
| a T-shirt | **το μπλουζάκι** toh bloo·zah·kee |
| a tie | **η γραβάτα** ee ghrah·vah·tah |
| underwear | **τα εσώρουχα** tah eh·soh·roo·khah |

## Fabric

| I'd like... | **Θα ήθελα...** thah ee·theh·lah... |
| cotton | **βαμβακερό** vahm·vah·keh·roh |
| denim | **τζιν** deh·neem jeen |
| lace | **δαντέλα** THahn·teh·lah |
| leather | **δερμάτινο** THehr·mah·tee·noh |
| linen | **λινό** lee·noh |
| silk | **μεταξωτό** meh·tah·ksoh·toh |
| wool | **μάλλινο** mah·lee·noh |
| Is it machine<br>washable? | **Πλένεται στο πλυντήριο;** pleh·neh·teh stoh<br>pleen·dee·ree·oh |

## Shoes

| I'd like... | **Θα ήθελα...** thah ee·theh·lah... |
| high-heeled/<br>flat shoes | **τα ψηλοτάκουνα/επίπεδα παπούτσια** tah psee·loh·<br>tah·koo·nah/ee·siah pah·poo·tsiah |
| boots | **οι μπότες** ee boh·tehs |
| loafers | **τα μοκασίνια** tah moh·kah·see·niah |
| sandals | **τα πέδιλα** tah peh·THee·lah |
| shoes | **τα παπούτσια** tah pah·poo·tsiah |
| slippers | **οι παντόφλες** ee pahn·dohf·lehs |
| sneakers | **τα αθλητικά παπούτσια** tah ahth·lee·tee·kah pah·<br>poo·tsiah |
| In size... | **Στο νούμερο...** stoh noo·meh·roh... |

For Numbers, see page 156.

## Sizes

| | |
|---|---|
| small (S) | **μικρό** meek·_roh_ |
| medium (M) | **μεσαίο** meh·_seh_·oh |
| large (L) | **μεγάλο** meh·_gha_·loh |
| extra large (XL) | **extra large** _eh_·xtrah lahrj |
| petite | **μικρό νούμερο** mee·_kroh_ noo·meh·roh |
| plus size | **μεγάλο νούμερο** meh·_ghah_·loh noo·meh·roh |

## Newsagent & Tobacconist

| | |
|---|---|
| Do you sell English-language books/newspapers? | **Πουλάτε αγγλικές εφημερίδες/περιοδικά;** poo·lah·teh ahng·lee·_kehs_ eh·fee·meh·_ree_·THes/peh·rioh·_THee_·_kah_ |
| I'd like... | **Θα ήθελα...** thah ee·theh·lah... |
| candy [sweets] | **γλυκά** ghlee·_kah_ |
| chewing gum | **τσίχλες** _tseekh_·lehs |
| a chocolate bar | **σοκολάτα** soh·koh·_lah_·tah |
| cigars | **πούρα** _poo_·rah |
| a pack/carton of cigarettes | **ένα πακέτο/μια κούτα τσιγάρα** _eh_·nah pah·_keh_·toh/miah _koo_·tah tsee·_ghah_·rah |
| a lighter | **έναν αναπτήρα** _eh_·nahn ah·nahp·_tee_·rah |
| a magazine | **ένα περιοδικό** _eh_·nah peh·ree·oh·_THee_·koh |
| matches | **σπίρτα** _speer_·tah |
| a newspaper | **μια εφημερίδα** miah eh·fee·meh·_ree_·THah |
| a pen | **ένα στυλό** _eh_·nah stee·_loh_ |
| a postcard | **μια καρτ ποστάλ** miah kahrt poh·_stahl_ |
| a road/town map of... | **έναν οδικό χάρτη/έναν χάρτη της πόλης για...** _eh_·nahn oh·_THee_·koh _khahr_·tee/_eh_·nahn _khahr_·tee tees _poh_·lees yah... |
| stamps | **γραμματόσημα** ghrah·mah·_toh_·see·mah |

## Photography

| | |
|---|---|
| I'm looking for…camera. | **Ψάχνω για…φωτογραφική μηχανή.** *psahkh·noh yah…foh·tohgh·rah·fee·kee mee·khah·nee* |
| an automatic | **μια αυτόματη** *miah ahf·toh·mah·tee* |
| a digital | **μια ψηφιακή** *miah psee·fee·ah·kee* |
| a disposable | **μια μιας χρήσεως** *miah miahs khree·seh·ohs* |
| I'd like… | **Θα ήθελα…** *thah ee·theh·lah…* |
| a battery | **μια μπαταρία** *miah bah·tah·ree·ah* |
| digital prints | **ψηφιακές εκτυπώσεις** *psee·fee·ah·kehs ehk·tee·poh·sees* |
| a memory card | **μια κάρτα μνήμης** *miah·kahr·tah mnee·mees* |
| Can I print digital photos here? | **Μπορώ να εκτυπώσω ψηφιακές φωτογραφίες εδώ;** *boh·roh nah ehk·tee·poh·soh psee·fee·ah·kehs foh·toh·ghrah·fee·ehs eh·THoh* |

## Souvenirs

| | |
|---|---|
| bottle of wine | **μπουκάλι κρασί** *boo·kah·lee krah·see* |
| box of pastries | **κουτί γλυκά** *koo·tee ghlee·kah* |
| dried Corinthian currants | **κορινθιακή σταφίδα** *koh·reen·thee·ah·kee stah·fee·THah* |
| ground Greek coffee | **ελληνικός καφές** *eh·lee·nee·kohs kah·fehs* |
| halva | **χαλβά** *khahl·vahs* |
| key ring | **μπρελόκ** *breh·lohk* |
| olives | **ελιές** *eh·liehs* |
| olive oil | **λάδι** *lah·THee* |
| pistachio nuts | **φυστίκια** *fees·tee·kiah* |
| postcard | **καρτποστάλ** *kahrt·pohs·tahl* |
| T-shirt | **μπλουζάκι** *bloo·zah·kee* |
| thyme honey | **θυμαρίσιο μέλι** *thee·mah·ree·sioh meh·lee* |
| Turkish delight | **λουκούμι** *loo·koo·mee* |
| Can I see this/that? | **Μπορώ να δω αυτό/εκείνο;** *boh·roh nah THoh ahf·toh/eh·kee·noh* |

| The one in the window/display case. | **Αυτό στη βιτρίνα.** *ahf·toh stee veet·ree·nah* |
|---|---|
| I'd like… | **Θα ήθελα…** *thah ee·theh·lah…* |
| a battery | **μια μπαταρία** *miah bah·tah·ree·ah* |
| a bracelet | **ένα βραχιόλι** *eh·nah vrah·khioh·lee* |
| a brooch | **μια καρφίτσα f** *miah kahr·fee·tsah* |
| earrings | **ένα ζευγάρι σκουλαρίκια** *eh·nah zehv·gah·ree skoo·lah·ree·kiah* |
| a necklace | **ένα κολλιέ** *eh·nah koh·lieh* |
| a ring | **ένα δαχτυλίδι** *eh·nah THahkh·tee·lee·THee* |
| a watch | **ένα ρολόι** *eh·nah roh·loh·ee* |
| copper | **χαλκό** *khahl·koh* |
| crystal | **κρύσταλλο** *krees·tah·loh* |
| diamond | **διαμάντι** *THiah·mahn·dee* |
| (white/yellow) gold | **λευκόχρυσο/χρυσό** *lehf·koh·khree·soh/khree·soh* |
| pearl | **μαργαριτάρι** *mahr·ghah·ree·tah·ree* |
| pewter | **κασσίτερο** *kah·see·teh·roh* |
| platinum | **πλατίνα** *plah·tee·nah* |
| sterling silver | **ασήμι** *ah·see·mee* |
| Is this real? | **Είναι αληθινό;** *ee·neh ah·lee·thee·noh* |
| Can you engrave it? | **Μπορείτε να το χαράξετε;** *boh·ree·teh nah toh khah·rah·kseh·teh* |

119

There is a vast choice of souvenirs to buy in Greece. In all major tourist locations, you will find shops selling jewelry, handmade goods and other typical souvenirs. In Athens, there are some very nice jewelry shops in Monastiraki. You can find anything from ancient Greek-style jewelry to pieces made by contemporary designers. Handicrafts range from re-creations of ancient Greek pottery to textiles, and handmade backgammon sets.

## Sport & Leisure

### ESSENTIAL

| | |
|---|---|
| When's the game? | **Πότε είναι ο αγώνας;** _poh·teh ee·neh oh ah·ghoh·nahs_ |
| Where's…? | **Πού είναι…;** _poo ee·neh…_ |
| the beach | **η παραλία** _ee pah·rah·lee·ah_ |
| the park | **το πάρκο** _toh pahr·koh_ |
| the pool | **η πισίνα** _ee pee·see·nah_ |
| Is it safe to swim/ dive here? | **Είναι ασφαλές εδώ για κολύμπι/κατάδυση;** _ee·neh ahs·fah·lehs eh·THoh yah koh·leem·bee/ kah·tah·THee·see_ |
| Can I hire golf clubs? | **Μπορώ να νοικιάσω μπαστούνια του γκόλφ;** _boh·roh nah nee·kiah·soh bahs·too·niah too gohlf_ |
| How much per hour? | **Πόσο χρεώνεται η ώρα;** _poh·soh khreh·oh·neh·teh ee oh·rah_ |
| How far is it to…? | **Πόσο μακριά είναι για…;** _poh·soh mahk·ree·ah ee· neh yah…_ |
| Can you show me on the map? | **Μπορείτε να μου δείξετε στο χάρτη;** _boh·ree·teh nah moo THee·kseh·teh stoh khahr·tee_ |

# Watching Sport

| | | |
|---|---|---|
| When's… | **Πότε είναι…** | _poh·teh ee·neh…_ |
| the baseball game | **ο αγώνας μπέιζμπολ** | _oh ah·ghoh·nahs beh·ee·zbohl_ |
| the basketball game | **ο αγώνας μπάσκετ** | _oh ah·ghoh·nahs bahs·keht_ |
| the boxing match | **ο αγώνας μποξ** | _oh ah·ghoh·nahs bohks_ |
| the cricket game | **ο αγώνας κρίκετ** | _oh ah·ghoh·nahs kree·keht_ |
| the cycling race | **ο αγώνας ποδηλασίας** | _oh ah·ghoh·nahs poh·THee·lah·see·ahs_ |
| the golf tournament | **το τουρνουά γκολφ** | _toh toor·noo·ah gohlf_ |
| the soccer [football] game | **ο αγώνας ποδοσφαίρου** | _oh ah·ghoh·nahs poh·THohs·feh·roo_ |
| the tennis match | **ο αγώνας τέννις** | _oh ah·ghoh·nahs teh·nees_ |
| the volleyball game | **ο αγώνας βόλεϊ** | _oh ah·ghoh·nahs voh·leh·ee_ |
| Which teams are playing? | **Ποιες ομάδες παίζουν;** | _pee·ehs oh·mah·THehs peh·zoon_ |
| Where's…? | **Πού είναι…;** | _poo ee·neh…_ |
| the horse track | **το ιπποδρόμιο** | _toh ee·poh·THroh·mee·oh_ |
| the racetrack | **ο ιππόδρομος** | _oh ee·poh·THroh·mohs_ |
| the stadium | **το στάδιο** | _toh stah·THee·oh_ |
| Where can I place a bet? | **Πού μπορώ να βάλω στοίχημα;** | _poo boh·roh nah vah·loh stee·khee·mah_ |

# Playing Sport

| | | |
|---|---|---|
| Where's…? | **Πού είναι…;** | _poo ee·neh…_ |
| the golf course | **το γήπεδο του γκόλφ** | _toh yee·peh·THoh too gohlf_ |
| the gym | **το γυμναστήριο** | _toh gheem·nahs·tee·ree·oh_ |
| the park | **το πάρκο** | _toh pahr·koh_ |
| Where are the tennis courts? | **Πού είναι τα γήπεδα του τέννις;** | _poo ee·neh tah ghee·peh·THah too teh·nees_ |

The most popular sport in Greece is **καλαθοσφαίρηση** *(kah·lah·thohs·feh·ree·see)*, basketball; even the smallest towns have their own basketball teams.

**Ποδόσφαιρο** *(poh·THohs·feh·roh)*, soccer, is also popular, and matches are usually played on Sunday.

Water sports are very popular on the islands and in coastal areas. However, you need a special permit to dive with oxygen tanks.

Winter skiing has gained popularity in the last few years — there are more than 15 ski resorts on the mainland. Contact the tourist information office for details on locations and snow conditions.

| | | |
|---|---|---|
| How much per…? | **Ποιο είναι το κόστος για…;** *pioh ee·neh toh kohs·tohs yah…* | |
| day | **την ημέρα** *teen ee·meh·rah* | |
| hour | **την ώρα** *teen oh·rah* | |
| game | **το παιχνίδι** *toh peh·khnee·THee* | |
| round | **το παιχνίδι** *toh peh·khnee·THee* | |
| Can I hire…? | **Μπορώ να νοικιάσω…;** *boh·roh nah nee·kiah·soh…* | |
| golf clubs | **μπαστούνια του γκόλφ** *bahs·too·niah too gohlf* | |
| equipment | **εξοπλισμό** *eh·ksohp·leez·moh* | |
| a racket | **μια ρακέτα** *miah rah·keh·tah* | |

## At the Beach/Pool

| | |
|---|---|
| Where's the beach/pool? | **Πού είναι η παραλία/πισίνα;** *poo ee·neh ee pah·rah·lee·ah/pee·see·nah* |
| Is there…? | **Υπάρχει…;** *ee·pahr·khee…* |
| a kiddie pool | **παιδική πισίνα** *peh·THee·kee pee·see·nah* |
| an indoor/outdoor pool | **εσωτερική/εξωτερική πισίνα** *eh·soh·teh·ree·kee/eh·ksoh·teh·ree·kee pee·see·nah* |
| a lifeguard | **ναυαγοσώστης** *nah·vah·ghoh·sohs·tees* |

| | |
|---|---|
| Is it safe…? | **Είναι ασφαλές…;** _ee_•neh ahs•fah•_lehs_… |
| to swim | **εδώ για κολύμπι** eh•_THoh_ yah koh•_leem_•bee |
| to dive | **εδώ για κατάδυση** eh•_THoh_ yah kah•tah•_THee_•see |
| for children | **για παιδιά** yah peh•_THyah_ |
| I want to hire… | **Θέλω να νοικιάσω…** _theh_•loh nah nee•_kiah_•soh… |
| a deck chair | **μια σεζ-λονγκ** miah _sehz_•lohng |
| diving equipment | **εξοπλισμό καταδύσεων** eh•ksoh•plee•_smoh_ kah•tah•_THee_•seh•ohn |
| a jet-ski | **ένα τζετ-σκι** _eh_•nah jeht skee |
| a motorboat | **μια εξωλέμβιο** miah eh•ksoh•_lehm_•vee•oh |
| a rowboat | **βάρκα** _vahr_•kah |
| a sailing boat | **ένα ιστιοπλοϊκό** _eh_•nah ees•tee•oh•ploh•ee•_koh_ |
| snorkeling equipment | **εξοπλισμό κατάδυσης με αναπνευστήρα** eh•ksoh•plee•_smoh_ kah•tah•_THee_•sees meh ah•nah•pnehf•_stee_•rah |
| a surfboard | **μιασανίδα του σέρφινγκ** miah sah•_nee_•THah too sehrf |
| a towel | **μια πετσέτα** miah peh•_tseh_•tah |
| an umbrella | **μια ομπρέλα θαλάσσης** miah ohm•_breh_•lah thah•_lah_•sees |
| water skis | **πέδιλα θαλάσσιου σκι** _peh_•THee•lah thah•_lah_•see•oo skee |
| For…hours. | **Για…ώρες.** yah… _oh_•rehs |

---

Greek beaches, which are usually free of charge, often offer a range of water sports. Beaches that are run by **EOT** require an entrance fee, but they tend to have more facilities. The use of jet-skis is restricted to a few beaches only, at a certain distance from the land and at specific times. Topless and nude sunbathing is acceptable at many island and mainland resorts, though it might be worth checking with a local beforehand if you're the only one!

## YOU MAY SEE...

| | |
|---|---|
| **ΤΕΛΕΣΚΙ** teh·leh·<u>skee</u> | ski lift |
| **ΤΕΛΕΣΕΖ** teh·leh·<u>sehz</u> | chair lift |
| **ΤΕΛΕΦΕΡΙΚ** teh·leh·feh·<u>reek</u> | cable car |
| **ΠΙΣΤΑ ΑΡΧΑΡΙΩΝ** | baby slope |
| <u>pees</u>·tah ahr·khahr·<u>ee</u>·ohn | |
| **ΜΕΣΑΙΑ ΠΙΣΤΑ** | intermediate slope |
| meh·<u>seh</u>·ah <u>pees</u>·tah | |
| **ΠΙΣΤΑ ΠΡΟΧΩΡΗΜΕΝΩΝ** | advanced slope |
| <u>pees</u>·tah proh·khoh·ree·<u>meh</u>·nohn | |
| **ΠΙΣΤΑ ΚΛΕΙΣΤΗ** pees·tah klees·tee | trail closed |

## Winter Sports

| | |
|---|---|
| A lift pass for a day/<br>few days, please. | **Μια άδεια για μια ημέρα/μερικές ημέρες,**<br>**παρακαλώ.** miah <u>ah</u>·THee·ah yah miah ee·<u>meh</u>·rah/<br>meh·ree·<u>kehs</u> ee·<u>meh</u>·rehs pah·rah·kah·<u>loh</u> |
| I'd like to hire... | **Θα ήθελα να νοικιάσω...** thah <u>ee</u>·theh·lah nah<br>nee·<u>kiah</u>·soh... |
| boots | **μπότες του σκι** <u>boh</u>·tehs too skee |
| a helmet | **ένα κράνος** <u>eh</u>·nah <u>krah</u>·nohs |
| poles | **μπαστούνια του σκι** bahs·<u>too</u>·niah too skee |
| skis | **πέδιλα του σκι** <u>peh</u>·THee·lah too skee |
| a snowboard | **μια σανίδα snowboard** miah sah·<u>nee</u>·THah snoh·<br>oo·<u>bohrd</u> |
| snowshoes | **παπούτσια χιονιού** pah·<u>poo</u>·tsiah khioh·<u>nioo</u> |
| These are too<br>big/small. | **Αυτά είναι πολυ μεγάλα/μικρά.** ahf·<u>tah</u><br>ee·neh poh·<u>lee</u> meh·<u>ghah</u>·lah/meek·<u>rah</u> |
| Are there lessons? | **Γίνονται μαθήματα;** <u>yee</u>·nohn·deh mah·<u>thee</u>·mah·tah |
| I'm a beginner. | **Είμαι αρχάριος.** <u>ee</u>·meh ahr·<u>khah</u>·ree·ohs |

| I'm experienced. | **Είμαι έμπειρος** *m* /**έμπειρη** *f* . *ee*·meh *ehm*·bee·rohs/ *ehm*·bee·ree |
|---|---|
| A trail [piste] map, please. | **Έναν χάρτη της πίστας.** *eh*·nahn *khahr*·tee tees *pees*·tahs |

## Out in the Country

| I'd like a map of… | **Θα ήθελα ένα χάρτη…** thah *ee*·theh·lah *eh*·nah *khahr*·tee… |
|---|---|
| this region | **αυτής της περιοχής** ahf·*tees* tees peh·ree·oh·*khees* |
| walking routes | **των διαδρομών περιήγησης** tohn THee·ah·THroh·*mohn* peh·ree·*ee*·yee·sees |
| cycle routes | **των ποδηλατόδρομων** tohn poh·THee·lah·*toh*·THroh·mohn |
| the trails | **των μονοπατιών** tohn moh·noh·pah·*tiohn* |

| Is it easy/difficult? | **Είναι εύκολο/δύσκολο;** *ee*·neh *ehf*·koh·loh/*ees*·koh·loh |
|---|---|
| Is it far/steep? | **Είναι μακριά/απότομο;** *ee*·neh mahk·ree·*ah*/ah·*poh*·toh·moh |
| How far is it to…? | **Πόσο μακριά είναι για…;** *poh*·soh mahk·ree·*ah* *ee*·neh yah… |
| Can you show me on the map? | **Μπορείτε να μου δείξετε στο χάρτη;** boh·*ree*·teh nah moo *THee*·kseh·teh stoh *khahr*·tee |
| I'm lost. | **Έχω χαθεί.** *eh*·khoh khah·*thee* |
| Where's…? | **Πού είναι…;** poo *ee*·neh… |
| the ancient temple | **ο αρχαίος ναός** oh ahr·*kheh*·ohs nah·*ohs* |
| the ancient theater | **το αρχαίο θέατρο** toh ahr·*kheh*·oh theh·ah·troh |
| the bridge | **η γέφυρα** ee *yeh*·fee·rah |
| the cave | **το σπήλαιο** toh *spee*·leh·oh |
| the desert | **η έρημος** ee *eh*·ree·mohs |
| the cliff | **ο γκρεμός** oh greh·*mohs* |
| the farm | **η φάρμα** ee *fahr*·mah |
| the field | **το χωράφι** toh khoh·*rah*·fee |

| | | |
|---|---|---|
| the forest | **το δάσος** | toh <u>THah</u>·sohs |
| the gorge | **το φαράγγι** | toh fah·<u>rah</u>·gee |
| the hill | **ο λόφος** | oh <u>loh</u>·fohs |
| the lake | **η λίμνη** | ee <u>leem</u>·nee |
| the mountain | **το βουνό** | toh voo·<u>noh</u> |
| the nature reserve | **ο εθνικός δρυμός** | oh ehth·nee·<u>kohs</u> THree·<u>mohs</u> |
| the viewpoint | **η πανοραμική θέση** | ee pah·noh·rah·mee·<u>kee</u> theh·seh |
| the park | **το πάρκο** | toh <u>pahr</u>·koh |
| the path | **το μονοπάτι** | toh moh·noh·<u>pah</u>·tee |
| the peak | **η κορυφή** | ee koh·ree·<u>fee</u> |
| the picnic area | **η περιοχή για πικ-νικ** | ee peh·ree·oh·<u>khee</u> yah peek·neek |
| the pond | **η λίμνη** | ee <u>lee</u>·mnee |
| the river | **ο ποταμός** | oh poh·tah·<u>mohs</u> |
| the sea | **η θάλασσα** | ee <u>thah</u>·lah·sah |
| the thermal bath | **τα ιαματικά λουτρα** | tah ee·ah·mah·tee·<u>kah</u> loot·<u>rah</u> |
| the hot spring | **τα ιαματικά λουτρα** | tah ee·ah·mah·tee·<u>kah</u> loot·<u>rah</u> |
| the stream | **το ρέμα** | toh <u>reh</u>·mah |
| the valley | **η κοιλάδα** | ee kee·<u>lah</u>·THah |
| the vineyard | **ο αμπελώνας** | oh ah·beh·<u>loh</u>·nahs |
| the volcano | **το ηφαίστειο** | toh ee·<u>feh</u>·stee·oh |
| the waterfall | **ο καταρράκτης** | oh kah·tah·<u>rahk</u>·tees |

# Going Out

## ESSENTIAL

| | |
|---|---|
| What's there to do in the evenings? | **Τι μπορώ να κάνω τα βράδια;** tee boh‑roh nah kah‑noh tah vrahTH‑yah |
| Do you have a program of events? | **Έχετε ένα πρόγραμμα εκδηλώσεων;** eh‑kheh‑teh eh‑nah prohgh‑rah‑mah ehk‑THee‑loh‑seh‑ohn |
| What's playing at the movies [cinema] tonight? | **Τι παίζει ο κινηματογράφος απόψε;** tee peh‑zee oh kee‑nee‑mah‑tohgh‑rah‑fohs ah‑poh‑pseh |
| Where's...? | **Πού είναι...;** poo ee‑neh... |
| the downtown area | **το κέντρο της πόλης** toh kehn‑droh tees poh‑lees |
| the bar | **το μπαρ** toh bahr |
| the dance club | **η ντισκοτέκ** ee dees‑koh‑tehk |
| Is there a cover charge? | **Υπάρχει κουβέρ;** ee‑pahr‑hee koo‑vehr |

## Entertainment

| | |
|---|---|
| Can you recommend...? | **Μπορείτε να συστήσετε...;** boh‑ree‑teh nah sees‑tee‑seh‑teh... |
| a concert | **μια συναυλία** miah see‑nahv‑lee‑ah |
| a movie | **μια ταινία** miah teh‑nee‑ah |
| an opera | **μια όπερα** miah oh‑peh‑rah |
| a play | **μια θεατρική παράσταση** miah theh‑aht‑ree‑kee pah‑rahs‑tah‑see |
| When does it start/end? | **Πότε αρχίζει/τελειώνει;** poh‑the ahr‑khee‑zee/teh‑lioh‑nee |
| What's the dress code? | **Πώς πρέπει να ντυθώ;** pohs preh‑pee nah dee‑thoh |
| I like... | **Μου αρέσει...** moo ah‑reh‑see... |
| classical music | **η κλασική μουσική** ee klah‑see‑kee moo‑see‑kee |

Nightlife in Greece is excellent. There are a great number of cafes, bars and dance and music clubs throughout cities and on the islands. Greeks will often start the evening around 10:00 p.m.; the evening will most likely go on well into the early hours at a nightclub or at **μπουζούκια** (*boo·zoo·kee·ah*), live music clubs. **Bouzoukia** are a big part of Greek nightlife, where Greeks often reserve a table and spend the evening listening, throwing flowers at their favorite singers and sometimes dancing on the tables. These clubs offer a range of musical genres: from traditional Greek music to contemporary pop. A typical evening there would end at around 5:00 a.m., when you will often encounter traffic jams along the main club strips. Clubbing is also very popular, with open-air summer clubs operating from about April to October.

| | | |
|---|---|---|
| folk music | **η δημοτική μουσική** | *ee THee·moh·tee·kee moo·see·kee* |
| jazz | **η τζαζ** | *ee jahz* |
| pop music | **η ποπ μουσική** | *ee pohp moo·see·kee* |
| rap | **η ραπ** | *ee rahp* |

## Nightlife

| | | |
|---|---|---|
| What's there to do in the evenings/at night? | **Τι μπορώ να κάνω τα βράδια;/τη νύχτα;** | *tee boh·roh nah kah·noh tah vrahTH·yah/tee nee·khtah* |

---

### YOU MAY HEAR...

**Παρακαλώ απενεργοποιήστε τα κινητά σας τηλέφωνα.** *pah·rah·kah·loh ah·peh·nehr·ghoh·pee·ees·teh tah kee·nee·tah sahs tee·leh·foh·nah*

Turn off your mobile phones, please.

| | |
|---|---|
| Can you recommend...? | **Μπορείτε να συστήσετε…;** *boh•ree•teh nah sees•tee•seh•teh…* |
| a bar | **ένα μπαρ** *eh•nah bahr* |
| a cabaret | **ένα καμπαρέ** *eh•nah kah•bah•reh* |
| a casino | **ένα καζίνο** *eh•nah kah•zee•noh* |
| a dance club | **μια ντισκοτέκ** *miah dees•koh•tehk* |
| a gay club | **ένα κλαμπ για γκέι** *eh•nah geh•ee klahb* |
| a jazz club | **ένα κλαμπ με τζαζ μουσική** *eh•nah klahb meh jahz moo•see•kee* |
| a club with local music | **ένα κλαμπ με τοπική μουσική** *eh•nah klahb meh toh•pee•kee moo•see•kee* |
| Is there live music? | **Παίζει live μουσική;** *peh•zee lah•eev moo•see•kee* |
| How do I get there? | **Πώς πάω εκεί;** *pohs pah•oh eh•kee* |
| Is there a cover charge? | **Το κουβέρ χρεώνεται;** *toh koo•vehr khreh•oh•neh•teh* |
| Let's go dancing. | **Πάμε για χορό.** *pah•meh yah khoh•roh* |
| Is this area safe at night? | **Η περιοχή είναι ασφαλής τη νύχτα;** *ee peh•ree•oh•khee ee•neh ah•sfah•lees tee nee•khtah* |

129

The Athens Festival takes place every summer and includes various concerts and theatrical performances particularly in the Odeion of Herod Atticus and the Epidaurus Ancient Theater, among other venues. Look out for feast days, especially on the islands. Some smaller villages or towns will often hold an amazing party with food, drink and music to celebrate the feast day of the patron saint of the local church or of the town.

Very useful information in English can be found in the Athens News, a newspaper which includes TV, movie, theater and other cultural listings. *Athens News* also includes information on where to buy tickets for various events.

# Special Requirements

### ESSENTIAL

| | |
|---|---|
| I'm here on business. | **Είμαι εδώ για δουλειά.** *ee·meh eh·THoh yah THoo·lee·ah* |
| Here's my business card. | **Ορίστε η κάρτα μου.** *oh·rees·teh ee kahr·tah moo* |
| Can I have your card? | **Μου δίνετε την κάρτα σας;** *moo THee·neh·the teen kahr·tah sahs* |
| I have a meeting with... | **Έχω μια συνάντηση με...** *eh·khoh miah see·nahn·dee·see me...* |
| Where's...? | **Πού είναι...;** *poo ee·neh...* |
| the business center | **το επαγγελματικό κέντρο** *toh eh·pah·gehl·mah·tee·koh kehn·droh* |
| the convention hall | **η αίθουσα συνεδριάσεων** *ee eh·thoo·sah see·nehTH·ree·ah·seh·ohn* |
| the meeting room | **η αίθουσα συσκέψεων** *ee eh·thoo·sah sees·keh·pseh·ohn* |

### On Business

| | |
|---|---|
| I'm here to attend... | **Είμαι εδώ για να συμμετάσχω...** *ee·meh eh·THoh yah nah see·meh·tahs·khoh...* |
| a seminar | **σε ένα σεμινάριο** *seh eh·nah seh·mee·nah·ree·oh* |
| a conference | **σε μια σύσκεψη** *seh miah sees·keh·psee* |
| a meeting | **σε μια συνάντηση** *seh miah see·nahn·dee·see* |
| My name is... | **Λέγομαι...** *leh·ghoh·meh...* |
| May I introduce my colleague...? | **Να σας συστήσω τον m /την f συνάδελφό μου...;** *nah sahs sees·tee·soh tohn/teen see·nah·THehl·foh moo...* |

## YOU MAY HEAR...

**Έχετε ραντεβού;** *eh·kheh·teh rahn·deh·voo* — Do you have an appointment?

**Με ποιον;** *meh piohn* — With whom?

**Είναι σε συνάντηση.** *ee·neh she see·nahn·dee·see* — He/She is in a meeting.

**Μισό λεπτό.** *mee·soh lehp·toh* — One moment, please.

**Κάτσε.** *kah·tseh* — Have a seat.

**Θέλεις να πιεις κάτι;** *theh·lees nah pye·ees kah·tee* — Would you like something to drink?

**Ευχαριστώ που ήρθατε.** *ehf·khah·rees·toh poo eer·thah·teh* — Thank you for coming.

| | |
|---|---|
| Pleasure to meet you. | **Χαίρω πολύ.** *kheh·roh poh·lee* |
| I'm sorry I'm late. | **Συγγνώμη που άργησα.** *seegh·noh·mee poo ahr·ghee·sah* |
| I'd like an interpreter. | **Θα ήθελα έναν m /μια f διερμηνέα.** *thah ee·theh·lal eh·nahn/miah THee·ehr·mee·neh·ah* |
| You can reach me at the...Hotel. | **Μπορείτε να με βρείτε στο...Ξενοδοχείο.** *boh·ree·teh nah meh vree·teh stoh... kseh·noh·THoh·khee·oh* |
| I'm here until... | **Θα είμαι εδώ μέχρι...** *thah ee·meh eh·THoh mekh·ree...* |
| I need to... | **Χρειάζομαι να...** *khree·ah·zoh·meh nah...* |
| make a call... | **κάνω ένα τηλέφωνο...** *kah·noh eh·nah tee·leh·foh·noh...* |
| make a photocopy | **βγάλω μια φωτοτυπία** *vghah·loh miah foh·toh·tee·pee·ah* |
| I need to... | **Χρειάζομαι να...** *khree·ah·zoh·meh nah...* |

| | | |
|---|---|---|
| send an e-mail | **στείλω ένα e-mail** _stee·loh eh·nah ee·meh·eel_ | |
| send a fax | **στείλω ένα φαξ** _stee·loh eh·nah fahks_ | |
| send a package | **στείλω ένα πακέτο (αυθημερόν)** _stee·loh_ | |
| (overnight) | _eh·nah pah·keh·toh (ahf·thee·meh·rohn)_ | |
| Nice to meet you. | **Χαίρω πολύ.** _kheh·roh poh·lee_ | |

For Communications, see page 48.

## Traveling with Children

### ESSENTIAL

| | |
|---|---|
| Is there a discount for children? | **Υπάρχει μειωμένο εισιτήριο για παιδιά;** _ee·pahr·khee mee·oh·meh·noh ee·see·tee·ree·oh yah peh·THyah_ |
| Can you recommend a babysitter? | **Μπορείτε να συστήσετε μια υπεύθυνη μπέιμπυ-σίτερ;** _boh·ree·teh nah sees·tee·seh·teh miah ee·pehf·thee·nee beh·ee·bee see·tehr_ |
| Could I have a child's seat/ highchair? | **Μπορούμε να έχουμε ένα παιδικό καθισματάκι/μια καρέκλα μωρού;** _boh·roo·meh naheh·khoo·meh eh·nah peh·THee·koh kah·theez·mah·tah·kee/miah kah·reh·klah moh·roo_ |
| Where can I change the baby? | **Πού μπορώ να αλλάξω το μωρό;** _poo boh·roh nah ah·lah·ksoh toh moh·roh_ |

### Out & About

| | |
|---|---|
| Can you recommend something for the kids? | **Μπορείτε να μας συστήσετε κάτι για τα παιδιά;** _boh·ree·teh nah mahs sees·tee·seh·the kah·tee yah tah peh·THyah_ |
| Where's...? | **Πού είναι...;** _poo ee·neh..._ |

| the amusement park | **το πάρκο ψυχαγωγίας** *toh pahr·koh psee·khah·ghoh·yee·ahs* |
| the arcade | **η αίθουσα ψυχαγωγίας** *ee eh·thoo·sah psee·khah·ghoh·yee·ahs* |
| the kiddie pool | **η παιδική πισίνα** *ee peh·THee·kee pee·see·nah* |
| the park | **το πάρκο** *toh pahr·koh* |
| the playground | **η παιδική χαρά** *ee peh·THee·kee khah·rah* |
| the zoo | **ο ζωολογικός κήπος** *oh zoh·oh·loh·yee·kohs kee·poh* |
| Are kids allowed? | **Επιτρέπονται τα παιδιά;** *eh·pee·treh·pohn·deh tah peh·THyah* |
| Is it safe for kids? | **Είναι ασφαλές για παιδιά;** *ee·neh ahs·fah·lehs yah tah peh·THyah* |
| Is it suitable for...year olds? | **Είναι κατάλληλο για παιδιά...ετών;** *ee·neh kah·tah·lee·loh yah peh·THyah...eh·tohn* |

For Numbers, see page 156.

## Baby Essentials

| Do you have...? | **Έχετε...;** *eh·kheh·teh...* |
| a baby bottle | **ένα μπιμπερό** *eh·nah bee·beh·roh* |
| baby food | **παιδικές τροφές** *peh·THee·kehs troh·fehs* |
| baby wipes | **υγρά μαντηλάκια** *eegh·rah mahn·dee·lah·kiah* |
| a car seat | **ένα παιδικό κάθισμα** *eh·nah peh·THee·koh kah·thee·smah* |
| a children's menu | **έναν παιδικό κατάλογο** *eh·nahn peh·THee·koh kah·tah·loh·ghoh* |

### YOU MAY HEAR...

| **Τι όμορφο!** *tee oh·mohr·foh* | How cute! |
| **Πως τον/την λένε;** *pohs tohn/teen leh·neh* | What's his/her name? |
| **Πόσο χρονών είναι;** *poh·soh khroh·nohn ee·neh* | How old is he/she? |

| a child's portion | **μια παιδική μερίδα** miah peh•THee•kee meh•ree•THah |
| a child's seat/ highchair | **ένα παιδικό κάθισμα/καρεκλάκι** eh•nah peh•ee•koh kah•theez•mah/kah•rehk•lah•kee moh•roo |
| a crib/cot | **μια κούνια/ένα παιδικό κρεβάτι** miah koo•niah/ eh•nah peh•THee•koh kreh•vah•tee |
| diapers [nappies] | **πάνες μωρού** ee pah•nehs moh•roo |
| formula | **βρεφικό γάλα** vreh•fee•koh ghah•lah |
| a pacifier [dummy] | **μια πιπίλα** miah pee•pee•lah |
| a playpen | **ένα παιδικό παρκάκι** eh•nah peh•THee•koh pahr•kah•kee |
| a stroller [pushchair] | **ένα καροτσάκι** eh•nah kah•roh•tsah•kee |
| Can I breastfeed the baby here? | **Μπορώ να θηλάσω το μωρό εδώ;** boh•roh nah thee•lah•soh toh moh•roh eh•THoh |
| Where can I change the baby? | **Πού μπορώ να αλλάξω το μωρό;** poo boh•roh nah ah•lah•ksoh toh moh•roh |

For Dining with Children, see page 63.

## Babysitting

| Can you recommend a reliable babysitter? | **Μπορείτε να συστήσετε μια υπεύθυνη μπέιμπυ-σίτερ;** boh•ree•teh nah sees•tee•seh•teh miah ee•pehf•thee•nee beh•ee•bee see•tehr |

| | |
|---|---|
| What's the charge? | **Ποιό είναι το κόστος;** *pioh ee·neh toh kohs·tohs* |
| I'll pick them up at... | **Θα τα πάρω στις...** *thah tah pah·roh stees...* |
| I can be reached at... | **Θα με βρείτε στο...** *thah meh vree·teh stoh...* |

For Time, see page 158.

## Health & Emergency

| | |
|---|---|
| Can you recommend a pediatrician? | **Μπορείτε να συστήσετε έναν παιδίατρο;** *boh·ree·teh nah sees·tee·seh·teh eh·nahn peh·THee·aht·roh* |
| My child is allergic to... | **Το παιδί μου είναι αλλεργικό σε...** *toh peh·THee moo ee·neh ah·lehr·ghee·koh seh...* |
| My child is missing. | **Λείπει το παιδί μου.** *lee·pee toh peh·THee moo* |
| Have you seen a boy/girl? | **Είδατε ένα αγόρι/κορίτσι;** *ee·THah·the eh·nah ah·ghoh·ree/koh·ree·tsee* |

# Disabled Travelers

## ESSENTIAL

| | |
|---|---|
| Is there...? | **Υπάρχει...;** *ee·pahr·khee...* |
| access for the disabled | **πρόσβαση για άτομα με ειδικές ανάγκες;** *prohz·vah·see yah ah·toh·mah meh ee·THee·kehs ah·nahn·gehs* |
| a wheelchair ramp | **ράμπα για αναπηρικό καρότσι** *rahm·bah yah ah·nah·pee·ree·koh kah·roh·tsee* |
| a disabled-accessible toilet | **προσβάσιμη τουαλέτα για ανάπηρους** *prohs·vah·see·mee too·ah·leh·tah yah ah·nah·pee·roos* |

| I need… | **Χρειάζομαι…** *khree·ah·zoh·meh…* |
| assistance | **βοήθεια** *voh·ee·thiah* |
| an elevator [lift] | **ασανσέρ** *ah·sahn·sehr* |
| a ground-floor room | **ισόγειο** *ee·soh·yee·oh* |

## Asking for Assistance

| I'm disabled. | **Είμαι ανάπηρος.** *ee·meh ah·nah·pee·rohs* |
| I'm deaf. | **Είμαι κουφός.** *ee·meh koo·fohs* |
| I'm visually/ hearing impaired. | **Έχω προβλήματα όρασης/ακοής.** *eh·khoh prohv·lee·mah·tah oh·rah·sees/ah·koh·ees* |
| I'm unable to walk far/ use the stairs. | **Δεν μπορώ να περπατήσω/χρησιμοποιήσω τις σκάλες.** *thehn boh·roh nah pehr·pah·tee·soh/ khree·see·moh·pee·ee·soh tees skah·lehs* |
| Please speak louder. | **Μιλήστε πιο δυνατά.** *mee·lee·steh pioh THee·nah·tah* |
| Can I bring my wheelchair? | **Μπορώ να φέρω την αναπηρική μου καρέκλα;** *boh·roh nah feh·roh teen ah·nah·pee·ree·kee moo kah·rehk·lah* |
| Are guide dogs permitted? | **Επιτρέπονται οι σκύλοι οδηγοί;** *eh·peet·reh·pohn·deh ee skee·lee oh·THee·ghee* |
| Can you help me? | **Μπορείτε να με βοηθήσετε;** *boh·ree·teh nah meh voh·ee·thee·seh·teh* |
| Please open/hold the door. | **Παρακαλώ ανοίξτε/κρατείστε την πόρτα.** *pah·rah·kah·loh ah·nee·ksteh/krah·tee·steh teen pohr·tah* |

# In an
# Emergency

# Emergencies

## ESSENTIAL

| | |
|---|---|
| Help! | **Βοήθεια!** voh·<u>ee</u>·thee·ah |
| Go away! | **Φύγετε!** <u>fee</u>·yeh·teh |
| Stop, thief! | **Σταματήστε τον κλέφτη!** stah·mah·<u>tees</u> teh tohn <u>klehf</u>·tee |
| Get a doctor! | **Φωνάξτε ένα γιατρό!** foh·<u>nahks</u>·teh <u>eh</u>·nah yaht·<u>roh</u> |
| Fire! | **Φωτιά!** foh·<u>tiah</u> |
| I'm lost. | **Έχω χαθεί.** <u>eh</u>·khoh khah·<u>thee</u> |
| Can you help me? | **Μπορείτε να με βοηθήσετε;** boh·<u>ree</u>·teh nah meh voh·ee·<u>thee</u>·seh·the |

139

In an emergency, dial: **100** for the police, **199** for the fire brigade and **166** for the ambulance. Or you can also dial the European SOS number: **112**

## YOU MAY HEAR...

| | |
|---|---|
| **Παρακαλώ συμπληρώστε αυτό το έντυπο.** pah·rah·kah·<u>loh</u> sehm·blee·<u>rohs</u>·teh ahf·<u>toh</u> toh <u>ehn</u>·tee·poh | Please fill out this form |
| **Την ταυτότητά σας, παρακαλώ.** teen tahf·<u>toh</u>·tee·<u>tah</u> sahs pah·rah·kah·<u>loh</u> | Your identification, please. |
| **Πότε/Πού έγινε;** <u>poh</u>·teh/poo <u>eh</u>·yee·neh | When/Where did it happen? |
| **Πώς είναι εμφανισιακά;** pohs <u>ee</u>·neh ehm·fah·nee·see·ah·<u>kah</u> | What does he/she look like? |

# Police

## ESSENTIAL

| | |
|---|---|
| Call the police! | **Φωνάξτε την αστυνομία!** foh-_nahks_-teh teen ahs-tee-noh-_mee_-ah |
| Where's the nearest police station? | **Πού είναι το κοντινότερο αστυνομικό τμήμα;** poo ee-neh toh kohn-dee-_noh_-teh-roh ahs-tee-noh-mee-_koh_ tmee-mah |
| There has been an accident. | **Έγινε ένα ατύχημα.** _eh_-yee-neh eh-nah ah-_tee_-khee-mah |
| My child is missing. | **Λείπει το παιδί μου.** _lee_-pee toh peh-_THee_ moo |
| I need... | **Χρειάζομαι...** khree-_ah_-zoh-meh... |
| an interpreter | **έναν διερμηνέα** _eh_-nahn THee-ehr-mee-_neh_-ah |
| I need... | **Χρειάζομαι...** khree-_ah_-zoh-meh... |
| to contact my lawyer | **να επικοινωνήσω με τον δικηγόρο μου** nah eh-pee-kee-noh-_nee_-soh meh tohn THee-kee-_ghoh_-roh moo |
| to make a phone call | **να κάνω ένα τηλέφωνο** nah _kah_-noh eh-nah tee-_leh_-foh-noh |
| I'm innocent. | **Είμαι αθώος m /αθώα f .** ee-meh ah-_thoh_-ohs/ ah-_thoh_-ah |

## Crime & Lost Property

| | |
|---|---|
| I want to report... | **Θέλω να αναφέρω...** _theh_-loh nah ah nah-_feh_-roh... |
| a mugging | **μια ληστεία** mlah lehs-_tee_-ah |
| a rape | **έναν βιασμό** _eh_-nahn vee-ahs-_moh_ |
| a theft | **μια κλοπή** miah kloh-_pee_ |
| I've been robbed/ mugged. | **Με έκλεψαν/λήστεψαν.** meh _ehk_-leh-psahn/ _lees_-teh-psahn |
| My...has/have been stolen. | **Μου έκλεψαν...μου.** moo _ehk_-leh-psahn...moo |

| I've lost my... | **Έχασα...** *eh·khah·sah...* |
| knapsack | **τον σάκκο** *tohn sah·koh* |
| bicycle | **το ποδήλατο** *toh poh·THee·lah·toh* |
| camera | **τη φωτογραφική μηχανή** *tee foh·tohgh·rah·fee·kee mee·khah·nee* |
| car | **το αυτοκίνητο ι** *toh ahf·toh·kee·nee·toh* |
| computer | **τον υπολογιστή** *tohn ee·poh·loh·yees·tee* |
| credit cards | **τις πιστωτικές κάρτες** *tees pees·toh·tee·kehs kahr·tehs* |
| jewelry | **τα κοσμήματα** *tah kohs·mee·mah·tah* |
| money | **τα χρήματα** *tah khree·mah·tah* |
| passport | **το διαβατήριο** *toh THiah·vah·tee·ree·oh* |
| purse | **την τσάντα** *teen tsahn·dah* |
| traveler's checks | **τις ταξιδιωτικές επιταγές** *tees tah·ksee·THee·oh·tee·kehs eh·pee·tah·yehs* |
| wallet | **το πορτοφόλι** *toh pohr·toh·foh·lee* |
| I need a police report. | **Θέλω να κάνω αναφορά στην αστυνομία.** *theh·loh nah kah·noh ah·nah·foh·rah steen ah·stee·noh·mee·ah* |
| Where is the British/American/Irish embassy? | **Πού είναι η αγγλική/αμερικάνικη/ιρλανδική πρεσβεία;** *poo ee·neh ee ag·lee·kee/ah·meh·ree·kah·nee·kee/eer·lahn·THee·kee preh·svee·ah* |

## Health

### ESSENTIAL

| | |
|---|---|
| I'm sick [ill]. | **Είμαι άρρωστος.** _ee_·meh _ah_·rohs·tohs |
| I need an English-speaking doctor. | **Χρειάζομαι έναν γιατρό που να μιλάει αγγλικά.** khree·_ah_·zoh·meh _eh_·nahn yaht·_roh_ poo nah mee·_lah_·ee ang·lee·_kah_ |
| It hurts here. | **Με πονάει εδώ.** meh poh·_nah_·ee eh·_THoh_ |
| I have a stomachache. | **Έχω στομαχόπονο.** _eh_·khoh stoh·mah·_khoh_·poh·noh |

### Finding a Doctor

| | |
|---|---|
| Can you recommend a doctor/dentist? | **Μπορείτε να συστήσετε έναν γιατρό/οδοντίατρο;** boh·_ree_·teh nah sees·_tee_·seh·the _eh_·nahn yaht·_roh_/oh·THohn·_dee_·aht·roh |
| Could the doctor come to see me here? | **Μπορεί να έρθει να με δει εδώ ο γιατρός;** boh·_ree_ nah _ehr_·thee nah meh THee eh·_THoh_ oh yaht·_rohs_ |
| I need an English-speaking doctor. | **Χρειάζομαι έναν γιατρό που να μιλάει αγγλικά.** khree·_ah_·zoh·meh _eh_·nahn yaht·_roh_ poo nah mee·_lah_·ee ahng·lee·_kah_ |
| What are the office hours? | **Ποιες ώρες δέχεται;** piehs _oh_·rehs _THeh_·kheh·teh |
| Can I make an appointment for...? | **Μπορώ να κλείσω ένα ραντεβού για...;** boh·_roh_ nah _klee_·soh _eh_·nah rahn·deh·_voo_ yah... |
| today | **σήμερα** _see_·meh·rah |
| tomorrow | **αύριο** _ahv_·ree·oh |
| as soon as possible | **όσο το δυνατό πιο σύντομα** _oh_·soh toh THee·nah·_toh_ pioh _seen_·doh·mah |
| It's urgent. | **Είναι επείγον.** _ee_·neh eh·_pee_·ghohn |

## Symptoms

| I'm... | **Έχω...** _eh_•khoh... |
| --- | --- |
| bleeding | **αιμορραγία** eh•moh•rah•_yee_•ah |
| constipated | **δυσκοιλιότητα** THees•kee•lee•_oh_•tee•tah |
| dizzy | **ζαλάδες** zah•_lah_•THehs |
| nauseous | **ναυτία** nahf•_tee_•ah |
| vomiting | **εμετούς** eh•meh•_toos_ |
| It hurts here. | **Με πονάει εδώ.** meh poh•_nah_•ee eh•_THoh_ |
| I have... | **Έχω...** _eh_•khoh... |
| an allergic | **αλλεργική αντίδραση** ah•lehr•yee•_kee_ |
| reaction | ahn•dee•_THrah_•see |
| a chest pain | **πόνο στο στήθος** _poh_•noh stoh _stee_•thohs |
| cramps | **κράμπες** _krah_•behs |
| diarrhea | **διάρροια** THee•_ah_•ree•ah |
| an earache | **πόνο στο αυτί** _poh_•noh stoh ahf•_tee_ |
| a fever | **πυρετό** pee•reh•_toh_ |
| a pain | **πόνο** _poh_•noh |
| a rash | **εξάνθημα** eh•_ksahn_•thee•mah |
| a sprain | **διάστρεμμα** THee•_ahs_•treh•mah |
| some swelling | **πρήξιμο** _pree_•ksee•moh |
| a sore throat | **πονόλαιμο** poh•_noh_•leh•moh |
| a stomachache | **στομαχόπονο** stoh•mah•_khoh_•poh•noh |
| sunstroke | **ηλίαση** ee•_lee_•ah•see |
| I've been sick [ill] | **Αισθάνομαι άρρωστος εδώ και...ημέρες.** |
| for...days. | ehs•_thah_•noh•meh _ah_•rohs•tohs eh•_THoh_ keh ee•_meh_•rehs |

For Numbers, see page 156.

## Conditions

| I'm... | **Έχω...** _eh_•khoh... |
| --- | --- |
| anemic | **αναιμία** ah•neh•_mee_•ah |
| asthmatic | **άσθμα** _ahs_•thmah |

| | |
|---|---|
| diabetic | **διαβήτη** THiah·<u>vee</u>·tee |
| epileptic | **επιληψία** eh·pee·lee·<u>psee</u>·ah |
| I'm allergic to antibiotics/ penicillin. | **Είμαι αλλεργικός στα αντιβιωτικά/στην πενικιλίν** <u>ee</u>·meh ah·lehr·yee·<u>kohs</u> stah ahn·dee·vee·oh·tee·<u>kah</u>, steen peh·nee·kee·<u>lee</u>·nee |
| I have arthritis/ (high/low) blood pressure. | **Έχω αρθρίτιδα/(υψηλή/χαμηλή) πίεση.** <u>eh</u>·khoh ahr·<u>three</u>·tee·THah/(ee·psee·<u>lee</u>/ khah·mee·<u>lee</u>) <u>pee</u>·eh·see |
| I have a heart condition. | **Έχω πρόβλημα καρδιάς.** <u>eh</u>·khoh <u>prohv</u>·lee·mah kahrTH·<u>yahs</u> |
| I'm on… | **Παίρνω…** <u>pehr</u>·noh… |

144

---

### YOU MAY HEAR...

| | |
|---|---|
| **Τι συμβαίνει;** tee seem·<u>veh</u>·nee | What's wrong? |
| **Πού πονάει;** poo poh·<u>nah</u>·ee | Where does it hurt? |
| **Πονάει εδώ;** poh·<u>nah</u>·ee eh·<u>THoh</u> | Does it hurt here? |
| **Παίρνετε άλλα φάρμακα;** <u>pehr</u>·neh·teh <u>ah</u>·lah <u>fahr</u>·mah·kah | Are you taking any other medication? |
| **Είστε αλλεργικός *m* /αλλεργική *f* σε κάτι;** <u>ees</u>·teh ah·lehr·yeek·<u>ohs</u>/ah·lehr·yeek·<u>ee</u> seh <u>kah</u>·tee | Are you allergic to anything? |
| **Ανοίξτε το στόμα σας.** ah·<u>nee</u>·ksteh toh <u>stoh</u>·mah sahs | Open your mouth. |
| **Πάρτε μια βαθιά αναπνοή.** <u>pahr</u>·teh miah vah·<u>thiah</u> ah·nahp·noh·<u>ee</u> | Breathe deeply. |
| **Βήξτε, παρακαλώ.** <u>vee</u>·ksteh, pah·rah·kah·<u>loh</u> | Cough, please. |
| **Θέλω να πάτε στο νοσοκομείο.** <u>theh</u>·loh nah <u>pah</u>·teh stoh noh·soh·koh·<u>mee</u>·oh | I want you to go to the hospital. |

## Treatment

| | |
|---|---|
| Do I need a prescription/medicine? | **Χρειάζομαι συνταγή/φάρμακο;** *khree•ah•zoh•meh see•ntah•ghee/fahr•mah•koh* |
| Can you prescribe a generic drug [unbranded medication]? | **Μπορείτε να γράψετε ένα γένιο φάρμακο;** *boh•ree•teh nah ghrah•pseh•teh eh•nah fahr•mah•koh* |
| Where can I get it? | **Από πού μπορώ να το πάρω;** *ah•poh poo boh•roh nah toh pah•roh* |

For Pharmacy, see page 147.

## Hospital

| | |
|---|---|
| Please notify my family. | **Παρακαλώ ειδοποιήστε την οικογένειά μου** *pah•rah•kah•loh ee•THoh•pee•ees•teh teen ee•koh•yeh•nee•ah moo* |
| I'm in pain. | **Πονάω.** *poh•nah•oh* |
| I need a doctor/nurse. | **Χρειάζομαι έναν γιατρό/μια νοσοκόμα.** *khree•ah•zoh• meh eh•nahn yaht•roh/miah noh•soh•koh•mah* |
| When are visiting hours? | **Ποιες είναι οι ώρες επισκεπτηρίου;** *pee•ehs ee•neh ee oh•rehs eh•pees•kehp•tee•ree•oo* |
| I'm visiting... | **Επισκέπτομαι...** *eh•pees•kehp•toh•meh...* |

## Dentist

| | |
|---|---|
| I've broken a tooth. | **Έσπασα ένα δόντι.** *ehs•pah•sah eh•nah THohn•dee* |
| I'm lost a filling. | **Μου έφυγε ένα σφράγισμα.** *moo eh•fee•gheh eh•nah sfrah•yees•mah* |
| This tooth hurts. | **Αυτό το δόντι με πονάει.** *ahf•toh toh THohn•dee meh poh•nah•ee* |
| Can you fix this denture? | **Μπορείτε να φτιάξετε αυτή την τεχνητή οδοντοστοιχία;** *boh•ree•teh nah ftee•ah•kseh•teh ahf•tee teen tehkh•nee•tee oh•THohn•dohs•tee•khee•ah* |

## Gynecologist

| | |
|---|---|
| I have menstrual cramps/a vaginal infection. | **Έχω πόνους περιόδου/κολπική μόλυνση.** *eh•khoh <u>poh</u>•noos peh•ree•<u>oh</u>•THoo/kohl•pee• <u>kee</u> moh•leen•see* |
| I missed my period. | **Έχω καθυστέρηση.** *eh•khoh kah•thees•<u>teh</u>•ree•see* |
| I'm on the Pill. | **Παίρνω αντισυλληπτικό χάπι.** *<u>pehr</u>•noh ahn•dee•see•leep•tee•<u>koh</u> <u>khah</u>•pee* |
| I'm (...months) pregnant. | **Είμαι (...μηνών) έγκυος.** *<u>ee</u>•meh (...mee•<u>nohn</u>) eh•gee•ohs* |
| I'm (not) pregnant. | **(Δεν) Είμαι έγκυος.** *(THehn) ee•meh ehn•gee•ohs* |
| I haven't had my period for...months. | **Δεν έχω περίοδο εδώ και...μήνες.** *THehn eh•khoh peh•<u>ree</u>•oh•THoh eh•<u>THoh</u> keh...<u>mee</u>•nehs* |

For Numbers, see page 156.

## Optician

| | |
|---|---|
| I've lost... | **Έχασα...** *eh•khah•sah...* |
| a contact lens | **έναν φακό επαφής** *eh•nahn fah•<u>koh</u> eh•pah•<u>fees</u>* |
| my glasses | **τα γυαλιά μου** *tah yah•lee•<u>ah</u> moo* |
| a lens | **έναν φακό** *eh•nahn fah•<u>koh</u>* |

## Payment & Insurance

| | |
|---|---|
| How much? | **Πόσο;** *poh•soh* |
| Can I pay by credit card? | **Μπορώ να πληρώσω με αυτή την πιστωτική κάρτα;** *boh•<u>roh</u> nah plee•<u>roh</u>•soh meh ahf•tee teen pees•toh•tee•<u>kee</u> kahr•tah* |
| I have insurance. | **Έχω ασφάλεια.** *eh•khoh ahs•<u>fah</u>•lee•ah* |
| Can I have a receipt for my insurance? | **Μπορώ να έχω μια απόδειξη για την ασφάλεια υγείας μου;** *boh•<u>roh</u> nah eh•khoh miah ah•<u>poh</u>•THee• ksee yah teen ahs•<u>fah</u>•lee•ah ee•<u>yee</u>•ahs moo* |

# Pharmacy

## ESSENTIAL

| | |
|---|---|
| Where's the nearest pharmacy? | **Πού είναι το κοντινότερο φαρμακείο;** *poo ee·neh toh kohn·dee·noh·teh·roh fahr·mah·kee·oh* |
| What time does the pharmacy [chemist] open/close? | **Τι ώρα ανοίγει/κλείνει το φαρμακείο;** *tee oh·rah ah·nee·yee/klee·nee toh fahr·mah·kee·oh* |
| What would you recommend for…? | **Τι συνιστάτε για…;** *tee see·nees·tah·teh yah…* |
| How much should I take? | **Πόσο πρέπει να πάρω;** *poh·soh preh·pee nah pah·roh* |
| Can you fill [make up] this prescription for me? | **Μπορείτε να μου φτιάξετε αυτή τη συνταγή;** *boh·ree·teh nah moo ftiah·kseh·teh ahf·tee tee seen·dah·yee* |
| I'm allergic to… | **Είμαι αλλεργικός _m_ /αλλεργική _f_ σε** … *ee·meh ah·lehr·yeek·ohs/ah·lehr·yeek·ee seh…* |

Many medications that are prescription-only in other countries can be bought over the counter in Greece. Pharmacies are open during normal working hours and on a rotating basis at all other times, so that there will always be one open 24 hours a day in any given area. Read the list on display in all pharmacy windows to find the one nearest to you.

## What to Take

| | | |
|---|---|---|
| How much should I take? | **Πόσο πρέπει να πάρω;** | _poh_-soh _preh_-pee nah _pah_-ro |
| How many times a day should I take it? | **Πόσες φορές την ημέρα πρέπει να το παίρνω;** | _poh_-sehs foh-_rehs_ teen ee-_meh_-rah _preh_-pee nah toh _pehr_-no |
| Is it suitable for children? | **Είναι κατάλληλο για παιδιά;** | _ee_-neh kah-_tah_-lee-loh yah peh-_THyah_ |
| I'm taking… | **Παίρνω…** | _pehr_-noh… |
| Are there side effects? | **Έχει παρενέργειες;** | _eh_-khee pah-reh-_nehr_-yee-ehs |
| I'd like some medicine for… | **Θα ήθελα ένα φάρμακο για…** | thah _ee_-theh-lah _eh_-nah _fahr_-mah-koh yah… |
| a cold | **το κρυολόγημα** | toh kree-oh-_loh_-yee-mah |
| a cough | **το βήχα** | toh _vee_-khah |
| diarrhea | **τη διάρροια** | tee THee-_ah_-ree-ah |
| a headache | **πονοκέφαλο** | poh-noh-_keh_-fah-loh |
| hay fever | **την αλλεργία σε γύρη** | teen ah-lehr-_yee_-ah seh _yee_-ree |
| insect bites | **το τσίμπημα από έντομο** | toh _tseem_-bee-mah ah-_poh_ ehn-doh-moh |
| motion sickness | **τη ναυτία** | tee nahf-_tee_-ah |
| a sore throat | **τον πονόλαιμο** | tohn poh-_noh_-leh-moh |
| sunburn | **τα εγκαύματα από τον ήλιο** | tah eh-_gkahv_-mah-tah ahpoh tohn _ee_-lioh |
| a toothache | **πονόδοντο** | poh-_noh_-THoh-doh |
| an upset stomach | **το στομαχόπονο** | toh stoh-mah-_khoh_-poh-noh |

## YOU MAY SEE...

| | |
|---|---|
| **ΧΑΠΙ(Α)** _khah·pee(ah)_ | tablet(s) |
| **ΣΤΑΓΟΝΕΣ** _stah·ghoh·nehs_ | drops |
| **ΠΡΙΝ/ΜΕΤΑ/ΜΕ ΤΟ ΓΕΥΜΑ** _preen/ me·tah/meh toh yehv·mah_ | before/after/with meals |
| **ΜΕ ΑΔΕΙΟ ΣΤΟΜΑΧΙ** _meh ah·THioh stoh·mah·khee_ | on an empty stomach |
| **ΜΟΝΟ ΓΙΑ ΕΞΩΤΕΡΙΚΗ ΧΡΗΣΗ** _moh·noh ya eh·ksoh·teh·ree·kee khree·see_ | for external use only |
| **ΜΙΑ/ΔΥΟ/ΤΡΕΙΣ ΦΟΡΕΣ ΤΗΝ ΗΜΕΡΑ** _miah/ee·oh/trees foh·rehs teen ee·meh·rah_ | once/twice/three times a day |

## Basic Supplies

| | |
|---|---|
| I'd like... | **Θα ήθελα...** _thah ee·theh·lah..._ |
| acetaminophen [paracetamol] | **παρακεταμόλη** _pah·rah·keh·tah·moh·lee_ |
| antiseptic cream | **μια αντισηπτική κρέμα** _miah ahn·dee·seep·tee·kee kreh·mah_ |
| aspirin | **ασπιρίνη** _ahs·pee·ree·nee_ |
| bandages | **επιδέσμους** _eh·pee·THehz·moos_ |
| a comb | **μια χτένα** _miah khteh·nah_ |
| condoms | **προφυλακτικά** _proh·fee·lahk·tee·kah_ |
| contact lens solution | **ένα υγρό καθαρισμού φακών επαφής** _eegh·roh kah·thah·rees·moo fah·kohn eh·pah·fees_ |
| deodorant | **ένα αποσμητικό** _eh·nah ah·pohz·mee·tee·koh_ |
| a hairbrush | **μια βούρτσα** _miah voor·tsah_ |
| hair spray | **μια λακ** _miah lahk_ |
| ibuprofen | **ιμπουπροφέν** _ee·boo·proh·fehn_ |

| | |
|---|---|
| insect repellent | **εντομοαπωθητικό** *ehn·doh·moh·ah·poh·thee·tee·ko* |
| a nail file | **μια λίμα για τα νύχια** *miah lee·mah yah tah nee·khia* |
| a (disposable) razor | **ένα ξυραφάκι (μιας χρήσης)** *eh·nah ksee·rah·fah·kee (miahs khree·sees)* |
| razor blades | **ξυραφάκια** *ksee·rah·fah·kiah* |
| sanitary napkins [towels] | **σερβιέτες** *sehr·vee·eh·tehs* |
| shampoo/ conditioner | **σαμπουάν/γαλάκτωμα για τα μαλλιά** *sahm·poo·ahn/ghah·lahk·toh·mah yah tah mah·liah* |
| soap | **ένα σαπούνι** *eh·nah sah·poo·nee* |
| I'd like… | **Θα ήθελα…** *thah ee·theh·lah…* |
| sunscreen | **αντιηλιακό** *ahn·dee·ee·lee·ah·koh* |
| tampons | **ταμπόν** *tahm·bohn* |
| tissues | **χαρτομάντηλα** *khahr·toh·mahn·dee·lah* |
| toilet paper | **χαρτί υγείας** *khahr·tee ee·yee·ahs* |
| a toothbrush | **οδοντόβουρτσα** *oh·THoh·ndoh·voor·tsah* |
| toothpaste | **μια οδοντόπαστα** *miah oh·THohn·doh·pah·stah* |

For Baby Essentials, see page 134.

# The Basics

## Grammar

Greeks generally use **εσείς** (*eh·sees*) the plural form of 'you' with people they do not know well. The familiar, singular form **εσύ** (*eh·see*), is used among friends and with children, but don't worry too much - you will not be considered rude, just friendly!

## Regular Verbs

Below are three of the main categories of regular verbs in the present tense. Using the endings indicated after the dash, you can use a large number of verbs competently.

Greek verbs are divided in categories that are formed by using certain endings and are conjugated accordingly. Some of the most popular endings are:

| | |
|---|---|
| **– ω** *oh* | **– έρνω** *ehr·noh* |
| **– νω** *noh* | **– αίνω** *eh·noh* |
| **– άζω** *ah·zoh* | **– ένω** *eh·noh* |
| **– άω** *ah·oh* | **– άσκω** *as·koh* |
| **– ήνω** *ee·noh* | **– όμαι** *oh·meh* |
| **– ώνω** *oh·noh* | **– άμαι** *ah·meh* |
| **– έλνω** *ehl·noh* | **– έμαι** *eh·meh* |

| Είμαι (to be) | Present |
|---|---|
| I am | **Εγώ είμαι** *eh·goh ee·meh* |
| You are | **Εσύ είσαι** *eh·see ee·seh* |
| He is | **Αυτός είναι** *ahf·tohs ee·neh* |
| She is | **Αυτή είναι** *ahf·tee ee·neh* |

| | |
|---|---|
| We are | **Εμείς είμαστε** *eh•mees eem•ah•steh* |
| You are | **Εσείς είστε** *eh•sees ee•steh* |
| They are | **Αυτοί είναι** *ahf•tee ee•neh* |

| Αφήνω (to let) | Present |
|---|---|
| I let | **Εγώ αφήνω** *ah•fee•noh* |
| You let | **Εσύ αφήνεις** *ah•fee•nees* |
| He lets | **Αυτός αφήνει** *ah•fee•nee* |
| She lets | **Αυτή αφήνει** *ah•fee•nee* |
| We let | **Εμείς αφήνουμε** *ah•fee•noo•meh* |
| You let | **Εσείς αφήνετε** *ah•fee•neh•teh* |
| They let | **Αυτοί αφήνουν** *ah•fee•noon* |

| Φέρνω (to bring) | Present |
|---|---|
| I bring | **Εγώ φέρνω** *fehr•noh* |
| You bring | **Εσύ φέρνεις** *fehr•nees* |
| He brings | **Αυτός φέρνει** *feh•rnee* |
| She brings | **Αυτή φέρνει** *fehr•nee* |
| We bring | **Εμείς φέρνουμε** *feh•rnoo•meh* |
| You bring | **Εσείς φέρνετε** *feh•neh•teh* |
| They bring | **Αυτοί φέρνουν** *fehr•noon* |

The infinitive/first person of most Greek verbs end in **ω**:

| | |
|---|---|
| to do | **κάνω** *kah•noh* |

To conjugate this verb, drop the final **ω**, and add the appropriate ending:

| Κάνω (to do) | Present |
|---|---|
| I do | **Εγώ κάνω** *eh•goh kahn•oh* |
| You do | **Εσύ κάνεις** *eh•see kahn•ees* |
| (familiar or sing.) | |
| He does | **Αυτός κάνει** *ahf•tohs kahn•ee* |
| She does | **Αυτή κάνει** *ahf•tee kahn•ee* |

| We do | **Εμείς κάνουμε** *eh·mees kahn·oo·meh* |
| You do (form., pl.) | **Εσείς κάνετε** *eh·sees kahn·eh·teh* |
| They do | **Αυτοί κάνουν** *ahf·tee kahn·oun* |

So, by applying this rule you can conjugate another verb ending in **ω**:

| Γράφω (to write) | Present |
| --- | --- |
| I write | **Εγώ γράφω** *eh·goh grahf·oh* |
| You write | **Εσύ γράφεις** *eh·see grahf·ees* |
| He writes | **Αυτός γράφει** *ahf·tohs grahf·ee* |
| She writes | **Αυτή γράφει** *ahf·tee grahf·ee* |
| We write | **Εμείς γράφουμε** *eh·mees grahf·oo·meh* |
| You write | **Εσείς γράφετε** *eh·sees grahf·eh·teh* |
| They write | **Αυτοί γράφουν** *ahf·ee grahf·oon* |

## Word Order

Syntax in Greek, especially in everyday spoken language, is very flexible. The standard word order is subject-verb-object, but you can change the order of sentence components to shift emphasis.

Example:

**Το τρένο φεύγει τώρα.** *toh treh·noh fehv·ghee toh·rah*

The train leaves now.

You can say the same thing by placing the verb at the beginning of the sentence:

**Φεύγει το τρένο τώρα.** *fehv·ghee toh treh·noh toh·rah*

The train leaves now.

Also, use an interrogatory intonation to turn this sentence into a question. The question form can work both with the verb in the beginning and at the end of the sentence.

**Τώρα φεύγει το τραίνο;** *toh·rah fehv·ghee toh treh·noh*

Is the train leaving now?

Note that, in Greek, the equivalent of a semi-colon (;) is used in place of a question mark.

## Negation

To form a negative sentence in Greek, add the word **δεν** (*THehn*) before the verb.

Example:

| | |
|---|---|
| **Θέλω** <u>theh</u>·loh | I want |
| **Δεν θέλω** *THehn* <u>theh</u>·loh | I don't want |

## Imperatives

Imperative sentences are formed by adding the appropriate ending to the stem of the verb. The endings used to form the imperative of a verb are mainly:

**α** (*ah*), **ε** (*eh*), **ήσου** (<u>ee</u>·soo), **άσου** (<u>ah</u>·soo).

| Examples: | **πηγαίνω** *pee·<u>yeh</u>·noh* | to go |
|---|---|---|
| | **Πήγαινε!** <u>pee</u>·yeh·neh | Go! |
| | **βιάζομαι** <u>viah</u>·zoh·meh | to hurry |
| | **Βιάσου!** <u>viah</u>·soo | Hurry! |

## Nouns & Articles

There are three genders in Greek: masculine, feminine and neuter; all nouns in Greek are assigned a specific gender. The gender of the article changes based on the gender of the noun it modifies. For example:

| She is tall. | **Είναι ψηλή.** <u>ee</u>·neh psee·<u>lee</u> |
|---|---|
| He is tall. | **Είναι ψηλός.** <u>ee</u>·neh psee·<u>lohs</u> |

The article **o** (oh) is used with masculine nouns, **η** (ee) with feminine nouns and **το** (toh) with neuter nouns.

| masculine | **ο καφές** *oh kah·<u>fehs</u>* | the coffee |
|---|---|---|
| feminine | **η μπίρα** *ee <u>bee</u>·rah* | the beer |
| neuter | **το τρένο** *toh <u>treh</u>·noh* | the train |

Greek nouns have four cases: nominative, genitive, accusative and vocative. A simple way to explain their use would be that the nominative indicates the subject, the genitive indicates possession, the accusative indicates the object and the vocative is used to address someone. Don't worry too much about this. In most cases, people will understand what you are saying even if you use a

noun with the wrong case. The words in the dictionary are in nominative.
There is no easy way to form the plural. Beginner speakers of Greek should
clearly state the number along with the noun to be easily understood.

## Adjectives

Adjectives agree with the noun they describe in gender, case and number.
The most common ending for a feminine adjective is **–η** *(ee)*, for a masculine
adjective it is **–ος** *(ohs)* and for the neuter **o** *(oh)*.

Example:

| | |
|---|---|
| **Είναι γρήγορος οδηγός.** | *ee·neh <u>ghree</u>·ghoh·rohs oh·THee·<u>ghohs</u>* |
| He is a fast driver. | |
| **Είναι γρήγορη οδηγός.** | *ee·neh <u>ghree</u>·ghoh·ree oh·THee·<u>ghohs</u>* |
| She is a fast driver. | |
| **Είναι γρήγορο αυτοκίνητο.** | *ee·neh <u>ghree</u>·ghoh·roh ah·ftoh·<u>kee</u>·nee·toh* |
| This is a fast car. | |

## Comparatives & Superlatives

The comparative form of adjectives is usually formed by adding the word
**πιο** *(pioh)* before the adjective. Also, in certain cases, the comparative may
be formed by adding the ending **–ερος** *m (eh·rohs)*, **–ερη** *f (eh·ree)*, **–ερο**
*(eh·roh) n* to the stem of an adjective, respectively. To form the superlative
of an adjective, add the ending **–ατος** *m (ah·tohs)*, **–ατη** *f (ah·tee)*, **–ατο**
*(ah·tee) (n* to the stem of the adjective.

## Possessive Pronouns

| | | |
|---|---|---|
| mine | **μου** | *moo* |
| yours | **σου** | *soo* |
| his/her/its | **του/της/του** | *too/tees/too* |
| ours | **μας** | *mahs* |
| yours | **σας** | *sahs* |
| theirs | **τους** | *toos* |

Example:

**Το βιβλίο είναι δικό μου.** *toh veev·lee·oh ee·neh thee·koh moo*

This book is mine.

## Adverbs

Adverbs are used to describe the action of verbs. Almost all adverbs are formed
by adding the ending **α** (*ah*) to the stem of the adjective.

Example:

**Οδηγεί γρήγορα.** *oh·THee·yee ghree·ghoh·rah*

He drives quickly.

## Numbers

### ESSENTIAL

| | | |
|---|---|---|
| 0 | **μηδέν** | *mee·THehn* |
| 1 | **ένας** | *eh·nahs* |
| 2 | **δύο** | *THee·oh* |
| 3 | **τρεις** | *trees* |
| 4 | **τέσσερις** | *teh·seh·rees* |
| 5 | **πέντε** | *pehn·deh* |
| 6 | **έξι** | *eh·ksee* |
| 7 | **επτά** | *eh·ptah* |
| 8 | **οκτώ** | *oh·ktoh* |
| 9 | **εννέα** | *eh·neh·ah* |
| 10 | **δέκα** | *THeh·kah* |
| 11 | **έντεκα** | *ehn·deh·kah* |
| 12 | **δώδεκα** | *THoh·THeh·kah* |
| 13 | **δεκατρία** | *THeh·kah·tree·ah* |
| 14 | **δεκατέσσερα** | *THeh·kah·teh·seh·rah* |
| 15 | **δεκαπέντε** | *THeh·kah·pehn·deh* |

| 16 | **δεκαέξι** *THeh·kah·eh·ksee* |
| 17 | **δεκαεπτά** *THeh·kah·eh·ptah* |
| 18 | **δεκαοκτώ** *THeh·kah·oh·ktoh* |
| 19 | **δεκαεννέα** *THeh·kah·eh·neh·ah* |
| 20 | **είκοσι** *ee·koh·see* |
| 21 | **είκοσι ένα** *ee·koh·see eh·nah* |
| 22 | **είκοσι δύο** *ee·koh·see THee·oh* |
| 30 | **τριάντα** *tree·ahn·dah* |
| 31 | **τριάντα ένα** *tree·ahn·dah eh·nah* |
| 40 | **σαράντα** *sah·rahn·dah* |
| 50 | **πενήντα** *peh·neen·dah* |
| 60 | **εξήντα** *eh·kseen·dah* |
| 70 | **εβδομήντα** *ehv·THoh·meen·dah* |
| 80 | **ογδόντα** *ohgh·THohn·dah* |
| 90 | **ενενήντα** *eh·neh·neen·dah* |
| 100 | **εκατό** *eh·kah·toh* |
| 101 | **εκατόν ένα** *eh·kah·tohn eh·nah* |
| 200 | **διακόσια** *THee·ah·koh·siah* |
| 500 | **πεντακόσια** *pehn·dah·koh·siah* |
| 1,000 | **χίλια** *khee·liah* |
| 10,000 | **δέκα χιλιάδες** *THeh·kah khee·liah·THehs* |
| 1,000,000 | **ένα εκατομμύριο** *eh·nah eh·kah·toh·mee·ree·oh* |

157

## Ordinal Numbers

| first | **πρώτος** *proh·tohs* |
| second | **δεύτερος** *THehf·teh·rohs* |
| third | **τρίτος** *tree·tohs* |
| fourth | **τέταρτος** *teh·tahr·tohs* |
| fifth | **πέμπτος** *pehm·ptohs* |
| once | **μια φορά** *miah foh·rah* |

| twice | **δύο φορές** _THee_·oh foh·_rehs_ |
| three times | **τρεις φορές** trees foh·_rehs_ |

## Time

### ESSENTIAL

| What time is it? | **Τι ώρα είναι;** tee _oh_·rah _ee_·neh |
| It's noon [midday]. | **Είναι μεσημέρι.** _ee_·neh meh·see·_meh_·ree |
| At midnight. | **Τα μεσάνυχτα.** tah meh·_sah_·neekh·tah |
| From nine o'clock. | **Από τις εννέα ως τις πέντε.** ah·_poh_ tees |
| to five o'clock | eh·_neh_·ah ohs tees _pehn_·deh |
| Twenty after [past] four. | **Τέσσερις και είκοσι.** _teh_·seh·rees keh _ee_·koh·see |
| A quarter to nine. | **Εννέα παρά τέταρτο.** eh·_neh_·ah pah·_rah_ _teh_·tahr·toh |
| 5:30 a.m./p.m. | **Πεντέμιση π.μ./μ.μ.** pehn·_deh_·mee·see proh meh·seem·_vree_·ahs/meh·_tah_ meh·seem·_vree_·ahs |

## Days

### ESSENTIAL

| Monday | **Δευτέρα** THehf·_teh_·rah |
| Tuesday | **Τρίτη** _tree_·tee |
| Wednesday | **Τετάρτη** teh·_tahr_·tee |
| Thursday | **Πέμπτη** _pehm_·tee |
| Friday | **Παρασκευή** pah·rahs·keh·_vee_ |
| Saturday | **Σάββατο** _sah_·vah·toh |
| Sunday | **Κυριακή** keer·yah·_kee_ |

## Dates

| | | |
|---|---|---|
| yesterday | **χτες** khtehs | |
| today | **σήμερα** <u>see</u>·meh·rah | |
| tomorrow | **αύριο** <u>ahv</u>·ree·oh | |
| day | **ημέρα** ee·<u>meh</u>·rah | |
| week | **εβδομάδα** ehv·THoh·<u>mah</u>·THah | |
| month | **μήνας** <u>mee</u>·nahs | |
| year | **χρόνος** <u>khroh</u>·nohs | |

Greece follows a day-month-year format instead of the month-day-year format used in the U.S.

E.g.: July 25, 2008; 25/07/08 = 7/25/2008 in the U.S.

## Months

| | | |
|---|---|---|
| January | **Ιανουάριος** ee·ah·noo·<u>ah</u>·ree·ohs | |
| February | **Φεβρουάριος** fehv·roo·<u>ah</u>·ree·ohs | |
| March | **Μάρτιος** <u>mahr</u>·tee·ohs | |
| April | **Απρίλιος** ahp·<u>ree</u>·lee·ohs | |
| May | **Μάιος** <u>mah</u>·ee·ohs | |
| June | **Ιούνιος** ee·<u>oo</u>·nee·ohs | |
| July | **Ιούλιος** ee·<u>oo</u>·lee·ohs | |
| August | **Αύγουστος** <u>ahv</u>·ghoo·stohs | |
| September | **Σεπτέμβριος** sehp·<u>tehm</u>·vree·ohs | |
| October | **Οκτώβριος** ohk·<u>toh</u>·vree·ohs | |
| November | **Νοέμβριος** noh·<u>ehm</u>·vree·ohs | |
| December | **Δεκέμβριος** THeh·<u>kehm</u>·vree·ohs | |

## Seasons

| | | |
|---|---|---|
| spring | **η άνοιξη** ee <u>ah</u>·nee·ksee | |
| summer | **το καλοκαίρι** toh kah·loh·<u>keh</u>·ree | |
| fall [autumn] | **το φθινόπωρο** toh fthee·<u>noh</u>·poh·roh | |
| winter | **ο χειμώνας** oh khee·<u>moh</u>·nahs | |

# Holidays

| | |
|---|---|
| January 1, New Year's Day | **Πρωτοχρονιά** *proh·toh·hroh·niah* |
| January 6, Epiphany | **Θεοφάνεια** *theh·oh·fah·nee·ah* |
| March 25, Annunciation | **Ευαγγελισμός** *eh·vahn·geh·lee·smohs* |
| March 25, National Holiday - Proclamation of the Greek War of Independence) | **Εθνική εορτή** *ehth·nee·kee eh·ohr·tee* |
| May 1, May Day | **Πρωτομαγιά** *proh·toh·mah·yah* |
| August 15, Assumption | **Κοίμηση της Θεοτόκου** *kee·mee·see tees theh·oh·toh·koo* |
| October 28, the OXI day | **Εθνική εορτή** *ehth·nee·kee eh·ohr·tee* |
| December 25, Christmas | **Χριστούγεννα** *khrees·too·yeh·nah* |

Moveable Holidays:

| | |
|---|---|
| Easter | **Πάσχα** *pahs·khah* |
| Shrove Monday (Greek Orthodox) | **Καθαρή Δευτέρα** *kah·thah·ree THeh·fteh·rah* |
| Pentecost | **Αγίου Πνεύματος** *ah·yee·oo pnehv·mah·tohs* |

Each city and town has a patron saint. The saint's holy day, also known as a name day, is a local public holiday.

The most important holidays in Greece are religious celebrations such as Easter and Christmas, with Easter being the most sacred holiday. The traditional celebrations usually start on Good Friday with a procession of the Epitaph (Bier) symbolizing the tomb of Christ. On Holy Saturday evening, the resurrection mass takes place when everyone goes to church at around 11:00 p.m. with unlit candles. At midnight the bells are rung and the priest comes out of the church to pass the Holy Light to the congregation. This is the largest religious gathering. In most places, the crowds fill the streets outside the church, traffic is blocked and there are usually fireworks right after midnight. After this, it is customary to eat a soup called **μαγειρίτσα** (*mah·ghee·ree·tsah*), made from the lamb's internal organs.

On Sunday the celebration is usually taken outdoors. Whole families come together to roast a lamb on the spit, a big feast lasting the whole day. If you are in the countryside you will see large parties of people roasting the lamb and you may even be invited to join them. Even in the big cities, don't be surprised if you see people doing the same on their rooftops!

Another major holiday is March 25th, which is a day of remembrance of the start of the Greek War of Independence. On this day there is a military parade in every major city.

## Conversion Tables

| When you know | Multiply by | To find |
| --- | --- | --- |
| ounces | 28.3 | grams |
| pounds | 0.45 | kilograms |
| inches | 2.54 | centimeters |
| feet | 0.3 | meters |
| miles | 1.61 | kilometers |
| square inches | 6.45 | sq. centimeters |
| square feet | 0.09 | sq. meters |
| square miles | 2.59 | sq. kilometers |
| pints (U.S./Brit) | 0.47/0.56 | liters |
| gallons (U.S./Brit) | 3.8/4.5 | liters |
| Fahrenheit | 5/9, after 32 | Centigrade |
| Centigrade | 9/5, then +32 | Fahrenheit |

### Kilometers to Miles Conversions

| 1 km – 0.62 mi | 20 km – 12.4 mi |
| --- | --- |
| 5 km – 3.10 mi | 50 km – 31.0 mi |
| 10 km – 6.20 mi | 100 km – 61.0 mi |

### Measurement

| 1 gram | **γραμμάριο** ghrah·_mah_·ree·oh | = 0.035 oz. |
| --- | --- | --- |
| 1 kilogram (kg) | **κιλό** kee·_loh_ | = 2.2 lb |
| 1 liter (l) | **λίτρο** _lee_·troh | = 1.06 U.S./0.88 Brit. quarts |
| 1 centimeter (cm) | **εκατοστό** eh·kah·toh·_stoh_ | = 0.4 inch |
| 1 meter (m) | **μέτρο** _meh_·troh | = 3.28 feet |
| 1 kilometer (km) | **χιλιόμετρο** khee·_lioh_·meh·troh | = 0.62 mile |

## Temperature

| | | |
|---|---|---|
| -40° C – -40° F | -1° C – 30° F | 20° C – 68° F |
| -30° C – -22° F | 0° C – 32° F | 25° C – 77° F |
| -20° C – -4° F | 5° C – 41° F | 30° C – 86° F |
| -10° C – 14° F | 10° C – 50° F | 35° C – 95° F |
| -5° C – 23° F | 15° C – 59° F | |

## Oven Temperature

| | |
|---|---|
| 100° C – 212° F | 177° C – 350° F |
| 121° C – 250° F | 204° C – 400° F |
| 149° C – 300° F | 260° C – 500° F |

# Dictionary

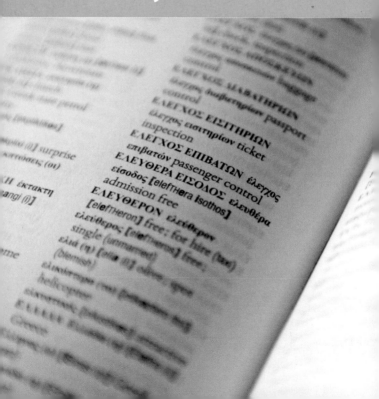

## GREEK ALPHABET

| Uppercase | Lowercase | Name of Greek Letter |
|-----------|-----------|----------------------|
| Α | α | Alpha |
| Β | β | Beta |
| Γ | γ | Gamma |
| Δ | δ | Delta |
| Ε | ε | Epsilon |
| Ζ | ζ | Zeta |
| Η | η | Eta |
| Θ | θ | Theta |
| Ι | ι | Iota |
| Κ | κ | Kappa |
| Λ | λ | Lambda |
| Μ | μ | Mu |
| Ν | ν | Nu |
| Ξ | ξ | Xi |
| Ο | ο | Omicron |
| Π | π | Pi |
| Ρ | ρ | Rho |
| Σ | σ | Sigma |
| Τ | τ | Tau |
| Υ | υ | Upsilon |
| Φ | φ | Phi |
| Χ | χ | Chi |
| Ψ | ψ | Psi |
| Ω | ω | Omega |

| | | |
|---|---|---|
| **adj** adjective | **BE** British English | **prep** preposition |
| **adv** adverb | **n** noun | **v** verb |

# English–Greek

## A

**access** n πρόσβαση <u>prohz</u>·vah·see
**accessory** αξεσουάρ ah·kseh·soo·<u>ahr</u>
**accident** ατύχημα ah·<u>tee</u>·khee·mah
**accompany** συνοδεύω
   see·noh·<u>THeh</u>·voh
**account** n λογαριασμός
   loh·ghahr·yahz·<u>mohs</u>
**adaptor** προσαρμοστής
   proh·sahr·moh·<u>stees</u>
**address** n διεύθυνση
   THee·<u>ehf</u>·theen·see
**admission** είσοδος <u>ee</u>·soh·Thohs
**adult** ενήλικας eh·<u>nee</u>·lee·kahs
**advance** προκαταβολή
   proh·kah·tah·voh·<u>lee</u>
**after** μετά meh·<u>tah</u>
**afternoon** απόγευμα
   ah·<u>poh</u>·yehv·mah
**after-sun lotion** λοσιόν μετά την
   ηλιοθεραπεία loh·<u>siohn</u> meh·<u>tah</u>
   teen ee·lioh·theh·rah·<u>pee</u>·ah
**age** n ηλικία ee·lee·<u>kee</u>·ah
**agree** συμφωνώ seem·foh·<u>noh</u>
**air conditioning** κλιματισμός
   klee·mah·teez·<u>mohs</u>
**air pump** n αντλία αέρος ahn·<u>dlee</u>·ah
   ah·<u>eh</u>·rohs
**airline** αεροπορική εταιρία
   ah·eh·roh·poh·ree·<u>kee</u> eh·the·<u>ree</u>·ah
**airmail** αεροπορικώς

ah·eh·roh·poh·ree·<u>kohs</u>
**airport** αεροδρόμιο
   ah·eh·roh·<u>THroh</u>·mee·oh
**aisle seat** διάδρομος
   THee·<u>ah</u>·Throh·mohs
**allergic** αλλεργικός ahl·ehr·yee·<u>kohs</u>
**allergy** αλλεργία ah·lehr·<u>yee</u>·ah
**alone** μόνος <u>moh</u>·nohs
**aluminum foil** αλουμινόχαρτο
   ah·loo·mee·<u>noh</u>·khah·rtoh
**amazing** καταπληκτικός
   kah·tahp·leek·tee·<u>kohs</u>
**ambassador** πρεσβευτής
   prehz·vehf·<u>tees</u>
**amber** κεχριμπάρι
   kehkh·reem·<u>bah</u>·ree
**ambulance** ασθενοφόρο
   ahs·theh·noh·<u>foh</u>·roh
**American** adj αμερικάνικος
   ah·meh·ree·<u>kah</u>·nee·kohs;
   (nationality) Αμερικανός
   ah·meh·ree·kah·<u>nohs</u>
**amount** n ποσό poh·<u>soh</u>
**amusement park** πάρκο
   ψυχαγωγίας <u>pahr</u>·koh
   psee·khah·ghoh·<u>yee</u>·ahs
**animal** ζώο <u>zoh</u>·oh
**another** άλλος <u>ah</u>·lohs
**antibiotic** αντιβιοτικό
   ahn·dee·vee·oh·tee·<u>koh</u>
**antiques store** κατάστημα με

**αντίκες** kah·tah·stee·mah meh
ahn·tee·kehs

**antiseptic cream αντισηπτική
κρέμα** ahn·dee·seep·tee·kee
kreh·mah

**anything οτιδήποτε**
oh·tee·THee·poh·teh

**apartment διαμέρισμα**
THee·ah·meh·reez·mah

**apologize ζητώ συγγνώμη** zee·toh
seegh·noh·mee

**appendix σκωληκοειδίτιδα**
skoh·lee·koh·ee·THee·tee·THah

**appointment ραντεβού**
rahn·deh·voo

**architecture αρχιτεκτονική**
ahr·khee·teh·ktoh·nee·kee

**area code κωδικός περιοχής**
koh·THee·kohs peh·ree·oh·khees

**arm** n **χέρι** kheh·ree

**arrange κανονίζω** kah·noh·nee·zoh

**arrest** v **συλλαμβάνω**
see·lahm·vah·noh

**arrive φτάνω** ftah·noh

**art τέχνη** tekh·nee

**art gallery γκαλερί τέχνης**
gah·leh·ree tekh·nees

**ashtray σταχτοδοχείο**
stakh·toh·THoh·khee·oh

**ask ζητώ** zee·toh

**aspirin ασπιρίνη** ahs·pee·ree·nee

**asthmatic ασθματικός**
ahsth·mah·tee·kohs

**ATM ATM** ehee·tee·ehm

**attack** n **επίθεση** eh·pee·theh·see; v
**επιτίθεμαι** eh·pee·tee·theh·meh

**attractive ελκυστικός**
ehl·kees·tee·kohs

**authenticity αυθεντικότητα**
ahf·thehn·dee·koh·tee·tah

## B

**baby μωρό** moh·roh

**baby food βρεφική τροφή**
vreh·fee·kee troh·fee

**baby seat καρέκλα μωρού**
kah·reh·klah moh·roo

**babysitter μπέιμπι σίτερ** beh·ee·bee
see·tehr

**back** n **πλάτη** plah·tee

**back ache πόνος στην πλάτη**
poh·nohs steen plah·tee

**backgammon τάβλι** tah·vlee

**bad κακός** kah·kohs

**baggage αποσκευές**
ah·pohs·keh·vehs

**baggage check φύλαξη αποσκευών**
fee·lah·ksee ah·poh·skeh·vohn

**baggage reclaim παραλαβή
αποσκευών** pah·rah·lah·vee
ah·poh·skeh·vohn

**bakery αρτοποιείο** ah·rtoh·pee·ee·oh

**balcony μπαλκόνι** bahl·koh·nee

**ballet μπαλέτο** bah·leh·toh

**bandage γάζα** ghah·zah

**bank τράπεζα** trah·peh·zah

**bank account λογαριασμός
τραπέζης** loh·ghahr·yahz·mohs

trah•**peh**•zees

**bank loan** τραπεζικό δάνειο
trah•peh•zee•**koh** THah•nee•oh

**bar** μπαρ bahr

**barber** κουρείο koo•**ree**•oh

**basket** καλάθι kah•**lah**•THee

**basketball** μπάσκετ **bah**•skeht

**bathing suit** μαγιό mah•**yoh**

**bathroom** μπάνιο **bah**•nioh

**battery** μπαταρία bah•tah•**ree**•ah

**beach** παραλία pah•rah•**lee**•ah

**beautiful** όμορφος **oh**•mohr•fohs

**bed** κρεβάτι kreh•**vah**•tee

**bed and breakfast** διαμονή με
πρωινό THiah•moh•**nee** meh
proh•ee•**noh**

**bedding** σεντόνια sehn•**doh**•niah

**bedroom** υπνοδωμάτιο
eep•noh•THoh•**mah**•tee•oh

**before** πριν preen

**beginner** αρχάριος ahr•**khah**•ree•ohs

**belong** ανήκω ah•**nee**•koh

**belt** ζώνη **zoh**•nee

**bicycle** ποδήλατο poh•**THee**•lah•toh

**big** μεγάλος meh•**ghah**•lohs

**bikini** μπικίνι bee•**kee**•nee

**bird** πουλί poo•**lee**

**bite** *n* (insect) τσίμπημα
**tsee**•bee•mah

**bladder** ουροδόχος κύστη
oo•roh•**THoh**•khohs **kee**•stee

**blanket** κουβέρτα koo•**veh**•rtah

**bleed** *n* αιμορραγία
eh•moh•rah•**yee**•ah; *v* αιμορραγώ
eh•moh•rah•**yoh**

**blinds** περσίδες peh•**rsee**•THehs

**blister** φουσκάλα foo•**skah**•lah

**blood** αίμα **eh**•mah

**blood group** ομάδα αίματος
oh•**mah**•THah **eh**•mah•tohs

**blood pressure** πίεση **pee**•eh•see

**blouse** μπλούζα **bloo**•zah

**boarding card** κάρτα επιβίβασης
**kah**•rtah eh•pee•**vee**•vah•sees

**boat** βάρκα **vahr**•kah

**boat trip** ταξίδι με πλοίο
tah•**ksee**•THee meh **plee**•oh

**body** σώμα **soh**•mah

**bone** οστό oh•**stoh**

**book** *n* βιβλίο veev•**lee**•oh; *v* κάνω
κράτηση **kah**•noh **krah**•tee•see

**bookstore** βιβλιοπωλείο
veev•lee•oh•poh•**lee**•oh

**boot** μπότα **boh**•tah

**border** (country) σύνορο **see**•noh•roh

**boring** βαρετός vah•reh•**tohs**

**borrow** δανείζομαι
THah•**nee**•zoh•meh

**botanical garden** βοτανικός κήπος
voh•tah•nee•**kohs kee**•pohs

**bottle** μπουκάλι boo•**kah**•lee

**bottle opener** τιρμπουσόν
teer•boo•**sohn**

**bowel** έντερο **ehn**•deh•roh

**box office** ταχυδρομική θυρίδα
tah•khee•THroh•mee•**kee**
THee•**ree**•THah

**boxing** *n* μποξ bohks

**boy αγόρι** ah·**ghoh**·ree
**boyfriend φίλος** **fee**·lohs
**bra σουτιέν** soo·**tiehn**
**break** *n* **διάλειμμα** THee·**ah**·lee·mah;
  *v* **σπάω** **spah**·oh
**breakdown** *n* (car) **βλάβη** **vlah**·vee
**breakfast πρωινό** proh·ee·**noh**
**break-in** *n* **διάρρηξη**
  THee·**ah**·ree·ksee
**breast στήθος** **stee**·THohs
**breathe αναπνέω** ah·nahp·**neh**·oh
**breathtaking φαντασμαγορικός**
  fahn·dahz·mah·ghoh·ree·**kohs**
**bridge** *n* (over water) **γέφυρα**
  **yeh**·fee·rah; (card game) **μπριτζ**
  breetz
**briefcase χαρτοφύλακας**
  khah·rtoh·**fee**·lah·kahs
**briefs (men's, women's) σλιπ**
  sleep (women's); **κυλοτάκι**
  kee·loh·**tah**·kee
**bring φέρνω** **fehr**·noh
**Britain Βρετανία** vreh·tah·**nee**·ah
**British** *adj* **βρετανικός**
  vreh·tah·nee·**kohs**; (nationality)
  **Βρετανός** vreh·tah·**nohs**
**brochure φυλλάδιο** fee·**lah**·THee·oh
**broken σπασμένος** spahz·**meh**·nohs
**broom** *n* **σκούπα** **skoo**·pah
**browse ξεφυλλίζω** kseh·fee·**lee**·zoh
**bruise** *n* **μελανιά** meh·lah·**niah**
**brush** *n* **βούρτσα** **voor**·tsah; *v*
  **βουρτσίζω** voor·**tsee**·zoh
**build κτίζω** **ktee**·zoh

**building κτίριο** **ktee**·ree·oh
**burn** *n* **έγκαυμα** **eh**·gahv·mah
**bus λεωφορείο** leh·oh·foh·**ree**·oh
**bus route διαδρομή λεωφορείων**
  THee·ah·THroh·**mee**
  leh·oh·foh·**ree**·ohn
**bus station σταθμός λεωφορείων**
  stahTH·**mohs** leh·oh·foh·**ree**·ohn
**bus stop στάση λεωφορείου**
  **stah**·see leh·oh·foh·**ree**·oo
**business class μπίζνες θέση**
  **bee**·znehs **theh**·see
**business trip επαγγελματικό**
  **ταξίδι** eh·pah·gehl·mah·tee·**koh**
  tah·**ksee**·THee
**busy (occupied) απασχολημένος**
  ah·pahs·khoh·lee·**meh**·nohs
**but αλλά** ah·**lah**
**butane gas υγραέριο**
  eegh·rah·**eh**·ree·oh
**butcher shop κρεοπωλείο**
  kreh·oh·poh·**lee**·oh
**button κουμπί** koo·**bee**
**buy αγοράζω** ah·ghoh·**rah**·zoh

## C

**cabaret καμπαρέ** kah·bah·**reh**
**cabin καμπίνα** kah·**bee**·nah
**cable car τελεφερίκ** teh·leh·feh·**reek**
**cafe καφετέρια** kah·feh·**teh**·ree·ah
**calendar ημερολόγιο**
  ee·meh·roh·**loh**·yee·oh
**call collect με χρέωση του**
  **καλούμενου** meh **khreh**·oh·see too

kah·loo·meh·noo

**call** *n* **κλήση** klee·see; *v* **καλώ** kah·loh

**camcorder φορητή βιντεοκάμερα**
foh·ree·tee vee·deh·oh·kah·meh·rah

**camera φωτογραφική μηχανή**
foh·tohgh·rah·fee·kee mee·khah·nee

**camera case θήκη μηχανής** thee·kee
mee·khah·nees

**camera store κατάστημα**
**με φωτογραφικά είδη**
kah·tah·stee·mah meh
foh·tohgh·rah·fee·kah ee·THee

**camp bed κρεβάτι εκστρατείας**
kreh·vah·tee ehk·strah·tee·ahs

**camping κάμπινγκ** kah·mpeeng

**camping equipment εξοπλισμός**
**κάμπιγκ** eh·ksohp·leez·mohs
kah·mpeeng

**campsite χώρος κάμπινγκ** khoh·rohs
kah·mpeeng

**can opener ανοιχτήρι**
ah·neekh·tee·ree

**Canada Καναδάς** kah·nah·THahs

**canal κανάλι** kah·nah·lee

**cancel** *v* **ακυρώνω** ah·kee·roh·noh

**cancer (disease) καρκίνος**
kahr·kee·nohs

**candle κερί** keh·ree

**canoe κανό** kah·noh

**car αυτοκίνητο** ahf·toh·kee·nee·toh

**car park [BE] χώρος στάθμευσης**
khoh·rohs stahth·mehf·sees

**car rental ενοικίαση**
**αυτοκινήτων** eh·nee·kee·ah·see

ahf·toh·kee·nee·tohn

**car wash πλύσιμο αυτοκινήτου**
plee·see·moh ahf·toh·kee·nee·too

**carafe καράφα** kah·rah·fah

**caravan τροχόσπιτο**
troh·khohs·pee·toh

**cards χαρτιά** khahr·tiah

**carpet (fitted) μοκέτα** moh·keh·tah

**carton κουτί** koo·tee

**cash desk [BE] ταμείο** tah·mee·oh

**cash** *n* **μετρητά** meht·ree·tah;
*v* **εξαργυρώνω**
eh·ksahr·ghee·roh·noh

**casino καζίνο** kah·see·noh

**castle κάστρο** kahs·troh

**catch** *v* (bus) **παίρνω** pehr·noh

**cathedral καθεδρικός ναός**
kah·theh·THree·kohs nah·ohs

**cave** *n* **σπήλαιο** spee·leh·oh

**CD σι ντι** see dee

**cell phone κινητό** kee·nee·toh

**change** *n* **αλλαγή** ah·lah·yee; *v*
**αλλάζω** ah·lah·zoh

**cheap φτηνός** ftee·nohs

**check** *n* (bank) **επιταγή**
eh·pee·tah·yee; (bill) **λογαριασμός**
loh·ghahr·yahz·mohs

**choose διαλέγω** THiah·leh·ghoh

**clean καθαρός** kah·thah·rohs

**cling film [BE] διαφανή μεμβράνη**
THee·ah·fah·nee mehm·vrah·nee

**clothing store κατάστημα ρούχων**
kah·tahs·tee·mah roo·khohn

**cold** *adj* (temperature) **κρύος**

kree•ohs; *n* (chill) **κρυολόγημα**
kree•oh•<u>loh</u>•yee•mah

**collapse** *v* **καταρρέω** kah•tah•<u>reh</u>•oh

**collect** *v* **παίρνω** <u>peh</u>•rnoh

**color** *n* **χρώμα** <u>khroh</u>•mah

**comb** *n* **χτένα** <u>khteh</u>•nah; *v* **χτενίζω**
khteh•<u>nee</u>•zoh

**come έρχομαι** <u>ehr</u>•khoh•meh

**come back** *v* (return) **επιστρέφω**
eh•pees•<u>treh</u>•foh

**commission** *n* (agent fee) **προμήθεια**
proh•<u>mee</u>•thee•ah

**company** *n* (business) **εταιρία**
eh•teh•<u>ree</u>•ah; (companionship)
**παρέα** pah•<u>reh</u>•ah

**complain παραπονιέμαι**
pah•rah•poh•<u>nieh</u>•meh

**computer υπολογιστής**
ee•poh•loh•yee•<u>stees</u>

**concert συναυλία** see•nahv•<u>lee</u>•ah

**concert hall αίθουσα συναυλιών**
<u>eh</u>•thoo•sah see•nahv•lee•<u>ohn</u>

**conditioner (hair) γαλάκτωμα για
τα μαλλιά** ghah•<u>lah</u>•ktoh•mah yah
tah mah•<u>liah</u>

**condom προφυλακτικό**
proh•fee•lah•ktee•<u>koh</u>

**conference συνέδριο**
see•<u>neh</u>•THree•oh

**confirm επιβεβαιώνω**
eh•pee•veh•veh•<u>oh</u>•noh

**constipation δυσκοιλιότητα**
thees•kee•lee•<u>oh</u>•tee•tah

**Consulate Προξενείο**

proh•kseh•<u>nee</u>•oh

**consult** *v* **συμβουλεύομαι**
seem•voo•<u>leh</u>•voh•meh

**contact** *v* **επικοινωνώ**
eh•pee•kee•noh•<u>noh</u>

**contact fluid υγρό για φακούς
επαφής** eegh•<u>roh</u> yah fah•<u>koos</u>
eh•pah•<u>fees</u>

**contact lens φακός επαφής** fah•<u>kohs</u>
eh•pah•<u>fees</u>

**contagious μεταδοτικός**
meh•tah•THoh•tee•<u>kohs</u>

**contain περιέχω** peh•ree•<u>eh</u>•khoh

**contraceptive pill αντισυλληπτικό
χάπι** ahn•dee•see•leep•tee•<u>koh</u>
<u>khah</u>•pee

**cook** *n* (chef) **μάγειρας** <u>mah</u>•yee•rahs;
*v* **μαγειρεύω** mah•yee•<u>reh</u>•voh

**copper χαλκός** khahl•<u>kohs</u>

**corkscrew τιρμπουσόν** teer•boo•<u>sohn</u>

**corner γωνία** ghoh•<u>nee</u>•ah

**correct** *v* **διορθώνω**
THee•ohr•<u>thoh</u>•noh

**cosmetics καλλυντικά**
kah•leen•dee•<u>kah</u>

**cot [BE] παιδικό κρεβάτι**
peh•THee•<u>koh</u> kreh•<u>vah</u>•tee

**cotton βαμβάκι** vahm•<u>vah</u>•kee

**cough** *n* **βήχας** <u>vee</u>•khahs; *v* **βήχω**
<u>vee</u>•khoh

**counter ταμείο** tah•<u>mee</u>•oh

**country (nation) χώρα** <u>khoh</u>•rah

**countryside εξοχή** eh•ksoh•<u>khee</u>

**couple** *n* (pair) **ζευγάρι** zehv•<u>ghah</u>•ree

**courier** n (messenger) **κούριερ**
koo·ree·ehr

**court house δικαστήριο**
THee·kahs·tee·ree·oh

**cramp** n **κράμπα** krahm·bah

**credit card πιστωτική κάρτα**
pees·toh·tee·kee kahr·tah

**crib [cot BE] παιδικό κρεβάτι**
peh·THee·koh kreh·vah·tee

**crown** n (dental, royal) **κορώνα**
koh·roh·nah

**cruise** n **κρουαζιέρα** kroo·ahz·yeh·rah

**crutch** n (walking support) **δεκανίκι**
THeh·kah·nee·kee

**crystal** n **κρύσταλλο** kree·stah·loh

**cup φλυτζάνι** flee·jah·nee

**cupboard ντουλάπα** doo·lah·pah

**currency νόμισμα** noh·meez·mah

**currency exchange office γραφείο**
**ανταλλαγής συναλλάγματος**
ghrah·fee·oh ahn·dah·lah·yees
see·nah·lahgh·mah·tohs

**customs (tolls) τελωνείο**
teh·loh·nee·oh

**customs declaration (tolls)**
**τελωνειακή δήλωση**
teh·loh·nee·ah·kee THee·loh·see

**cut** n (wound) **κόψιμο** koh·psee·moh

**cut glass** n **σκαλιστό γυαλί**
skah·lees·toh yah·lee

**cycle helmet κράνος ποδηλάτη**
krah·nohs poh·THee·lah·tee

**cyclist ποδηλάτης** poh·THee·lah·tees

**Cypriot** adj **κυπριακός**

keep·ree·ah·kohs; (nationality)
**Κύπριος** kee·pree·ohs

**Cyprus Κύπρος** kee·prohs

# D

**damage** n **ζημιά** zee·miah; v
**καταστρέφω** kah·tah·streh·foh

**dance** v **χορεύω** khoh·reh·voh

**dangerous επικίνδυνος**
eh·pee·keen·THee·nohs

**dark** adj (color) **σκούρος** skoo·rohs

**dawn** n **ξημερώματα**
ksee·meh·roh·mah·tah

**day trip ημερήσια εκδρομή**
ee·meh·ree·see·ah ehk·THroh·mee

**deaf κουφός** koo·fohs

**decide αποφασίζω**
ah·poh·fah·see·zoh

**deck** n **κατάστρωμα**
kah·tah·stroh·mah

**deck chair σεζ-λονγκ** sehz lohng

**declare δηλώνω** THee·loh·noh

**deduct** (money) **αφαιρώ** ah·feh·roh

**defrost ξεπαγώνω**
kseh·pah·ghoh·noh

**degrees (temperature) βαθμοί**
vahth·mee

**delay** n **καθυστέρηση**
kah·thee·steh·ree·see; v **καθυστερώ**
kah·thee·steh·roh

**delicious νόστιμος** nohs·tee·mohs

**deliver παραδίδω**
pah·rah·THee·THoh

**dental floss οδοντικό νήμα**

oh·THohn·dee·<u>koh</u> nee·mah

**dentist** οδοντίατρος
oh·THohn·<u>dee</u>·ah·trohs

**deodorant** αποσμητικό
ah·pohz·mee·tee·<u>koh</u>

**department store** πολυκατάστημα
poh·lee·kah·<u>tahs</u>·tee·mah

**departure (travel)** αναχώρηση
ah·nah·<u>khoh</u>·ree·see

**departure lounge** αίθουσα
αναχωρήσεων <u>eh</u>·thoo·sah
ah·nah·khoh·<u>ree</u>·seh·ohn

**depend** εξαρτώμαι eh·ksahr·<u>toh</u>·meh

**deposit** n (down payment)
προκαταβολή proh·kah·tah·voh·<u>lee</u>

**describe** περιγράφω
peh·reegh·<u>rah</u>·foh

**designer** σχεδιαστής
skheh·THee·ahs·<u>tees</u>

**detergent** απορρυπαντικό
ah·poh·ree·pahn·dee·<u>koh</u>

**develop (photos)** εμφανίζω
ehm·fah·<u>nee</u>·zoh

**diabetes** διαβήτης THee·ah·<u>vee</u>·tees

**diabetic** διαβητικός
THee·ah·vee·tee·<u>kohs</u>

**diagnosis** διάγνωση
THee·<u>ahgh</u>·noh·see

**dialing code** κωδικός koh·THee·<u>kohs</u>

**diamond** n διαμάντι THiah·<u>mahn</u>·dee

**diaper** πάνα μωρού pah·nah moh·<u>roo</u>

**diarrhea** διάρροια THee·<u>ah</u>·ree·ah

**dice** n ζάρια <u>zah</u>·riah

**dictionary** λεξικό leh·ksee·<u>koh</u>

**diesel** ντήζελ <u>dee</u>·zehl

**diet** n δίαιτα THee·eh·tah

**difficult** δύσκολος <u>THee</u>·skoh·lohs

**dining room** τραπεζαρία
trah·peh·zah·<u>ree</u>·ah

**dinner** βραδινό vrah·THee·<u>noh</u>

**direct** v κατευθύνω
kah·tehf·<u>thee</u>·noh

**direction** n (instruction) οδηγία
oh·THee·<u>yee</u>·ah

**dirty** adj βρώμικος <u>vroh</u>·mee·kohs

**disabled** άτομο με ειδικές ανάγκες
<u>ah</u>·toh·moh meh ee··<u>nahn</u>
THee·<u>kehs</u> ah ·gehs

**discounted ticket** μειωμένο
εισιτήριο mee·oh·<u>meh</u>·noh
ee·see·<u>tee</u>·ree·oh

**dishwashing liquid** λίγο υγρό
πιάτων <u>lee</u>·ghoh ee·<u>ghroh</u> piah·tohn

**district** περιφέρεια
peh·ree·<u>feh</u>·ree·ah

**disturb** ενοχλώ eh·noh·<u>khloh</u>

**diving equipment** καταδυτικός
εξοπλισμός kah·tah·THee·tee·<u>kohs</u>
eh·ksoh·pleez·<u>mohs</u>

**divorced** διαζευγμένος
THee·ah·zehv·<u>ghmeh</u>·nohs

**dock** προκυμαία proh·kee·<u>meh</u>·ah

**doctor** γιατρός yah·<u>trohs</u>

**doll** κούκλα <u>kook</u>·lah

**dollar** δολάριο THoh·<u>lah</u>·ree·oh

**door** πόρτα <u>pohr</u>·tah

**dosage** δοσολογία
THoh·soh·loh·<u>yee</u>·ah

**double** *adj* **διπλός** THeep·<u>lohs</u>

**double bed διπλό κρεβάτι** THeep·<u>loh</u> kreh·<u>vah</u>·tee

**double room δίκλινο δωμάτιο** <u>THeek</u>·lee·noh THoh·<u>mah</u>·tee·oh

**downtown area κέντρο της πόλης** <u>kehn</u>·droh tees <u>poh</u>·lees

**dozen ντουζίνα** doo·<u>zee</u>·nah

**dress** *n* **φόρεμα** <u>foh</u>·reh·mah

**drink** *n* **ποτό** poh·<u>toh</u>; *v* **πίνω** <u>pee</u>·noh

**drive** *v* **οδηγώ** oh·THee·<u>ghoh</u>

**drugstore φαρμακείο** fahr·mah·<u>kee</u>·oh

**dry cleaner καθαριστήριο** kah·thah·rees·<u>tee</u>·ree·oh

**dubbed μεταγλωττισμένος** meh·tahgh·loh·teez·<u>meh</u>·nohs

**dusty σκονισμένος** skoh·neez·<u>meh</u>·nohs

**duty (customs) φόρος** <u>foh</u>·rohs; (obligation) **καθήκον** kah·<u>thee</u>·kohn

**duty-free goods αφορολόγητα είδη** ah·foh·roh·<u>loh</u>·yee·tah <u>ee</u>·THee

**duty-free shop κατάστημα αφορολόγητων** kah·<u>tahs</u>·tee·mah ah·foh·roh·<u>loh</u>·yee·tohn

**E**

**each κάθε ένα** <u>kah</u>·theh <u>eh</u>·nah

**ear αυτί** ahf·<u>tee</u>

**earache πόνος στο αυτί** <u>poh</u>·nohs stoh ahf·<u>tee</u>

**early νωρίς** noh·<u>rees</u>

**east ανατολικά** ah·nah·toh·lee·<u>kah</u>

**easy** *adj* **εύκολος** <u>ehf</u>·koh·lohs

**eat τρώω** <u>troh</u>·oh

**economical οικονομικός** ee·koh·noh·mee·<u>kohs</u>

**economy class τουριστική θέση** too·ree·stee·<u>kee</u> <u>theh</u>·see

**elastic ελαστικός** eh·lahs·tee·<u>kohs</u>

**electrical outlet πρίζα** <u>pree</u>·zah

**e-mail ηλεκτρονικό ταχυδρομείο** (e-mail) ee·lehk·troh·nee·<u>koh</u> tah·hee·dro·<u>mee</u>·oh (ee·<u>meh</u>·eel)

**embassy πρεσβεία** prehz·<u>vee</u>·ah

**emerald σμαράγδι** zmah·<u>rahgh</u>·THe

**emergency έκτακτη ανάγκη** <u>ehk</u>·tahk·tee ah·<u>nah</u>·gee

**emergency exit έξοδος κινδύνου** <u>eh</u>·ksoh·THohs keen·<u>THee</u>·noo

**empty** *adj* **άδειος** <u>ahTH</u>·yohs

**end** *n* **τέλος** <u>teh</u>·lohs; *v* **τελειώνω** teh·lee·<u>oh</u>·noh

**engine μηχανή** mee·khah·<u>nee</u>

**England Αγγλία** ahng·<u>lee</u>·ah

**English** *adj* **αγγλικός** ahng·lee·<u>kohs</u>; (nationality) **Άγγλος** <u>ahng</u>·lohs; (language) **αγγλικά** ahng·lee·<u>kah</u>

**enjoy ευχαριστιέμαι** ehf·khah·rees·<u>tieh</u>·meh

**enough αρκετά** ahr·keh·<u>tah</u>

**entertainment guide οδηγός ψυχαγωγίας** oh·THee·<u>ghohs</u> psee·khah·ghoh·<u>yee</u>·ahs

**entrance fee τιμή εισόδου** tee·<u>mee</u> ee·<u>soh</u>·THoo

**epileptic επιληπτικός**

eh·pee·leep·tee·<u>kohs</u>
**error λάθος** <u>lah</u>·thohs
**escalator κυλιόμενες σκάλες**
kee·lee·<u>oh</u>·meh·nehs <u>skah</u>·lehs
**essential απαραίτητος**
ah·pah·<u>reh</u>·tee·tohs
**e-ticket ηλεκτρονικό εισιτήριο**
ee·leh·ktroh·nee·<u>koh</u>
ee·see·<u>tee</u>·ree·oh
**European Union Ευρωπαϊκή Ένωση**
ehv·roh·pah·ee·<u>kee</u> eh·noh·see
**euro ευρώ** ehv·<u>roh</u>
**evening βράδυ** <u>vrah</u>·THee
**examination (medical) ιατρική
εξέταση** ee·ah·tree·<u>kee</u>
eh·<u>kseh</u>·tah·see
**example παράδειγμα**
pah·<u>rah</u>·THeegh·mah
**excess baggage υπέρβαρο**
ee·<u>pehr</u>·vah·roh
**exchange** v (money) **αλλάζω**
ah·<u>lah</u>·zoh
**exchange rate τιμή συναλλάγματος**
tee·<u>mee</u> see·nah·<u>lahgh</u>·mah·tohs
**excursion εκδρομή** ehk·THroh·<u>mee</u>
**exhibition έκθεση** <u>ehk</u>·theh·see
**exit** n **έξοδος** <u>eh</u>·ksoh·THohs
**expensive ακριβός** ahk·ree·<u>vohs</u>
**expiration date ημερομηνία
λήξεως** ee·meh·roh·mee·<u>nee</u>·ah
<u>lee</u>·kseh·ohs
**exposure (photos) στάση** <u>stah</u>·see
**express (mail) εξπρές** ehk·<u>sprehs</u>
**extension (number) εσωτερική**

**γραμμή** eh·soh·theh·ree·<u>kee</u>
ghrah·<u>mee</u>
**extra (additional) άλλο ένα** <u>ah</u>·loh
eh·nah
**eye** n **μάτι** <u>mah</u>·tee

## F

**fabric (cloth) ύφασμα** ee·fahs·mah
**face** n **πρόσωπο** proh·soh·poh
**facial καθαρισμός προσώπου**
kah·thah·reez·<u>mohs</u> proh·<u>soh</u>·poo
**facility εξυπηρέτηση**
eh·ksee·pee·<u>reh</u>·tee·see
**faint λιποθυμώ** lee·poh·thee·<u>moh</u>
**fall** v **πέφτω** <u>pehf</u>·toh
**family οικογένεια** ee·koh·<u>yeh</u>·nee·ah
**famous διάσημος** THee·<u>ah</u>·see·mohs
**fan** n (air) **ανεμιστήρας**
ah·neh·mees·<u>tee</u>·rahs
**far** adv **μακριά** mahk·ree·<u>ah</u>
**fare εισιτήριο** ee·see·<u>tee</u>·ree·oh
**farm** n **φάρμα** <u>fahr</u>·mah
**fast** adv **γρήγορα** <u>ghree</u>·ghoh·rah
**fat** adj (person) **παχύς** pah·<u>khees</u>
**faucet βρύση** <u>vree</u>·see
**fault λάθος** <u>lah</u>·thohs
**favorite αγαπημένος**
ah·ghah·pee·<u>meh</u>·nohs
**fax facility υπηρεσία φαξ**
ee·pee·reh·<u>see</u>·ah fahks
**feed** v **ταΐζω** tah·<u>ee</u>·zoh
**female θηλυκός** thee·lee·<u>kohs</u>
**fence** n **φράχτης** <u>frahkh</u>·tees
**ferry φέρυ-μπωτ** <u>feh</u>·ree·boht

**festival** **φεστιβάλ** fehs·tee·<u>vahl</u>
**fever** **πυρετός** pee·reh·<u>tohs</u>
**fiancé** **αρραβωνιαστικός**
  ah·rah·voh·niahs·tee·<u>kohs</u>
**fiancée** **αρραβωνιαστικιά**
  ah·rah·voh·niahs·tee·<u>kiah</u>
**filling (dental)** **σφράγισμα**
  <u>sfrah</u>·yeez·mah
**film** *n* (camera) **φιλμ** feelm
**filter** *n* **φίλτρο** <u>feel</u>·troh
**fine** *adv* **καλά** kah·<u>lah</u>; *n* **πρόστιμο**
  <u>prohs</u>·tee·moh
**finger** *n* **δάχτυλο** <u>THakh</u>·tee·loh
**fire** *n* **φωτιά** foh·<u>tiah</u>
**fire brigade [BE]** **πυροσβεστική**
  pee·rohz·vehs·tee·<u>kee</u>
**fire escape** **έξοδος κινδύνου**
  <u>eh</u>·ksoh·THohs keen·<u>THee</u>·noo
**fire extinguisher** **πυροσβεστήρας**
  pee·rohz·vehs·<u>tee</u>·rahs
**first class** **πρώτη θέση** <u>proh</u>·tee
  <u>theh</u>·see
**first-aid kit** **κουτί πρώτων**
  **βοηθειών** koo·<u>tee</u> <u>proh</u>·tohn
  voh·ee·thee·<u>ohn</u>
**fishing** **ψάρεμα** <u>psah</u>·reh·mah
**flag** *n* **σημαία** see·<u>meh</u>·ah
**flashlight** **φακός** fah·<u>kohs</u>
**flat** *adj* **επίπεδος** eh·<u>pee</u>·peh·Thohs; *n*
  **διαμέρισμα** THee·ah·<u>mehr</u>·ees·mah
**flea** **ψύλλος** <u>psee</u>·lohs
**flight** **πτήση** <u>ptee</u>·see
**flight number** **αριθμός πτήσεως**
  ah·reeth·<u>mohs</u> <u>ptee</u>·seh·ohs

**flip-flops** **σαγιονάρες**
  sah·yoh·<u>nah</u>·rehs
**flood** *n* **πλημμύρα** plee·<u>mee</u>·rah
**florist** **ανθοπωλείο**
  ahn·thoh·poh·<u>lee</u>·oh
**flower** *n* **λουλούδι** loo·<u>loo</u>·THee
**flu** **γρίππη** <u>ghree</u>·pee
**flush** **τραβώ το καζανάκι** trah·<u>voh</u>
  toh kah·zah·<u>nah</u>·kee
**fly** *n* **μύγα** <u>mee</u>·ghah; *v* **πετάω**
  peh·<u>tah</u>·oh
**follow** *v* **ακολουθώ** ah·koh·loo·<u>thoh</u>
**foot** **πόδι** <u>poh</u>·THee
**football [BE]** **ποδόσφαιρο**
  poh·<u>THohs</u>·feh·roh
**footpath** **μονοπάτι** moh·noh·<u>pah</u>·te
**forecast** *n* **πρόβλεψη** <u>prohv</u>·leh·psee
**foreign** **ξένος** <u>kseh</u>·nohs
**foreign currency** **ξένο συνάλλαγμα**
  <u>kseh</u>·noh see·<u>nah</u>·lahgh·mah
**forest** *n* **δάσος** <u>THah</u>·sohs
**forget** **ξεχνώ** ksehkh·<u>noh</u>
**form** *n* **έντυπο** <u>ehn</u>·dee·poh
**fortunately** **ευτυχώς** ehf·tee·<u>khohs</u>
**forward** **προωθώ** proh·oh·<u>thoh</u>
**fountain** **συντριβάνι**
  seen·dree·<u>vah</u>·nee
**free** *adj* (available) **ελεύθερος**
  eh·<u>lehf</u>·theh·rohs
**freezer** **κατάψυξη** kah·<u>tah</u>·psee·ksee
**frequent** *adj* **συχνός** seekh·<u>nohs</u>
**fresh** *adj* **φρέσκος** <u>frehs</u>·kohs
**friend** *n* **φίλος** <u>fee</u>·lohs
**frightened** **φοβισμένος**

foh·veez·<u>meh</u>·nohs

**from** **από** ah·<u>poh</u>

**front** *n* **προκυμαία** proh·kee·<u>meh</u>·ah

**full** *adj* **γεμάτος** yeh·<u>mah</u>·tohs

**furniture** **έπιπλα** <u>eh</u>·peep·lah

**fuse** *n* **ασφάλεια** ahs·<u>fah</u>·lee·ah

## G

**gambling** **τζόγος** <u>joh</u>·ghohs

**game (toy)** **παιχνίδι** pehkh·<u>nee</u>·THee

**garage** **γκαράζ** gah·<u>rahz</u>

**garden** *n* **κήπος** <u>kee</u>·pohs

**gas** **βενζίνη** vehn·<u>zee</u>·nee

**gas station** **βενζινάδικο**
vehn·zee·<u>nah</u>·THee·koh

**gastritis** **γαστρίτιδα**
ghahs·<u>tree</u>·tee·THah

**gate (airport)** **έξοδος** <u>eh</u>·ksoh·THohs

**genuine** **αυθεντικός**
ahf·thehn·dee·<u>kohs</u>

**get off (transport)** **κατεβαίνω**
kah·teh·<u>veh</u>·noh

**get out (of vehicle)** **βγαίνω**
<u>vyeh</u>·noh

**gift** **δώρο** <u>THoh</u>·roh

**gift store** **κατάστημα με είδη
δώρων** kah·<u>tahs</u>·tee·mah meh
ee·THee <u>THoh</u>·rohn

**girl** **κορίτσι** koh·<u>ree</u>·tsee

**girlfriend** **φίλη** <u>fee</u>·lee

**give** **δίνω** <u>THee</u>·noh

**glass (container)** **ποτήρι** poh·<u>tee</u>·ree

**glasses (optical)** **γυαλιά** yah·<u>liah</u>

**glove** *n* **γάντι** <u>ghahn</u>·dee

**go** **πηγαίνω** pee·<u>yeh</u>·noh

**gold** *n* **χρυσός** khree·<u>sohs</u>

**golf** **γκόλφ** gohlf

**golf course** **γήπεδο γκολφ**
<u>yee</u>·peh·THoh gohlf

**good** **καλός** kah·<u>lohs</u>

**grass** **γρασίδι** ghrah·<u>see</u>·THee

**gratuity** **φιλοδώρημα**
fee·loh·<u>THoh</u>·ree·mah

**greasy (hair, skin)** **λιπαρός**
lee·pah·<u>rohs</u>

**Greece** **Ελλάδα** eh·<u>lah</u>·THah

**Greek** *adj* **ελληνικός** eh·lee·nee·<u>kohs</u>;
**(nationality)** **Έλληνας** <u>eh</u>·lee·nahs

**greengrocer [BE]** **οπωροπωλείο**
oh·poh·roh·poh·<u>lee</u>·oh

**ground (earth)** **έδαφος** <u>eh</u>·THah·fohs

**group** *n* **γκρουπ** groop

**guarantee** *n* **εγγύηση** eh·<u>gee</u>·ee·see;
*v* **εγγυώμαι** eh·gee·<u>oh</u>·meh

**guide book** **τουριστικός οδηγός**
too·ree·stee·<u>kohs</u> oh·THee·<u>ghohs</u>

**guided tour** **ξενάγηση**
kseh·<u>nah</u>·yee·see

**guitar** **κιθάρα** kee·<u>thah</u>·rah

**gynecologist** **γυναικολόγος**
yee·neh·koh·<u>loh</u>·ghohs

## H

**hair** **μαλλιά** mah·<u>liah</u>

**hairbrush** **βούρτσα** <u>voor</u>·tsah

**hair dresser** **κομμωτήριο**
koh·moh·<u>tee</u>·ree·oh

**hair dryer** **σεσουάρ** seh·soo·<u>ahr</u>

**half** μισός mee-<u>sohs</u>
**hammer** σφυρί sfee-<u>ree</u>
**hand** n χέρι <u>kheh</u>-ree
**hand luggage** αποσκευές χειρός
ah-pohs-keh-<u>vehs</u> khee-<u>rohs</u>
**handbag** τσάντα <u>tsahn</u>-dah
**handicraft** λαϊκή τέχνη lah-ee-<u>kee</u>
<u>tehkh</u>-nee
**handicapped-accessible toilet**
προσβάσιμη τουαλέτα για
ανάπηρους prohs-<u>vah</u>-see-mee
too-ah-<u>leh</u>-tah yah ah-<u>nah</u>-pee-roos
**handkerchief** χαρτομάντηλο
khah-rtoh-<u>mahn</u>-dee-loh
**handle** n πόμολο <u>poh</u>-moh-loh
**hanger** κρεμάστρα kreh-<u>mahs</u>-trah
**harbor** n λιμάνι lee-<u>mah</u>-nee
**hat** καπέλο kah-<u>peh</u>-loh
**have** (possession) έχω <u>eh</u>-khoh
**have to** (obligation) οφείλω
oh-<u>fee</u>-loh
**head** n κεφάλι keh-<u>fah</u>-lee
**headache** πονοκέφαλος
poh-noh-<u>keh</u>-fah-lohs
**health food store** κατάστημα με
υγιεινές τροφές kah-<u>tahs</u>-tee-mah
meh ee-yee-ee-<u>nehs</u> troh-<u>fehs</u>
**health insurance** ασφάλεια υγείας
ahs-<u>fah</u>-lee-ah ee-<u>yee</u>-ahs
**hearing aid** ακουστικό βαρυκοΐας
ah-koo-stee-<u>koh</u> vah-ree-koh-<u>ee</u>-ahs
**heart** v καρδιά kahr-THee-<u>ah</u>
**heart attack** καρδιακό έμφραγμα
kahr-THee-ah-<u>koh</u> <u>ehm</u>-frahgh-mah

**heat wave** καύσωνας <u>kahf</u>-soh-nahs
**heater (water)** θερμοσίφωνας
thehr-moh-<u>see</u>-foh-nahs
**heating** θέρμανση <u>thehr</u>-mahn-see
**heavy** βαρύς vah-<u>rees</u>
**height** ύψος <u>ee</u>-psohs
**helicopter** ελικόπτερο
eh-lee-<u>kohp</u>-teh-roh
**help** n βοήθεια voh-<u>ee</u>-thee-ah; v
βοηθώ voh-ee-<u>thoh</u>
**here** εδώ eh-<u>THoh</u>
**highway** εθνική οδός ehth-nee-<u>kee</u>
oh-<u>THohs</u>
**hike** v κάνω πεζοπορία <u>kah</u>-noh
peh-zoh-poh-<u>ree</u>-ah
**hill** λόφος <u>loh</u>-fohs
**hire [BE]** v νοικιάζω nee-<u>kiah</u>-zoh
**history** ιστορία ee-stoh-<u>ree</u>-ah
**hitchhiking** οτοστόπ oh-toh-<u>stohp</u>
**hobby (pastime)** χόμπυ <u>khoh</u>-bee
**hold on** περιμένω peh-ree-<u>meh</u>-noh
**hole (in clothes)** τρύπα <u>tree</u>-pah
**holiday [BE]** διακοπές
THee-ah-koh-<u>pehs</u>
**honeymoon** μήνας του μέλιτος
<u>mee</u>-nahs too <u>meh</u>-lee-tohs
**horse track** ιπποδρόμιο
ee-poh-<u>THroh</u>-mee-oh
**hospital** νοσοκομείο
noh-soh-koh-<u>mee</u>-oh
**hot (weather)** ζεστός zehs-<u>tohs</u>
**hot spring** θερμή πηγή thehr-<u>mee</u>
pee-<u>yee</u>
**hotel** ξενοδοχείο

kseh·noh·THoh·<u>khee</u>·oh

**household articles είδη οικιακής χρήσεως** <u>ee</u>·THee ee·kee·ah·<u>kees</u> khree·seh·ohs

**husband σύζυγος** <u>see</u>·zee·ghohs

---

**ice** *n* **πάγος** <u>pah</u>·ghohs

**identification ταυτότητα** tahf·<u>toh</u>·tee·tah

**illegal παράνομος** pah·<u>rah</u>·noh·mohs

**illness αρρώστεια** ahr·<u>ohs</u>·tee·ah

**imitation απομίμηση** ah·poh·<u>mee</u>·mee·see

**immediately αμέσως** ah·<u>meh</u>·sohs

**impressive εντυπωσιακός** ehn·dee·poh·see·ah·<u>kohs</u>

**included συμπεριλαμβάνεται** seem·beh·ree·lahm·<u>vah</u>·neh·teh

**indigestion δυσπεψία** THehs·peh·<u>psee</u>·ah

**indoor εσωτερικός** eh·soh·teh·ree·<u>kohs</u>

**indoor pool εσωτερική πισίνα** eh·soh·teh·ree·<u>kee</u> pee·<u>see</u>·nah

**inexpensive φτηνός** ftee·<u>nohs</u>

**infected μολυσμένος** moh·leez·<u>meh</u>·nohs

**inflammation φλεγμονή** flegh·moh·<u>nee</u>

**information πληροφορίες** plee·roh·foh·<u>ree</u>·ehs

**information office γραφείο πληροφοριών** ghrah·<u>fee</u>·oh

plee·roh·foh·ree·<u>ohn</u>

**injection ένεση** <u>eh</u>·neh·see

**injured τραυματισμένος** trahv·mah·teez·<u>meh</u>·nohs

**innocent αθώος** ah·<u>thoh</u>·ohs

**insect bite τσίμπημα από έντομο** <u>tseem</u>·bee·mah ah·<u>poh</u> ehn·doh·moh

**insect repellent εντομοαπωθητικό** ehn·doh·moh·ah·poh·thee·tee·<u>koh</u>

**inside μέσα** <u>meh</u>·sah

**insist επιμένω** eh·pee·<u>meh</u>·noh

**insomnia αϋπνία** ah·eep·<u>nee</u>·ah

**instruction οδηγία** oh·THee·<u>yee</u>·ah

**insulin ινσουλίνη** een·soo·<u>lee</u>·nee

**insurance ασφάλεια** ahs·<u>fah</u>·lee·ah

**insurance certificate πιστοποιητικό ασφάλειας** pees·toh·pee·ee·tee·<u>koh</u> ahs·<u>fah</u>·lee·ahs

**insurance claim ασφάλεια αποζημίωσης** ahs·<u>fah</u>·lee·ah ah·poh·zee·<u>mee</u>·oh·sees

**insurance company ασφαλιστική εταιρία** ahs·fah·lees·tee·<u>kee</u> eh·teh·<u>ree</u>·ah

**interest rate επιτόκιο** eh·pee·<u>toh</u>·kee·oh

**interesting ενδιαφέρων** ehn·THee·ah·<u>feh</u>·rohn

**international διεθνής** THee·eth·<u>nees</u>

**International Student Card διεθνής φοιτητική κάρτα** THee·ehth·<u>nees</u> fee·tee·tee·<u>kee</u> <u>kahr</u>·tah

**internet ίντερνετ** <u>ee</u>·nteh·rnet

**internet cafe** ίντερνετ καφέ
ee‑nteh‑rnet kah‑<u>feh</u>

**interpreter** διερμηνέας
THee‑ehr‑mee‑<u>neh</u>‑ahs

**interval** διάλειμμα THee‑<u>ah</u>‑lee‑mah

**introduce** συστήνω see‑<u>stee</u>‑noh

**introductions** συστάσεις
see‑<u>stah</u>‑sees

**invitation** πρόσκληση <u>prohs</u>‑klee‑see

**invite** v προσκαλώ prohs‑kah‑<u>loh</u>

**iodine** ιώδειο ee‑<u>oh</u>‑THee‑oh

**iron** n σίδερο <u>see</u>‑THeh‑roh; v
σιδερώνω see‑THeh‑<u>roh</u>‑noh

**itemized bill** αναλυτικός
λογαριασμός ah‑nah‑lee‑tee‑<u>kohs</u>
loh‑ghahr‑yahz‑<u>mohs</u>

## J

**jacket** σακάκι sah‑<u>kah</u>‑kee

**jammed** σφηνωμένος
sfee‑noh‑<u>meh</u>‑nohs

**jar** n βάζο <u>vah</u>‑zoh

**jaw** σαγόνι sah‑<u>ghoh</u>‑nee

**jeans** μπλου‑τζην bloo‑<u>jeen</u>

**jellyfish** μέδουσα <u>meh</u>‑THoo‑sah

**jet‑ski** τζετ‑σκι jeht‑skee

**jeweler** κοσμηματοπωλείο
kohz‑mee‑mah‑toh‑poh‑<u>lee</u>‑oh

**job** δουλειά THoo‑<u>liah</u>

**jogging** τζόγκιγκ joh‑geeng

**joke** n ανέκδοτο ah‑<u>nehk</u>‑THoh‑toh

**journey** ταξίδι tah‑<u>ksee</u>‑THee

**junction** (intersection) κόμβος
<u>kohm</u>‑vohs

## K

**keep** v κρατώ krah‑<u>toh</u>

**key** n κλειδί klee‑<u>THee</u>

**key card** κάρτα‑κλειδί
<u>kahr</u>‑tah‑klee‑dee

**key ring** μπρελόκ breh‑<u>lohk</u>

**kidney** νεφρό nehf‑<u>roh</u>

**kind** είδος ee‑THohs

**king** βασιλιάς vah‑see‑<u>liahs</u>

**kiosk** περίπτερο peh‑<u>ree</u>‑pteh‑roh

**kiss** n φιλί fee‑<u>lee</u>; v φιλώ fee‑<u>loh</u>

**kitchen** χαρτί κουζίνας khah‑<u>rtee</u>
koo‑<u>zee</u>‑nahs

**knapsack** σάκκος <u>sah</u>‑kohs

**knee** γόνατο <u>ghoh</u>‑nah‑toh

**knife** μαχαίρι mah‑<u>kheh</u>‑ree

**know** γνωρίζω ghnoh‑<u>ree</u>‑zoh

## L

**label** n ετικέτα eh‑tee‑<u>keh</u>‑tah

**ladder** σκάλα <u>skah</u>‑lah

**lake** λίμνη <u>leem</u>‑nee

**lamp** λάμπα <u>lahm</u>‑bah

**land** n γη ghee; v προσγειώνομαι
prohz‑yee‑<u>oh</u>‑noh‑meh

**language course** μάθημα ξένης
γλώσσας <u>mah</u>‑thee‑mah <u>kseh</u>‑nees
<u>ghloh</u>‑sahs

**large** adj μεγάλος meh‑<u>ghah</u>‑lohs

**last** τελευταίος teh‑lehf‑<u>teh</u>‑ohs

**late** adv αργά ahr‑<u>ghah</u>

**laugh** v γελώ yeh‑<u>loh</u>

**laundry facility** πλυντήριο
pleen‑<u>dee</u>‑ree‑oh

**lavatory μπάνιο** bah·nioh

**lawyer δικηγόρος**
THee·kee·ghoh·rohs

**laxative καθαρτικό**
kah·thahr·tee·koh

**learn μαθαίνω** mah·theh·noh

**leave** v (depart) **φεύγω** fehv·ghoh;
(let go) **αφήνω** ah·fee·noh

**left** adj **αριστερός** ah·rees·teh·rohs;
adv **αριστερά** ah·rees·teh·rah

**leg πόδι** poh·THee

**legal νόμιμος** noh·mee·mohs

**lend δανείζω** THah·nee·zoh

**length μήκος** mee·kohs

**lens φακός** fah·kohs

**lens cap κάλυμμα φακού**
kah·lee·mah fah·koo

**less λιγότερο** lee·ghoh·teh·roh

**letter γράμμα** ghrah·mah

**level (even) επίπεδο**
eh·pee·peh·THoh

**library βιβλιοθήκη**
veev·lee·oh·thee·kee

**lie down ξαπλώνω** ksah·ploh·noh

**life boat ναυαγοσωστική λέμβος**
nah·vah·ghoh·sohs·tee·kee
lehm·vohs

**lifeguard ναυαγοσώστης**
nah·vah·ghoh·sohs·tees

**life jacket σωσίβιο** soh·see·vee·oh

**lift [BE]** n (elevator) **ασανσέρ**
ah·sahn·sehr

**lift pass άδεια σκι** ah·THee·ah skee

**light** adj (color) **ανοιχτός**

ah·neekh·tohs; n (electric) **φως** fohs

**light bulb λάμπα** lahm·bah

**lighter** adj **ανοιχτότερος**
ah·neekh·toh·teh·rohs; n
**αναπτήρας** ah·nahp·tee·rahs

**lighthouse φάρος** fah·rohs

**lights (car) φώτα** foh·tah

**line** n (subway) **γραμμή** ghrah·mee

**lips χείλη** khee·lee

**lipstick κραγιόν** krah·yohn

**liter λίτρο** lee·troh

**little μικρός** meek·rohs

**liver συκώτι** see·koh·tee

**living room σαλόνι** sah·loh·nee

**local τοπικός** toh·pee·kohs

**location (space) θέση** theh·see

**lock** n (door) **κλειδαριά**
klee·THahr·yah; (river, canal)
**φράγμα** frahgh·mah; v **κλειδώνω**
klee·THoh·noh

**long** adj **μακρύς** mak·rees

**long-distance bus υπεραστικό
λεωφορείο** ee·peh·rahs·tee·koh
leh·oh·foh·ree·oh

**long-distance call υπεραστικό
τηλεφώνημα** ee·pehr·ahs·tee·koh
tee·leh·foh·nee·mah

**long-sighted [BE] πρεσβύωπας**
prehz·vee·oh·pahs

**look** v **κοιτάω** kee·tah·oh

**look for ψάχνω** psahkh·noh

**loose (fitting) φαρδύς** fahr·THees

**loss** n **απώλεια** ah·poh·lee·ah

**lotion λοσιόν** loh·siohn

**loud** *adj* **δυνατός** THee·nah·<u>tohs</u>
**love** *v* **αγαπώ** ah·ghah·<u>poh</u>
**lower** *adj* (berth) **κάτω** kah·toh
**lubricant λιπαντικό**
  lee·pahn·dee·<u>koh</u>
**luck τύχη** <u>tee</u>·khee
**luggage αποσκευές**
  ah·pohs·keh·<u>vehs</u>
**luggage cart καροτσάκι**
  **αποσκευών** kah·roh·<u>tsah</u>·kee
  ah·pohs·keh·<u>vohn</u>
**luggage locker θυρίδα**
  thee·<u>ree</u>·THah
**lukewarm χλιαρός** khlee·ah·<u>rohs</u>
**lump** *n* **σβώλος** <u>svoh</u>·lohs; (medical)
  **εξόγκωμα** eh·<u>ksoh</u>·goh·mah
**lunch** *n* **μεσημεριανό**
  meh·see·mehr·yah·<u>noh</u>
**lung πνεύμονας** <u>pnehv</u>·moh·nahs
**luxury πολυτέλεια** poh·lee·<u>teh</u>·lee·ah

# M

**magazine περιοδικό**
  peh·ree·oh·THee·<u>koh</u>
**magnificent μεγαλοπρεπής**
  meh·ghah·lohp·reh·<u>pees</u>
**mailbox ταχυδρομικό κουτί**
  tah·kheeTH·roh·mee·<u>koh</u> koo·<u>tee</u>
**mail** *n* **αλληλογραφία**
  ah·lee·lohgh·rah·<u>fee</u>·ah
**main κύριος** <u>kee</u>·ree·ohs
**make-up μακιγιάζ** mah·kee·<u>yahz</u>
**man** (male) **άνδρας** <u>ahn</u>·THrahs
**manager διευθυντής**
  THee·ehf·theen·<u>dees</u>
**manicure μανικιούρ** mah·nee·<u>kioor</u>
**manual** (car) **χειροκίνητος**
  khee·roh·<u>kee</u>·nee·tohs
**map** *n* **χάρτης** <u>khahr</u>·tees
**market** *n* **αγορά** ah·ghoh·<u>rah</u>
**married παντρεμένος**
  pahn·dreh·<u>meh</u>·nohs
**mask** *n* (diving) **μάσκα** <u>mahs</u>·kah
**mass** *n* (church) **λειτουργία**
  lee·toor·<u>yee</u>·ah
**massage** *n* **μασάζ** mah·<u>sahz</u>
**match** *n* (sport) **αγώνας**
  ah·<u>ghoh</u>·nahs; (fire starter) **σπίρτο**
  <u>speer</u>·toh
**maybe ίσως** <u>ee</u>·sohs
**meal γεύμα** <u>yehv</u>·mah
**mean** *v* **σημαίνω** see·<u>meh</u>·noh
**measure** *v* **μετρώ** meht·<u>roh</u>
**measurement μέτρηση**
  <u>meh</u>·tree·see
**medication φάρμακα** <u>fahr</u>·mah·kah
**meet συναντώ** see·nahn·<u>doh</u>
**memorial μνημείο** mnee·<u>mee</u>·oh
**mend διορθώνω** THee·ohr·<u>thoh</u>·noh
**menstrual cramp πόνος περιόδου**
  poh·nohs peh·ree·<u>oh</u>·THoo
**mention αναφέρω** ah·nah·<u>feh</u>·roh
**message** *n* **μήνυμα** <u>mee</u>·nee·mah
**metal** *n* **μέταλλο** <u>meh</u>·tah·loh
**microwave (oven) φούρνος**
  **μικροκυμάτων** <u>foor</u>·nohs
  mee·kroh·kee·<u>mah</u>·tohn
**migraine ημικρανία**

ee•mee•krah•<u>nee</u>•ah

**mileage χιλιόμετρα**
khee•<u>lioh</u>•meh•trah

**mini-bar μινι-μπαρ** <u>mee</u>•nee•bahr

**minimart παντοπωλείο**
pahn•doh•poh•<u>lee</u>•oh

**minimum ελάχιστος**
eh•<u>lah</u>•khees•tohs

**minute** n (time) **λεπτό** lehp•<u>toh</u>

**mirror** n **καθρέφτης** kah•<u>threhf</u>•tees

**mistake λάθος** <u>lah</u>•thohs

**misunderstanding παρεξήγηση**
pah•reh•<u>ksee</u>•yee•see

**mobile phone [BE] κινητό**
kee•nee•<u>toh</u>

**modern μοντέρνος** moh•<u>deh</u>•rnohs

**moisturizer** (cream) **ενυδατική
κρέμα** eh•nee•THah•tee•<u>kee</u>
kreh•mah

**money χρήματα** <u>khree</u>•mah•tah

**money order ταχυδρομική
επιταγή** tah•kheeTH•roh•mee•<u>kee</u>
eh•pee•tah•<u>yee</u>

**money-belt ζώνη για χρήματα**
<u>zoh</u>•nee yah <u>khree</u>•mah•tah

**monument μνημείο** mnee•<u>mee</u>•oh

**moped μοτοποδήλατο**
moh•toh•poh•<u>THee</u>•lah•toh

**more παραπάνω** pah•rah•<u>pah</u>•noh

**morning πρωί** proh•<u>ee</u>

**mosquito κουνούπι** koo•<u>noo</u>•pee

**mosquito bite τσίμπημα
κουνουπιού** <u>tseem</u>•bee•mah
koo•noo•<u>piooh</u>

**motorboat εξωλέμβιο**
eh•ksoh•<u>lehm</u>•vee•oh

**motorway [BE] εθνική οδός**
ehth•nee•<u>kee</u> oh•<u>THohs</u>

**mountain βουνό** voo•<u>noh</u>

**moustache μουστάκι** moos•<u>tah</u>•kee

**mouth** n **στόμα** <u>stoh</u>•mah

**move** v (room) **μετακομίζω**
meh•tah•koh•<u>mee</u>•zoh

**movie ταινία** teh•<u>nee</u>•ah

**movie theater κινηματογράφος**
kee•nee•mah•tohgh•<u>rah</u>•fohs

**much πολύ** poh•<u>lee</u>

**muscle** n **μυς** mees

**museum μουσείο** moo•<u>see</u>•oh

**music μουσική** moo•see•<u>kee</u>

**musician μουσικός** moo•see•<u>kohs</u>

**must** v **πρέπει** <u>preh</u>•pee

183

# N

**nail salon σαλόνι νυχιών** sah•<u>loh</u>•nee
nee•<u>khiohn</u>

**name** n **όνομα** <u>oh</u>•noh•mah

**napkin πετσέτα** peh•<u>tseh</u>•tah

**nappy [BE] πάνα μωρού** <u>pah</u>•nah
moh•<u>roo</u>

**narrow στενός** steh•<u>nohs</u>

**national εθνικός** eth•nee•<u>kohs</u>

**nationality υπηκοότητα**
ee•pee•koh•<u>oh</u>•tee•tah

**nature φύση** <u>fee</u>•see

**nature reserve εθνικός δρυμός**
eth•nee•<u>kohs</u> THree•<u>mohs</u>

**nature trail μονοπάτι**

moh·noh·**pah**·tee

**nausea** ναυτία nahf·**tee**·ah

**near** *adv* κοντά kohn·**dah**

**nearby** εδώ κοντά eh·**THoh** kohn·**dah**

**necessary** απαραίτητος
ah·pah·**reh**·tee·tohs

**necklace** κολλιέ koh·**lieh**

**need** v χρειάζομαι khree·**ah**·zoh·meh

**neighbor** n γείτονας **yee**·toh·nahs

**nerve** νεύρο **nehv**·roh

**never** ποτέ poh·**teh**

**new** καινούργιος keh·**noor**·yohs

**newspaper** εφημερίδα
eh·fee·meh·**ree**·THah

**newsstand** περίπτερο
peh·**ree**·pteh·roh

**next** επόμενος eh·**poh**·meh·nohs

**next to** δίπλα **THeep**·lah

**night** νύχτα neekh·tah

**night club** νυχτερινό κέντρο
neekh·teh·ree·**noh** kehn·droh

**noisy** θορυβώδης
thoh·ree·**voh**·THees

**none** *adj* κανένας kah·**neh**·nahs

**non-smoking** μη καπνίζοντες mee
kap·**nee**·zohn·dehs

**north** βόρεια **voh**·ree·ah

**nose** n μύτη **mee**·tee

**nudist beach** παραλία γυμνιστών
pah·rah·**lee**·ah yeem·nees·**tohn**

**nurse** n νοσοκόμα noh·soh·**koh**·mah

**O**

**occupied** κατειλημένος

kah·tee·lee·**meh**·nohs

**office** γραφείο ghrah·**fee**·oh

**old** *adj* (thing) παλιός pah·**liohs**;
(person) γέρικος **yeh**·ree·kohs

**old town** παλιά πόλη pah·**liah**
poh·lee

**old-fashioned** ντεμοντέ
deh·mohn·**deh**

**once** μια φορά miah foh·**rah**

**one-way ticket** απλό εισιτίριο
ahp·**loh** ee·see·**tee**·ree·oh

**open** *adj* ανοιχτός ah·neekh·**tohs**; v
ανοίγω ah·**nee**·ghoh

**opening hours** ώρες λειτουργίας
**oh**·rehs lee·toor·**yee**·ahs

**opera** όπερα **oh**·peh·rah

**opposite** απέναντι ah·**peh**·nahn·dee

**optician** οφθαλμίατρος
ohf·thahl·**mee**·aht·rohs

**orchestra** ορχήστρα ohr·**khees**·trah

**order** v παραγγέλνω
pah·rah·**gehl**·noh

**organized** οργανωμένος
ohr·ghah·noh·**meh**·nohs

**others** άλλα **ah**·lah

**out** *adv* έξω **eh**·ksoh

**outdoor** εξωτερικός
eh·ksoh·teh·ree·**kohs**

**outside** *adj* έξω **eh**·ksoh

**oval** οβάλ oh·**vahl**

**oven** φούρνος **foor**·nohs

**over there** εκεί eh·**kee**

**overnight (package)** ένα βράδυ
**eh**·nah vrah·THee

**owe** χρωστώ khroh·<u>stoh</u>
**owner** κάτοχος <u>kah</u>·toh·khohs

## P

**pacifier** πιπίλα pee·<u>pee</u>·lah
**pack** *v* (baggage) **φτιάχνω τις**
  **βαλίτσες** ftee·<u>ahkh</u>·noh tees
  vah·<u>lee</u>·tsehs
**paddling pool [BE]** ρηχή πισίνα
  ree·<u>khee</u> pee·<u>see</u>·nah
**padlock** λουκέτο loo·<u>keh</u>·toh
**pain** *n* πόνος <u>poh</u>·nohs
painkiller **παυσίπονο**
  pahf·<u>see</u>·poh·noh
**paint** *v* ζωγραφίζω
  zohgh·rah·<u>fee</u>·zoh
**pair** ζευγάρι zehv·<u>ghah</u>·ree
**pajamas** πιτζάμες pee·<u>jah</u>·mehs
**palace** ανάκτορα ah·<u>nahk</u>·toh·rah
**panorama** πανόραμα
  pah·<u>noh</u>·rah·mah
**pants** παντελόνι pahn·deh·<u>loh</u>·nee
**paper** χαρτί khar·<u>tee</u>
**paralysis** παραλυσία
  pah·rah·lee·<u>see</u>·ah
**parcel** πακέτο pah·<u>keh</u>·toh
**parents** γονείς ghoh·<u>nees</u>
**park** *n* πάρκο <u>pahr</u>·koh
**parking lot** χώρος στάθμευσης
  <u>khoh</u>·rohs <u>stahth</u>·mehf·sees
**parking meter** παρκόμετρο
  pahr·<u>koh</u>·meht·roh
**party** *n* (social gathering) **πάρτυ**
  <u>pah</u>·rtee

**pass** *v* περνώ pehr·<u>noh</u>
**passenger** επιβάτης eh·pee·<u>vah</u>·tees
**passport** διαβατήριο
  THiah·vah·<u>tee</u>·ree·oh
**pastry store** ζαχαροπλαστείο
  zah·khah·rohp·lahs·<u>tee</u>·oh
**path** μονοπάτι moh·noh·<u>pah</u>·tee
**pay** *v* πληρώνω plee·<u>roh</u>·noh
**payment** πληρωμή plee·roh·<u>mee</u>
**peak** *n* κορυφή koh·ree·<u>fee</u>
**pearl** μαργαριτάρι
  mahr·ghah·ree·<u>tah</u>·ree
**pebbly (beach)** με χαλίκια meh
  khah·<u>lee</u>·kiah
**pedestrian crossing** διάβαση πεζών
  THee·<u>ah</u>·vah·see peh·<u>zohn</u>
**pedestrian zone** πεζόδρομος
  peh·<u>zohTH</u>·roh·mohs
**pen** *n* στυλό stee·<u>loh</u>
**per** την teen
**perhaps** ίσως ee·sohs
**period (menstrual)** περίοδος
  peh·<u>ree</u>·oh·THohs; **(time)**
  **χρονική περίοδος** khroh·nee·<u>kee</u>
  peh·<u>ree</u>·oh·Thohs
**permit** *n* άδεια <u>ah</u>·THee·ah
**petrol [BE]** βενζίνη vehn·<u>zee</u>·nee
**pewter** κασσίτερος kah·<u>see</u>·teh·rohs
**phone** *n* τηλέφωνο tee·<u>leh</u>·foh·noh
**phone call** τηλεφώνημα
  tee·leh·<u>foh</u>·nee·mah
**phone card** τηλεκάρτα
  tee·leh·<u>kahr</u>·tah
**photo** *v* φωτογραφία

foh·tohgh·rah·<u>fee</u>·ah

**photocopier φωτοτυπικό**
foh·toh·tee·pee·<u>koh</u>

**phrase** n **φράση** <u>frah</u>·see

**pick up παίρνω** <u>pehr</u>·noh

**picnic area περιοχή για πικνίκ**
peh·ree·oh·<u>khee</u> yah peek·neek

**piece τεμάχιο** teh·<u>mah</u>·khee·oh

**pillow μαξιλάρι** mah·ksee·<u>lah</u>·ree

**pillow case μαξιλαροθήκη**
mah·ksee·lah·roh·<u>thee</u>·kee

**pipe (smoking) πίπα** <u>pee</u>·pah

**piste [BE] μονοπάτι**
moh·noh·<u>pah</u>·tee

**pizzeria πιτσαρία** pee·tsah·<u>ree</u>·ah

**plan** n **σχέδιο** <u>skheh</u>·THee·oh

**plane** n **αεροπλάνο**
ah·eh·rohp·<u>lah</u>·noh

**plant** n **φυτό** fee·<u>toh</u>

**plastic wrap διαφανή μεμβράνη**
THee·ah·fah·<u>nee</u> mehm·<u>vrah</u>·nee

**platform αποβάθρα**
ah·poh·<u>vahth</u>·rah

**platinum πλατίνα** plah·<u>tee</u>·nah

**play** v **(games) παίζω** <u>peh</u>·zoh;
(music) **παίζω** <u>peh</u>·zoh

**playground παιδική χαρά**
peh·THee·<u>kee</u> khah·<u>rah</u>

**pleasant ευχάριστος**
ehf·<u>khah</u>·rees·tohs

**plug** n **πρίζα** <u>pree</u>·zah

**point** n **σημείο** see·<u>mee</u>·oh; v **δείχνω**
<u>THeekh</u>·noh

**poison** n **δηλητήριο**

THee·lee·<u>tee</u>·ree·oh

**poisonous δηλητηριώδης**
THee·lee·tee·ree·<u>oh</u>·THees

**police** n **αστυνομία**
ah·stee·noh·<u>mee</u>·ah

**police station αστυνομικό τμήμα**
ah·stee·noh·mee·<u>koh</u> <u>tmee</u>·mah

**pond** n **λιμνούλα** leem·<u>noo</u>·lah

**popular δημοφιλής**
THee·moh·fee·<u>lees</u>

**porter αχθοφόρος**
ahkh·thoh·<u>foh</u>·rohs

**portion** n **μερίδα** meh·<u>ree</u>·THah

**possible πιθανός** pee·thah·<u>nohs</u>

**postbox [BE] ταχυδρομικό κουτί**
tah·kheeTH·roh·mee·<u>koh</u> koo·<u>tee</u>

**post card καρτποστάλ**
kahrt·poh·<u>stahl</u>

**post office ταχυδρομείο**
tah·kheeTH·roh·<u>mee</u>·oh

**pottery αγγειοπλαστική**
ahn·gee·ohp·lahs·tee·<u>kee</u>

**pound (sterling) λίρα** <u>lee</u>·rah

**pregnant έγκυος** <u>eh</u>·gee·ohs

**prescribe συνταγογραφώ**
seen·dah·ghoh·ghrah·<u>foh</u>

**prescription συνταγή γιατρού**
seen·dah·<u>yee</u> yaht·<u>roo</u>

**present δώρο** <u>THoh</u>·roh

**press** v **σιδερώνω** see·THeh·<u>roh</u>·noh

**pretty** adj **όμορφος** <u>oh</u>·mohr·fohs

**prison** n **φυλακή** fee·lah·<u>kee</u>

**private bathroom ιδιωτικό μπάνιο**
ee·THee·oh·tee·<u>koh</u> <u>bah</u>·nioh

**problem** πρόβλημα <u>prohv</u>·lee·mah
**program** n πρόγραμμα
   <u>prohgh</u>·rah·mah
**program of events** πρόγραμμα
   θεαμάτων <u>proh</u>·ghrah·mah
   theh·ah·<u>mah</u>·tohn
**prohibited** απαγορευμένος
   ah·pah·ghoh·rehv·<u>meh</u>·nohs
**pronounce** προφέρω proh·<u>feh</u>·roh
**public** δημόσιος THee·<u>moh</u>·see·ohs
**public holiday** αργία ahr·<u>yee</u>·ah
**pump** n τρόμπα <u>troh</u>·mbah
**purpose** σκοπός skoh·<u>pohs</u>
**put** v βάζω <u>vah</u>·zoh

## Q

**quality** ποιότητα pee·<u>oh</u>·tee·tah
**quantity** ποσότητα poh·<u>soh</u>·tee·tah
**quarantine** n καραντίνα
   kah·rahn·<u>dee</u>·nah
**quarter (quantity)** ένα τέταρτο
   eh·nah teh·tah·rtoh
**quay** αποβάθρα ah·poh·<u>vath</u>·rah
**question** n ερώτηση eh·<u>roh</u>·tee·see
**queue [BE]** v περιμένω στην ουρά
   peh·ree·<u>meh</u>·noh steen oo·<u>rah</u>
**quick** γρήγορος <u>ghree</u>·ghoh·rohs
**quiet** adj ήσυχος <u>ee</u>·see·khohs

## R

**racket (tennis, squash)** ρακέτα
   rah·<u>keh</u>·tah
**radio** n ραδιόφωνο
   rah·THee·<u>oh</u>·foh·noh

**railway station [BE]**
   σιδηροδρομικός σταθμός
   see·THee·rohTH·roh·mee·<u>kohs</u>
   stahth·<u>mohs</u>
**rain** n βροχή vroh·<u>khee</u>; v βρέχει
   <u>vreh</u>·khee
**raincoat** αδιάβροχο
   ah·THee·<u>ahv</u>·roh·khoh
**rapids** ρεύμα ποταμού <u>rehv</u>·mah
   poh·tah·<u>moo</u>
**rare (unusual)** σπάνιος <u>spah</u>·nee·ohs
**rash** n εξάνθημα eh·<u>ksahn</u>·thee·mah
**ravine** ρεματιά reh·mah·<u>tiah</u>
**razor** ξυραφάκι ksee·rah·<u>fah</u>·kee
**razor blade** ξυραφάκι
   ksee·rah·<u>fah</u>·kee
**ready** adj έτοιμος eh·<u>tee</u>·mohs
**real (genuine)** γνήσιος <u>ghee</u>·see·ohs;
   **(true)** αληθινός ah·lee·thee·nohs
**receipt** απόδειξη ah·<u>poh</u>·THee·ksee
**reception (hotel)** ρεσεψιόν
   reh·seh·<u>psiohn</u>
**recommend** συστήνω sees·<u>tee</u>·noh
**reduction** έκπτωση <u>ehk</u>·ptoh·see
**refund** n επιστροφή χρημάτων
   eh·pees·troh·<u>fee</u> khree·<u>mah</u>·tohn
**region** περιοχή peh·ree·oh·<u>khee</u>
**registration number** αριθμός
   κυκλοφορίας ah·reeth·<u>mohs</u>
   kee·kloh·foh·<u>ree</u>·ahs
**religion** θρησκεία three·<u>skee</u>·ah
**remember** θυμάμαι thee·<u>mah</u>·meh
**rent** v νοικιάζω nee·<u>kiah</u>·zoh
**repair** n επισκευή eh·pee·skeh·<u>vee</u>; v

**repeat** *v* επαναλαμβάνω
eh•pah•nah•lahm•<u>vah</u>•noh

**replacement part** ανταλλακτικό
ahn•dah•lahk•tee•<u>koh</u>

**report** *v* αναφέρω ah•nah•<u>feh</u>•roh

**restaurant** εστιατόριο
ehs•tee•ah•<u>toh</u>•ree•oh

**restroom** τουαλέτα too•ah•<u>leh</u>•tah

**retired** συνταξιούχος
seen•dah•ksee•<u>oo</u>•khohs

**return ticket** [BE] εισιτήριο με
επιστροφή ee•see•<u>tee</u>•ree•oh meh
eh•pee•stroh•<u>fee</u>

**reverse the charges** με χρέωση του
καλούμενου meh <u>khreh</u>•oh•see too
kah•<u>loo</u>•meh•noo

**revolting** αηδιαστικός
ah•ee•THee•ah•stee•<u>kohs</u>

**rib** πλευρό plehv•<u>roh</u>

**right** *adj* (correct) σωστός soh•<u>stohs</u>;
(side) δεξιός THeh•ksee•<u>ohs</u>

**river** ποταμός poh•tah•<u>mohs</u>

**road** δρόμος <u>THroh</u>•mohs

**road assistance** οδική βοήθεια
oh•THee•<u>kee</u> voh•<u>ee</u>•thee•ah

**road sign** πινακίδα pee•nah•<u>kee</u>•Thah

**robbery** ληστεία lees•<u>tee</u>•ah

**rock** *n* βράχος <u>vrah</u>•khohs

**rock climbing** αναρρίχηση
ah•nah•<u>ree</u>•khee•see

**romantic** ρομαντικός
roh•mahn•dee•<u>kohs</u>

**roof** *n* στέγη <u>steh</u>•yee

**room** *n* δωμάτιο THoh•<u>mah</u>•tee•oh

**room service** υπηρεσία δωματίου
ee•pee•reh•<u>see</u>•ah THoh•mah•<u>tee</u>•oo

**rope** *n* σχοινί skhee•<u>nee</u>

**round** *adj* στρογγυλός
strohn•gkee•<u>lohs</u>; *n* (of golf) παιχνίδι
pehkh•<u>nee</u>•THee

**round-trip ticket** εισιτήριο με
επιστροφή ee•see•<u>tee</u>•ree•oh meh
eh•pee•stroh•<u>fee</u>

**route** *n* διαδρομή THee•ahTH•roh•<u>mee</u>

**rowing** κωπηλασία
koh•pee•lah•<u>see</u>•ah

**rubbish** [BE] σκουπίδια
skoo•<u>peeTH</u>•yah

**rude** αγενής ah•yeh•<u>nees</u>

**rug** χαλί khah•<u>lee</u>

**run** *v* τρέχω <u>treh</u>•khoh

**rush hour** ώρα αιχμής <u>oh</u>•rah
ehkh•<u>mees</u>

## S

**safe** *adj* (not dangerous) ασφαλής
ahs•fah•<u>lees</u>

**sailing boat** ιστιοπλοϊκό
ees•tee•oh•ploh•ee•<u>koh</u>

**sales tax** ΦΠΑ fee•pee•<u>ah</u>

**same** ίδιος <u>ee</u>•THee•ohs

**sand** άμμος <u>ah</u>•mohs

**sandals** πέδιλα <u>peh</u>•THee•lah

**sandy (beach)** με άμμο meh <u>ah</u>•moh

**sanitary napkin** σερβιέτα
sehr•vee•<u>eh</u>•tah

**satin** σατέν sah•<u>tehn</u>

**saucepan** κατσαρόλα

kah·tsah·<u>roh</u>·lah

**sauna** σάουνα <u>sah</u>·oo·nah

**scarf** κασκόλ kahs·<u>kohl</u>

**scissors** ψαλίδι psah·<u>lee</u>·THee

**scratch** γρατζουνιά ghrah·joo·<u>niah</u>

**screw** n βίδα vee·<u>THah</u>

**screwdriver** κατσαβίδι
  kah·tsah·<u>vee</u>·THee

**sea** θάλασσα <u>thah</u>·lah·sah

**seafront** προκυμαία
  proh·kee·<u>meh</u>·ah

**seat** n θέση <u>theh</u>·see

**second-hand shop** κατάστημα
  μεταχειρισμένων
  ειδών kah·<u>tah</u>·stee·mah
  meh·tah·khee·reez·<u>meh</u>·nohn
  ee·<u>THohn</u>

**sedative** ηρεμιστικό
  ee·reh·mee·stee·<u>koh</u>

**see** βλέπω <u>vleh</u>·poh

**send** στέλνω <u>stehl</u>·noh

**senior citizen** ηλικιωμένος
  ee·lee·kee·oh·<u>meh</u>·nohs

**separately** ξεχωριστά
  kseh·khoh·ree·<u>stah</u>

**service** n (business) υπηρεσία
  ee·pee·reh·<u>see</u>·ah; (mass)
  λειτουργία lee·toor·<u>yee</u>·ah

**service charge** χρέωση υπηρεσίας
  <u>khreh</u>·oh·see ee·pee·reh·<u>see</u>·ahs

**sewer** υπόνομος ee·<u>poh</u>·noh·mohs

**shade (color)** απόχρωση ah·<u>pohkh</u>·r
  oh·see; (darkness) σκιά skee·<u>ah</u>

**shampoo** n σαμπουάν sahm·poo·<u>ahn</u>

**shape** n σχήμα <u>skhee</u>·mah

**shaving cream** κρέμα ξυρίσματος
  <u>kreh</u>·mah ksee·<u>reez</u>·mah·tohs

**shelf** n ράφι <u>rah</u>·fee

**ship** n πλοίο <u>plee</u>·oh

**shirt** πουκάμισο poo·<u>kah</u>·mee·soh

**shock (electric)** ηλεκτροπληξία
  ee·leh·ktroh·plee·<u>ksee</u>·ah

**shoe** παπούτσι pah·<u>poo</u>·tsee

**shoe polish** βερνίκι παπουτσιών
  vehr·<u>nee</u>·kee pah·poo·<u>tsiohn</u>

**shoe repair** επισκευή παπουτσιών
  eh·pee·skeh·<u>vee</u> pah·poo·<u>tsiohn</u>

**shoe store** κατάστημα
  υποδημάτων kah·<u>tah</u>·stee·mah
  ee·poh·<u>THee</u>·<u>mah</u>·tohn

**shop (store)** κατάστημα
  kah·<u>tah</u>·stee·mah

**shopping mall** εμπορικό κέντρο
  ehm·boh·ree·<u>koh</u> keh·ntroh

**shore** n ακτή ahk·<u>tee</u>

**short** adj κοντός kohn·<u>dohs</u>

**shorts** n σορτς sohrts

**short-sighted [BE]** μύωπας
  <u>mee</u>·oh·pahs

**shoulder** n (anatomy) ώμος <u>oh</u>·mohs

**show** δείχνω <u>THeekh</u>·noh

**shower** n ντουζ dooz

**shower gel** αφρόλουτρο για ντουζ
  ahf·<u>roh</u>·loot·roh yah dooz

**shut** adj κλειστός klees·<u>tohs</u>

**sick** adj άρρωστος <u>ah</u>·rohs·tohs

**side (of road)** μεριά mehr·<u>yah</u>

**sightseeing sight** αξιοθέατο

ah·ksee·oh·theh·ah·toh

**sightseeing tour** ξενάγηση στα αξιοθέατα kseh·nah·yee·see stah ah·ksee·oh·theh·ah·tah

**sign (road)** σήμα see·mah

**silk** μετάξι meh·tah·ksee

**silver** ασήμι ah·see·mee

**simple** απλός ahp·lohs

**single (not married)** ελεύθερος eh·lehf·theh·rohs

**single room** μονόκλινο δωμάτιο moh·noh·klee·noh THoh·mah·tee·oh

**single ticket [BE]** απλό εισιτήριο ahp·loh ee·see·tee·ree·oh

**sink (bathroom)** νιπτήρας nee·ptee·rahs

**sit** κάθομαι kah·thoh·meh

**size** n μέγεθος meh·yeh·thohs

**skates** παγοπέδιλα pah·ghoh·peh·THee·lah

**skating rink** παγοδρόμιο pah·ghohTH·roh·mee·oh

**ski boots** μπότες του σκι boh·tehs too skee

**ski poles** μπαστούνια του σκι bahs·too·niah too skee

**ski school** σχολή σκι skhoh·lee skee

**skiing** σκι skee

**skin** n δέρμα Thehr·mah

**skirt** φούστα foo·stah

**sleep** v κοιμάμαι kee·mah·meh

**sleeping bag** υπνόσακκος ee·pnoh·sah·kohs

**sleeping car** βαγκόν-λι vah·gohn·lee

**sleeping pill** υπνωτικό χάπι eep·noh·tee·koh khah·pee

**slippers** παντόφλες pahn·dohf·lehs

**slope (ski)** πλαγιά plah·yah

**slow** adj αργός ahr·ghohs

**small** μικρός meek·rohs

**smell** v μυρίζω mee·ree·zoh

**smoke** v καπνίζω kahp·nee·zoh

**smoking area** περιοχή για καπνίζοντες peh·ree·oh·khee yah kahp·nee·zohn·dehs

**snack bar** κυλικείο kee·lee·kee·oh

**sneakers** αθλητικά παπούτσια ath·lee·tee·kah pah·poo·tsiah

**snorkeling equipment** εξοπλισμό για ελεύθερη κατάδυση eh·ksohp·leez·moh yah eh·lehf·theh·ree kah·tah·THee·see

**snow** v χιονίζει khioh·nee·zee

**soap** n σαπούνι sah·poo·nee

**soccer** ποδόσφαιρο poh·THohs·feh·roh

**socket** πρίζα pree·zah

**socks** κάλτσες kahl·tsehs

**sofa** καναπές kah·nah·pehs

**sole (shoes)** σόλα soh·lah

**something** κάτι kah·tee

**sometimes** μερικές φορές meh·ree·kehs foh·rehs

**soon** σύντομα seen·doh·mah

**soother [BE]** πιπίλα pee·pee·lah

**sore throat** πονόλαιμος poh·noh·leh·mohs

**sort** n είδος ee·THohs; v διαλέγω

THiah·**leh**·ghoh

**south** *adj* **νότιος** noh·tee·ohs

**souvenir σουβενίρ** soo·veh·**neer**

**souvenir store κατάστημα σουβενίρ**
kah·**tahs**·tee·mah soo·veh·**neer**

**spa σπα** spah

**space** *n* **(area) χώρος** khoh·rohs

**spare (extra) επιπλέον**
eh·peep·**leh**·ohn

**speak μιλώ** mee·**loh**

**special requirement ειδική ανάγκη**
ee·THee·**kee** ah·**nahn**·gkee

**specialist ειδικός** ee·THee·**kohs**

**specimen δείγμα** THeegh·mah

**speed** *v* **τρέχω** treh·khoh

**spend ξοδεύω** ksoh·**THeh**·voh

**spine σπονδυλική στήλη**
spohn·THee·lee·**kee** stee·lee

**spoon** *n* **κουτάλι** koo·**tah**·lee

**sport αθλητισμός** ahth·lee·teez·**mohs**

**sporting goods store κατάστημα**
**αθλητικών ειδών** kah·**tahs**·tee·mah
ath·lee·tee·**kohn** ee·**THohn**

**sports massage αθλητικό μασάζ**
ahth·lee·tee·**koh** mah·**sahz**

**sports stadium αθλητικό στάδιο**
ahth·lee·tee·**koh** stah·THee·oh

**square τετράγωνος**
teht·**rah**·ghoh·nohs

**stadium στάδιο** stah·THee·oh

**stain** *n* **λεκές** leh·**kehs**

**stairs σκάλες** skah·lehs

**stale μπαγιάτικος** bah·**yah**·tee·kohs

**stamp** *n* **(postage) γραμματόσημο**

**start** *v* **αρχίζω** ahr·**khee**·zoh

**statement (legal) δήλωση**
THee·loh·see

**statue άγαλμα** ah·ghahl·mah

**stay** *v* **μένω** meh·noh

**sterilizing solution αποστειρωτικό**
**διάλυμα** ah·pohs·tee·roh·tee·**koh**
THee·**ah**·lee·mah

**sting** *n* **(insect) τσίμπημα**
tsee·bee·mah

**stolen κλεμένος** kleh·**meh**·nohs

**stomach** *n* **στομάχι** stoh·**mah**·khee

**stomachache στομαχόπονος**
stoh·mah·**khoh**·poh·nohs

**stop** *n* **(bus) στάση** stah·see; *v*
**σταματώ** stah·mah·**toh**

**store guide [BE] οδηγός**
**καταστήματος** oh·THee·**ghohs**
kah·tahs·**tee**·mah·tohs

**stove κουζίνα** koo·**zee**·nah

**straight ahead ευθεία** ehf·**thee**·ah

**strange παράξενος**
pah·**rah**·kseh·nohs

**straw (drinking) καλαμάκι**
kah·lah·**mah**·kee

**stream** *n* **ρυάκι** ree·**ah**·kee

**street δρόμος** THroh·mohs

**string** *n* **(cord) σπάγγος** spah·gohs

**student φοιτητής** fee·tee·**tees**

**study** *v* **σπουδάζω** spoo·**THah**·zoh

**style** *n* **στυλ** steel

**subtitled με υπότιτλους** meh
ee·**poh**·teet·loos

**subway** μετρό meh·<u>troh</u>

**subway station** σταθμός μετρό
stahth·<u>mohs</u> meh·<u>troh</u>

**suggest** προτείνω proh·<u>tee</u>·noh

**suit (men's)** κουστούμι
koos·<u>too</u>·mee; **(women's)** ταγιέρ
tah·<u>yehr</u>

**suitable** κατάλληλος
kah·<u>tah</u>·lee·lohs

**sunburn** *n* έγκαυμα ηλίου
<u>ehn</u>·gahv·mah ee·<u>lee</u>·oo

**sunglasses** γυαλιά ηλίου yah·<u>liah</u>
ee·<u>lee</u>·oo

**sunshade [BE]** ομπρέλλα
ohm·<u>breh</u>·lah

**sunstroke** ηλίαση ee·<u>lee</u>·ah·see

**sun tan lotion** λοσιόν μαυρίσματος
loh·<u>siohn</u> mahv·<u>rees</u>·mah·tohs

**sunscreen** αντιηλιακό
ahn·dee·ee·lee·ah·<u>koh</u>

**superb** έξοχος eh·ksoh·khohs

**supermarket** σουπερμάρκετ
soo·pehr·<u>mahr</u>·keht

**supervision** επίβλεψη
eh·<u>peev</u>·leh·psee

**surname** επίθετο eh·<u>pee</u>·theh·toh

**sweatshirt** φούτερ <u>foo</u>·tehr

**swelling** πρήξιμο <u>pree</u>·ksee·moh

**swimming** κολύμβηση
koh·<u>leem</u>·vee·see

**swimming pool** πισίνα pee·<u>see</u>·nah

**swimming trunks** μαγιό mah·<u>yoh</u>

**swimsuit** μαγιό mah·<u>yoh</u>

**switch** *n* διακόπτης THiah·<u>koh</u>·ptees

**swollen** πρησμένος preez·<u>meh</u>·noh

**symptom** σύμπτωμα <u>seem</u>·ptoh·mɑ

**T**

**table** τραπέζι trah·<u>peh</u>·zee

**tablecloth** τραπεζομάντηλο
trah·peh·zoh·<u>mahn</u>·dee·loh

**tablet** χάπι <u>khah</u>·pee

**take** παίρνω <u>pehr</u>·noh

**take a photograph** βγάζω
φωτογραφία <u>vghah</u>·zoh
foh·tohgh·rah·<u>fee</u>·ah

**take away [BE]** πακέτο για το σπίτι
pah·<u>keh</u>·toh yah toh <u>spee</u>·tee

**tall** ψηλός psee·<u>lohs</u>

**tampon** ταμπόν tahm·<u>bohn</u>

**tax** *n* φόρος <u>foh</u>·rohs

**taxi** ταξί tah·<u>ksee</u>

**taxi driver** ταξιτζής tah·ksee·<u>jees</u>

**taxi rank [BE]** πιάτσα ταξί piah·tsah
tah·<u>ksee</u>

**teaspoon** κουταλάκι koo·tah·<u>lah</u>·kee

**team** *n* ομάδα oh·<u>mah</u>·THah

**teenager** έφηβος <u>eh</u>·fee·vohs

**telephone** *n* τηλέφωνο
tee·<u>leh</u>·foh·noh

**telephone booth** τηλεφωνικός
θάλαμος tee·leh·foh·nee·<u>kohs</u>
<u>thah</u>·lah·mohs

**telephone call** κλήση <u>klee</u>·see

**telephone directory** τηλεφωνικός
κατάλογος tee·leh·foh·nee·<u>kohs</u>
kah·<u>tah</u>·loh·ghohs

**telephone number** αριθμός

**τηλεφώνου** ah‑reeth‑<u>mohs</u>
tee‑leh‑<u>foh</u>‑noo

**tell** λέω <u>leh</u>‑oh

**temperature (body)** θερμοκρασία
theh‑rmohk‑rah‑<u>see</u>‑ah

**temple** ναός nah‑<u>ohs</u>

**temporary** προσωρινός
proh‑soh‑ree‑<u>nohs</u>

**tennis** τέννις <u>teh</u>‑nees

**tennis court** γήπεδο τέννις
yee‑peh‑THoh <u>teh</u>‑nees

**tent** σκηνή skee‑<u>nee</u>

**terrible** φοβερός foh‑veh‑<u>rohs</u>

**theater** θέατρο <u>theh</u>‑aht‑roh

**theft** κλοπή kloh‑<u>pee</u>

**there** εκεί eh‑<u>kee</u>

**thermal bath** ιαματικό λουτρό
ee‑ah‑mah‑tee‑<u>koh</u> loot‑roh

**thermos flask** θερμός thehr‑<u>mohs</u>

**thick** χοντρός khohn‑<u>drohs</u>

**thief** κλέφτης <u>klehf</u>‑tees

**thin** adj λεπτός lehp‑<u>tohs</u>

**think** νομίζω noh‑<u>mee</u>‑zoh

**thirsty** διψάω THee‑<u>psah</u>‑oh

**those** εκείνα eh‑<u>kee</u>‑nah

**throat** λαιμός leh‑<u>mohs</u>

**thumb** αντίχειρας ahn‑<u>dee</u>‑khee‑rahs

**ticket** εισιτήριο ee‑see‑<u>tee</u>‑ree‑oh

**ticket office** γραφείο εισιτηρίων
ghrah‑<u>fee</u>‑oh ee‑see‑tee‑<u>ree</u>‑ohn

**tie** n γραβάτα ghrah‑<u>vah</u>‑tah

**tight** adj στενός steh‑<u>nohs</u>

**tights [BE]** n καλσόν kahl‑<u>sohn</u>

**timetable [BE]** δρομολόγιο

THroh‑moh‑<u>loh</u>‑yee‑oh

**tire** λάστιχο <u>lahs</u>‑tee‑khoh

**tired** κουρασμένος
koo‑rahz‑<u>meh</u>‑nohs

**tissue** χαρτομάντηλο
khahr‑toh‑<u>mahn</u>‑dee‑loh

**toaster** τοστιέρα toh‑<u>stieh</u>‑rah

**tobacco** καπνός kahp‑<u>nohs</u>

**tobacconist** καπνοπωλείο
kahp‑noh‑poh‑<u>lee</u>‑oh

**toilet [BE]** τουαλέτα too‑ah‑<u>leh</u>‑tah

**toilet paper** χαρτί υγείας khahr‑<u>tee</u>
ee‑<u>yee</u>‑ahs

**toiletries** καλλυντικά
kah‑leen‑dee‑<u>kah</u>

**tongue** γλώσσα <u>ghloh</u>‑sah

**too (extreme)** πάρα πολύ <u>pah</u>‑rah
poh‑<u>lee</u>

**tooth** δόντι THohn‑dee

**toothache** πονόδοντος
poh‑<u>noh</u>‑THohn‑dohs

**toothbrush** οδοντόβουρτσα
oh‑THohn‑<u>doh</u>‑voor‑tsah

**toothpaste** οδοντόπαστα
oh‑THohn‑<u>doh</u>‑pahs‑tah

**top** adj πάνω <u>pah</u>‑noh

**torn** σχισμένος skheez‑<u>meh</u>‑nohs

**tour guide** ξεναγός kseh‑nah‑<u>ghohs</u>

**tourist** τουρίστας too‑<u>rees</u>‑tahs

**towards** προς prohs

**tower** πύργος <u>peer</u>‑ghohs

**town** πόλη <u>poh</u>‑lee

**town hall** δημαρχείο
THee‑mahr‑<u>khee</u>‑oh

**toy store** κατάστημα παιχνιδιών
  kah·tahs·tee·mah peh·khnee·THiohn

**traditional** παραδοσιακός
  pah·rah·THoh·see·ah·kohs

**traffic** κίνηση kee·nee·see

**trail** μονοπάτι moh·noh·pah·tee

**trailer** τροχόσπιτο
  troh·khohs·pee·toh

**train** τρένο treh·noh

**train station** σταθμός των τρένων
  stahth·mohs tohn treh·nohn

**tram** τραμ trahm

**transfer** μεταφέρω meh·tah·feh·roh

**transit** n μεταφορά meh·tah·foh·rah

**translate** μεταφράζω
  meh·tah·frah·zoh

**translation** μετάφραση
  meh·tah·frah·see

**translator** μεταφραστής
  meh·tah·frah·stees

**trash** σκουπίδια skoo·peeTH·yah

**trash can** κάδος απορριμμάτων
  kah·THohs ah·poh·ree·mah·tohn

**travel agency** ταξιδιωτικό
  γραφείο tah·ksee·THyoh·tee·koh
  ghrah·fee·oh

**travel sickness [BE]** ναυτία
  nahf·tee·ah

**traveler's check** ταξιδιωτική
  επιταγή tah·ksee·THee·oh·tee·kee
  eh·pee·tah·yee

**tray** δίσκος THees·kohs

**tree** δέντρο THehn·droh

**trim** n διόρθωμα THee·ohr·thoh·mah

**trolley [BE] (cart)** καροτσάκι
  kah·roh·tsah·kee

**trolley-bus** τρόλλεϋ troh·leh·ee

**trousers [BE]** παντελόνι
  pahn·deh·loh·nee

**try on** δοκιμάζω THoh·kee·mah·zoh

**T-shirt** μπλουζάκι bloo·zah·kee

**tunnel** τούνελ too·nehl

**turn** v γυρίζω yee·ree·zoh

**turn down** v (volume, heat)
  χαμηλώνω khah·mee·loh·noh

**turn off** v σβήνω svee·noh

**turn on** v ανάβω ah·nah·voh

**turn up** v (volume, heat) ανεβάζω
  ah·neh·vah·zoh

**TV** τηλεόραση tee·leh·oh·rah·see

**twin bed** διπλό κρεβάτι THeep·loh
  kreh·vah·tee

**typical** τυπικός tee·pee·kohs

**U**

**ugly** άσχημος ahs·khee·mohs

**unconscious** αναίσθητος
  ah·nehs·thee·tohs

**underground [BE]** υπόγειος
  ee·poh·ghee·ohs

**underpants [BE]** κυλοτάκι
  kee·loh·tah·kee

**understand** καταλαβαίνω
  kah·tah·lah·veh·noh

**uneven (ground)** ανώμαλος
  ah·noh·mah·lohs

**unfortunately** δυστυχώς
  THees·tee·khohs

**uniform** *n* στολή stoh-<u>lee</u>

**unique μοναδικός**
moh-nah-<u>THee</u>-<u>kohs</u>

unit **μονάδα** moh-<u>nah</u>-THah

**United Kingdom Ηνωμένο Βασίλειο**
ee-noh-<u>meh</u>-noh vah-<u>see</u>-lee-oh

**United States Ηνωμένες Πολιτείες**
ee-noh-<u>meh</u>-nehs poh-lee-<u>tee</u>-ehs

**university Πανεπιστήμιο**
pah-neh-pees-<u>tee</u>-mee-oh

**unlimited mileage απεριόριστα**
**χιλιόμετρα** ah-peh-ree-<u>ohr</u>-ees-tah
khee-<u>lioh</u>-meht-rah

**unpleasant δυσάρεστος**
THee-<u>sah</u>-reh-stohs

**upper (berth) πάνω (κουκέτα)**
<u>pah</u>-noh (koo-<u>keh</u>-tah)

**upstairs επάνω** eh-<u>pah</u>-noh

**urgent επείγον** eh-<u>pee</u>-ghohn

**use** *v* **χρησιμοποιώ**
khree-see-moh-pee-<u>oh</u>

**useful χρήσιμος** <u>khree</u>-see-mohs

## V

**vacancy ελεύθερο δωμάτιο**
eh-<u>lehf</u>-theh-roh THoh-<u>mah</u>-tee-oh

**vacant ελεύθερος** eh-<u>lehf</u>-theh-rohs

**vacation διακοπές** THee-ah-koh-<u>pehs</u>

**vacation resort θέρετρο διακοπών**
<u>theh</u>-reh-troh THee-ah-koh-<u>pohn</u>

**vaccination εμβόλιο** ehm-<u>voh</u>-lee-oh

**valid ισχύει** ee-<u>skhee</u>-ee

**valley κοιλάδα** kee-<u>lah</u>-THah

**valuable πολύτιμος**

poh-<u>lee</u>-tee-mohs

**value** *n* **αξία** ah-<u>ksee</u>-ah

**VAT [BE] ΦΠΑ** fee-pee-<u>ah</u>

**vegetarian χορτοφάγος**
khohr-toh-<u>fah</u>-ghohs

**vein φλέβα** <u>fleh</u>-vah

**velvet βελούδο** veh-<u>loo</u>-THoh

**very πολύ** poh-<u>lee</u>

**video βιντεοκασέτα**
vee-deh-oh-kah-<u>seh</u>-tah

**video game παιχνίδι βίντεο**
pehkh-<u>nee</u>-THee <u>vee</u>-deh-oh

**village χωριό** khohr-<u>yoh</u>

**visa βίζα** <u>vee</u>-zah

**visit** *n* **επίσκεψη** eh-<u>pees</u>-keh-psee

**volleyball βόλεϊ** <u>voh</u>-leh-ee

**vomit** *v* **κάνω εμετό** <u>kah</u>-noh
eh-meh-<u>toh</u>

## W

**wait** *v* **περιμένω** peh-ree-<u>meh</u>-noh

**waiter** *n* **γκαρσόν** gahr-<u>sohn</u>

**waitress δεσποινίς** THehs-pee-<u>nees</u>

**wake** *v* **ξυπνώ** kseep-<u>noh</u>

**walk** *v* **περπατώ** pehr-pah-<u>toh</u>

**walking route διαδρομή**
**περιήγησης** THee-ah-THroh-<u>mee</u>
peh-ree-<u>ee</u>-yee-sees

**wall τοίχος** <u>tee</u>-khohs

**wallet πορτοφόλι** pohr-toh-<u>foh</u>-lee

**want θέλω** <u>theh</u>-loh

**warm ζεστός** zehs-<u>tohs</u>

**washing machine πλυντήριο**
pleen-<u>deer</u>-ee-oh

**watch** n **ρολόι** roh·loh·ee
**watch strap** **λουρί ρολογιού** loo·ree
roh·loh·yioo
**water** n **νερό** neh·roh
**waterfall** **καταρράχτης**
kah·tah·rahkh·tees
**waterproof** **αδιάβροχος**
ah·THee·ahv·roh·khohs
**wave** n **κύμα** kee·mah
**way** **δρόμος** THroh·mohs
**wear** v **φορώ** foh·roh
**weather** **καιρός** keh·rohs
**weather forecast** **πρόβλεψη καιρού**
prohv·leh·psee keh·roo
**wedding** **γάμος** ghah·mohs
**west** **δυτικά** THee·tee·kah
**wetsuit** **στολή δύτη** stoh·lee
THee·tee
**wheelchair** **αναπηρική καρέκλα**
ah·nah·pee·ree·kee kah·rehk·lah
**wide** **φαρδύς** fahr·THees
**wife** **σύζυγος** see·zee·ghohs
**window** **παράθυρο** pah·rah·thee·roh
**window seat** **θέση δίπλα στο**
**παράθυρο** theh·see THeep·lah stoh
pah·rah·thee·roh
**winery** **οινοποιείο** ee·noh·pee·ee·oh
**wireless internet** **ασύρματο**
**ίντερνετ** ah·see·rmah·toh
ee·nteh·rnet
**with** **με** meh
**withdraw** **κάνω ανάληψη** kah·noh

ah·nah·lee·psee
**without** **χωρίς** khoh·rees
**witness** **μάρτυρας** mahr·tee·rahs
**wood (forest)** **δάσος** THah·sohs;
(material) **ξύλο** ksee·loh
**work** **δουλεύω** THoo·leh·voh
**worry** **ανησυχώ** ah·nee·see·khoh
**worse** **χειρότερος** khee·roh·teh·rohs
**wound (cut)** **πληγή** plee·yee
**write (down)** **γράφω** ghrah·foh
**wrong** **λάθος** lah·thohs

**X**
**x-ray** **ακτινογραφία**
ahk·tee·nohgh·rah·fee·ah

**Y**
**yacht** **γιωτ** yoht
**yellow** **κίτρινος** keet·ree·nohs
**young** **νέος** neh·ohs
**youth hostel** **ξενώνας νεότητας**
kseh·noh·nahs neh·oh·tee·tahs

**Z**
**zoo** **ζωολογικός κήπος**
zoh·oh·loh·yee·kohs kee·pohs

**A**

**ATM** ehee·tee·<u>ehm</u> **ATM**

**άγαλμα** <u>ah</u>·ghahl·mah **statue**

**αγαπημένος** ah·ghah·pee·<u>meh</u>·nohs **favorite**

**αγαπώ** ah·ghah·<u>poh</u> v **love**

**αγγειοπλαστική** ahn·gee·ohp·lahs·tee·<u>kee</u> **pottery**

**Αγγλία** ahng·<u>lee</u>·ah **England**

**αγγλικά** ahng·lee·<u>kah</u> **English language**

**αγγλικός** ahng·lee·<u>kohs</u> adj **English**

**Άγγλος** <u>ahng</u>·lohs **English (nationality)**

**αγενής** ah·yeh·<u>nees</u> **rude**

**αγορά** ah·ghoh·<u>rah</u> n **market**

**αγοράζω** ah·ghoh·<u>rah</u>·zoh **buy**

**αγόρι** ah·<u>ghoh</u>·ree **boy**

**αγώνας** ah·<u>ghoh</u>·nahs n **match (sport)**

**άδεια** <u>ah</u>·THee·ah n **permit**

**άδεια σκι** <u>ah</u>·THee·ah skee **lift pass**

**άδειος** <u>ahTH</u>·yohs adj **empty**

**αδιάβροχο** ah·THee·<u>ahv</u>·roh·khoh **raincoat**

**αδιάβροχος** ah·THee·<u>ahv</u>·roh·khohs **waterproof**

**αδύναμος** ah·<u>THee</u>·nah·mohs **weak**

**αεροδρόμιο** ah·eh·roh·<u>THroh</u>·mee·oh **airport**

**αεροπλάνο** ah·eh·rohp·<u>lah</u>·noh n **plane**

**αεροπορική εταιρία** ah·eh·roh·poh·ree·<u>kee</u> eh·teh·<u>ree</u>·ah **airline**

**αεροπορικώς** ah·eh·roh·poh·ree·<u>kohs</u> **airmail**

**αηδιαστικός** ah·ee·THee·ah·stee·<u>kohs</u> **revolting**

**αθλητικά παπούτσια** ath·lee·tee·<u>kah</u> pah·<u>poo</u>·tsiah **sneakers**

**αθλητικό στάδιο** ahth·lee·tee·<u>koh</u> <u>stah</u>·THee·oh **sports stadium**

**αθλητικός όμιλος** ahth·lee·tee·<u>kohs</u> <u>oh</u>·mee·lohs **sports club**

**αθλητισμός** ahth·lee·teez·<u>mohs</u> **sport**

**αθώος** ah·<u>thoh</u>·ohs **innocent**

**αιμορραγία** eh·moh·rah·<u>yee</u>·ah n **bleed**

**αιμορραγώ** eh·moh·rah·<u>yoh</u> v **bleed**

**αίθουσα συναυλιών** <u>eh</u>·thoo·sah see·nahv·lee·<u>ohn</u> **concert hall**

**ακολουθώ** ah·koh·loo·<u>thoh</u> v **follow**

**ακουστικό βαρυκοΐας** ah·koo·stee·<u>koh</u> vah·ree·koh·<u>ee</u>·ahs **hearing aid**

**ακριβός** ahk·ree·<u>vohs</u> **expensive**

**ακτή** ahk·<u>tee</u> n **shore**

**ακτινογραφία** ahk·tee·nohgh·rah·<u>fee</u>·ah **x-ray**

**ακυρώνω** ah·kee·<u>roh</u>·noh v **cancel**

**αληθινός** ah·lee·thee·<u>nohs</u> **real (genuine)**

**αλλά** ah·<u>lah</u> conj **but**

**άλλα** ah·lah **others**

**αλλαγή** ah·lah·<u>yee</u> n **change**

**αλλάζω** ah·<u>lah</u>·zoh v **exchange (money)**

**αλλεργικός** ahl·ehr·yee·<u>kohs</u> **allergic**

**αλληλογραφία** ah·lee·lohgh·rah·<u>fee</u>·ah n **mail**

**άλλο ένα** ah·loh eh·nah **extra (additional)**

**άλλος** ah·lohs **another**

**αλουμινόχαρτο** ah·loo·mee·<u>noh</u>·khah·rtoh **aluminum foil**

**Αμερικανός** ah·meh·ree·kah·<u>nohs</u> n **American**

**αμέσως** ah·<u>meh</u>·sohs **immediately**

**άμμος** <u>ah</u>·mohs **sand**

**ανάβω** ah·<u>nah</u>·voh v **turn on**

**αναίσθητος** ah·<u>nehs</u>·thee·tohs **unconscious**

**ανάκτορα** ah·<u>nahk</u>·toh·rah **palace**

**αναλυτικός λογαριασμός** ah·nah·lee·tee·<u>kohs</u> loh·ghahr·yahz·<u>mohs</u> **itemized bill**

**αναπηρική καρέκλα** ah·nah·pee·ree·<u>kee</u> kah·<u>rehk</u>·lah **wheelchair**

**αναπνευστήρας** ah·nahp·nehf·<u>stee</u>·rahs **snorkel**

**αναπνέω** ah·nahp·<u>neh</u>·oh **breathe**

**αναπτήρας** ah·nahp·<u>tee</u>·rahs n **lighter (cigarette)**

**αναρρίχηση** ah·nah·<u>ree</u>·khee·see **rock climbing**

**ανατολικά** ah·nah·toh·lee·<u>kah</u> **east**

**αναφέρω** ah·nah·<u>feh</u>·roh **mention (report)**

**αναχώρηση** ah·nah·<u>khoh</u>·ree·see **departure (travel)**

**άνδρας** <u>ahn</u>·THrahs n **male (man)**

**ανεμιστήρας** ah·neh·mees·<u>tee</u>·rahs n **fan (air)**

**ανεβάζω** ah·neh·<u>vah</u>·zoh v **turn up (volume, heat)**

**ανέκδοτο** ah·<u>nehk</u>·THoh·toh n **joke**

**ανησυχώ** ah·nee·see·<u>khoh</u> **worry**

**ανθοπωλείο** ahn·thoh·poh·<u>lee</u>·oh **florist**

**ανοίγω** ah·<u>nee</u>·ghoh v **open**

**ανοιχτήρι** ah·neekh·<u>tee</u>·ree **can opener**

**ανοιχτός** ah·neekh·<u>tohs</u> adj **light (color), open**

**ανοιχτότερος** ah·neekh·<u>toh</u>·teh·rohs adj **lighter (color)**

**ανταλλακτικό** ahn·dah·lahk·tee·<u>koh</u> **replacement part**

**αντιβιοτικό** ahn·dee·vee·oh·tee·<u>koh</u> **antibiotic**

**αντιηλιακό** ahn·dee·ee·lee·ah·<u>koh</u> **sunscreen**

**αντισηπτική κρέμα** ahn·dee·seep·tee·<u>kee</u> <u>kreh</u>·mah **antiseptic cream**

**αντίχειρας** ahn·<u>dee</u>·khee·rahs **thumb**

**ανώμαλος** ah·<u>noh</u>·mah·lohs **uneven (ground)**

**αξεσουάρ** ah·kseh·soo·<u>ahr</u> **accessory**

**αξία** ah·<u>ksee</u>·ah n **value**

**αξιοθέατο** ah·ksee·oh·<u>theh</u>·ah·tah

**sightseeing sight**

**απαγορευμένος** ah·pah·ghoh·rehv·<u>meh</u>·nohs **prohibited**

**απαραίτητος** ah·pah·<u>reh</u>·tee·tohs **essential, necessary**

**απασχολημένος** ah·pahs·khoh·lee·meh·nohs *adj* **busy (occupied)**

**απέναντι** ah·<u>peh</u>·nahn·dee **opposite**

**απεριόριστα χιλιόμετρα** ah·peh·ree·<u>ohr</u>·ees·tah khee·<u>lioh</u>·meht·rah **unlimited mileage**

**απλό εισιτήριο** ahp·<u>loh</u> ee·see·<u>tee</u>·ree·oh **one-way [single BE] ticket**

**απλός** ahp·<u>lohs</u> **simple**

**από** ah·<u>poh</u> **from**

**απομίμηση** ah·poh·<u>mee</u>·mee·see **imitation**

**αποβάθρα** ah·poh·<u>vahth</u>·rah **platform, quay**

**απόγευμα** ah·<u>poh</u>·yehv·mah **afternoon**

**απόδειξη** ah·<u>poh</u>·THee·ksee **receipt**

**απορρυπαντικό** ah·poh·ree·pahn·dee·<u>koh</u> **detergent**

**αποσμητικό** ah·pohz·mee·tee·<u>koh</u> **deodorant**

**αποσκευές** ah·pohs·keh·<u>vehs</u> **baggage [BE]**

**αποσκευές χειρός** ah·pohs·keh·<u>vehs</u> khee·<u>rohs</u> **hand luggage**

**αποστειρωτικό διάλυμα** ah·pohs·tee·roh·tee·<u>koh</u> THee·<u>ah</u>·lee·mah **sterilizing solution**

**απόχρωση** ah·<u>pohkh</u>·roh·see **shade (color)**

**απώλεια** ah·<u>poh</u>·lee·ah *n* **loss**

**αργά** ahr·<u>ghah</u> *adv* **late**

**αργία** ahr·<u>yee</u>·ah **public holiday**

**αργός** ahr·<u>ghohs</u> *adj* **slow**

**αριθμός κυκλοφορίας** ah·reeth·<u>mohs</u> kee·kloh·foh·<u>ree</u>·ahs **registration number**

**αριθμός πτήσεως** ah·reeth·<u>mohs</u> ptee·seh·ohs **flight number**

**αριθμός τηλεφώνου** ah·reeth·<u>mohs</u> tee·leh·<u>foh</u>·noo **telephone number**

**αριστερός** ah·rees·teh·<u>rohs</u> **left** (*adj*)

**αριστερά** ah·rees·teh·<u>rah</u> **left** (*adv*)

**αρκετά** ahr·keh·<u>tah</u> **enough**

**αρραβωνιαστικιά** ah·rah·voh·niahs·tee·<u>kiah</u> **fiancée**

**αρραβωνιαστικός** ah·rah·voh·niahs·tee·<u>kohs</u> **fiancé**

**αρρώστεια** ahr·<u>ohs</u>·tee·ah **illness**

**άρρωστος** <u>ah</u>·rohs·tohs *adj* **sick**

**αρτοποιείο** ah·rtoh·pee·<u>ee</u>·oh **bakery**

**αρχάριος** ahr·<u>khah</u>·ree·ohs **beginner**

**αρχίζω** v ahr·<u>khee</u>·zoh **start**

**ασανσέρ** ah·sahn·<u>sehr</u> *n* **lift (elevator)**

**ασήμι** ah·<u>see</u>·mee **silver**

**ασύρματο ίντερνετ** ah·<u>see</u>·rmah·toh ee·nteh·rnet **wireless internet**

**ασθενοφόρο** ahs·theh·noh·<u>foh</u>·roh **ambulance**

**ασθματικός** ahsth·mah·tee·<u>kohs</u>

**asthmatic**

**ασπιρίνη** ahs·pee·<u>ree</u>·nee **aspirin**

**αστυνομία** ah·stee·noh·<u>mee</u>·ah *n* **police**

**αστυνομικό τμήμα** ah·stee·noh·mee·<u>koh</u> <u>tmee</u>·mah **police station**

**ασφάλεια** ahs·<u>fah</u>·lee·ah *n* **fuse; insurance**

**ασφάλεια αποζημίωσης** ahs·<u>fah</u>·lee·ah ah·poh·zee·<u>mee</u>·oh·sees **insurance claim**

**ασφάλεια υγείας** ahs·<u>fah</u>·lee·ah ee·<u>yee</u>·ahs **health insurance**

**ασφαλής** ahs·fah·<u>lees</u> *adj* **safe (not dangerous)**

**ασφαλιστική εταιρία** ahs·fah·lees·tee·<u>kee</u> eh·teh·<u>ree</u>·ah **insurance company**

**άσχημος** <u>ahs</u>·khee·mohs **ugly**

**άτομο με ειδικές ανάγκες** <u>ah</u>·toh·moh meh ee·THee·<u>kehs</u> ah·<u>nahn</u>·gehs **disabled**

**ατύχημα** ah·<u>tee</u>·khee·mah **accident**

**αυθεντικός** ahf·thehn·dee·<u>kohs</u> **genuine**

**αυθεντικότητα** ahf·thehn·dee·<u>koh</u>·tee·tah **authenticity**

**αϋπνία** ah·eep·<u>nee</u>·ah **insomnia**

**αυτοκίνητο** ahf·toh·<u>kee</u>·nee·toh **car**

**αυχένας** ahf·<u>kheh</u>·nahs **neck (part of body)**

**αφήνω** ah·<u>fee</u>·noh *v* **leave (let go)**

**αφορολόγητα είδη** ah·foh·roh·<u>loh</u>·yee·tah ee·<u>THee</u> **duty-free goods**

**αφρόλουτρο για ντουζ** ahf·<u>roh</u>·loot·roh yah dooz **shower gel**

**αχθοφόρος** ahkh·thoh·<u>foh</u>·rohs **porter**

# B

**βαμβάκι** vahm·<u>vah</u>·kee **cotton**

**βαγκόν-λι** vah·<u>gohn</u>·lee **sleeping car**

**βάζο** <u>vah</u>·zoh *n* **jar**

**βάζω** <u>vah</u>·zoh *v* **put**

**βαλές** vah·<u>lehs</u> **jack**

**βαρετός** vah·reh·<u>tohs</u> **boring**

**βάρκα** <u>vahr</u>·kah **boat**

**βαρύς** vah·<u>rees</u> **heavy**

**βασιλιάς** vah·see·<u>liahs</u> **king**

**βγαίνω** <u>vyeh</u>·noh **get out (of vehicle)**

**βελούδο** veh·<u>loo</u>·THoh **velvet**

**βενζινάδικο** vehn·zee·<u>nah</u>·THee·koh **gas [petrol BE] station**

**βενζίνη** vehn·<u>zee</u>·nee **gasoline [petrol BE]**

**βερνίκι παπουτσιών** vehr·<u>nee</u>·kee pah·poo·<u>tsiohn</u> **shoe polish**

**βήχας** <u>vee</u>·khahs *n* **cough**

**βήχω** <u>vee</u>·khoh *v* **cough**

**βιβλίο** veev·<u>lee</u>·oh *n* **book**

**βιβλιοθήκη** veev·lee·oh·<u>thee</u>·kee **library**

**βιβλιοπωλείο** veev·lee·oh·poh·<u>lee</u>·oh **bookstore**

**βίδα** <u>vee</u>·THah *n* **screw**

**βίζα** <u>vee</u>·zah **visa**

**βιντεοκασέτα** vee·deh·oh·

kah·seh·tah **video**

**βλάβη** vlah·vee **breakdown** n (car)

**βλέπω** vleh·poh **see**

**βοήθεια** voh·ee·thee·ah n **help**

**βοηθώ** voh·ee·thoh v **help**

**βόλεϊ** voh·leh·ee **volleyball**

**βόρεια** voh·ree·ah **north**

**βοτανικός κήπος** voh·tah·nee·kohs kee·pohs **botanical garden**

**βουνό** voo·noh **mountain**

**βουρτσίζω** voor·tsee·zoh v **brush**

**βραδινό** vrah·THee·noh **dinner**

**βράδυ** vrah·THee **evening**

**βράζω** vrah·zoh **boil**

**βράχος** vrah·khohs n **rock**

**βρετανικός** vreh·tah·nee·kohs **British** adj

**Βρετανός** vreh·tah·nohs **British (nationality)**

**βρέχει** vreh·khee v **rain**

**βροχή** vroh·khee n **rain**

**βρύση** vree·see **faucet**

**βρώμικος** vroh·mee·kohs adj **dirty**

## Γ

**γάμος** ghah·mohs **wedding**

**γάζα** ghah·zah **bandage**

**γαλάκτωμα για τα μαλλιά** ghah·lah·ktoh·mah yah tah mah·liah **conditioner (hair)**

**γάντι** ghahn·dee n **glove**

**γαστρίτιδα** ghahs·tree·tee·THah **gastritis**

**γεμάτος** yeh·mah·tohs adj **full**

**γείτονας** yee·toh·nahs n **neighbor**

**γελώ** yeh·loh v **laugh**

**γεμιστή** yeh·mees·tee **stuffed olive**

**γέρικος** yeh·ree·kohs **old (person)**

**γεύμα** yehv·mah **meal**

**γέφυρα** yeh·fee·rah n **bridge (over water)**

**γη** ghee n **land**

**γήπεδο γκολφ** yee·peh·THoh gohlf **golf course**

**γήπεδο τένις** yee·peh·THoh teh·nees **tennis court**

**γιατρός** yah·trohs **doctor**

**γιωτ** yoht **yacht**

**γκαράζ** gah·rahz **garage**

**γκαρσόν** gahr·sohn **waiter**

**γκόλφ** gohlf **golf**

**γκρουπ** groop n **group**

**γλώσσα** ghloh·sah **tongue**

**γνωρίζω** ghnoh·ree·zoh **know**

**γόνατο** ghoh·nah·toh **knee**

**γονείς** ghoh·nees **parents**

**γράμμα** ghrah·mah **letter**

**γραμματόσημο** ghrah·mah·toh·see·moh n **stamp (postage)**

**γραμμή** ghrah·mee n **line (subway)**

**γραβάτα** ghrah·vah·tah n **tie**

**γρασίδι** ghrah·see·THee **grass**

**γραφείο** ghrah·fee·oh **office**

**γραφείο ανταλλαγής συναλλάγματος** ghrah·fee·oh ahn·dah·lah·yees see·nah·lahgh·mah·tohs **currency exchange office**

**γραφείο εισιτηρίων** ghrah·<u>fee</u>·oh ee·see·tee·<u>ree</u>·ohn **ticket office**

**γραφείο πληροφοριών** ghrah·<u>fee</u>·oh plee·roh·foh·ree·<u>ohn</u> **information office**

**γράφω** <u>ghrah</u>·foh **write (down)**

**γρήγορα** <u>ghree</u>·ghoh·rah *adv* **fast**

**γρήγορος** <u>ghree</u>·ghoh·rohs **quick**

**γρίππη** <u>ghree</u>·pee **flu**

**γυαλιά** yah·<u>liah</u> **glasses (optical)**

**γυαλιά ηλίου** yah·<u>liah</u> ee·<u>lee</u>·oo **sun glasses**

**γυναικολόγος** yee·neh·koh·<u>loh</u>·ghohs **gynecologist**

**γυρίζω** yee·<u>ree</u>·zoh *v* **turn**

**γωνία** ghoh·<u>nee</u>·ah **corner**

## Δ

**δανείζω** THah·<u>nee</u>·zoh **lend**

**δάσος** <u>THah</u>·sohs *n* **forest (wood)**

**δάχτυλο** <u>THakh</u>·tee·loh *n* **finger**

**δείγμα** <u>THeegh</u>·mah **specimen**

**δείχνω** <u>THeekh</u>·noh *v* **point (show)**

**δέντρο** <u>THehn</u>·droh **tree**

**δεξιός** THeh·ksee·<u>ohs</u> *adj* **right (not left)**

**δέρμα** <u>THehr</u>·mah *n* **skin**

**δημαρχείο** THee·mahr·<u>khee</u>·oh **town hall**

**δημοφιλής** THee·moh·fee·<u>lees</u> **popular**

**δηλητήριο** THee·lee·<u>tee</u>·ree·oh *n* **poison**

**δηλητηριώδης** THee·lee·tee·ree·<u>oh</u>·THees **poisonous**

**δηλώνω** THee·<u>loh</u>·noh **declare**

**δήλωση** <u>THee</u>·loh·see **statement (legal)**

**δημόσιος** THee·<u>moh</u>·see·ohs **public**

**διαμάντι** THiah·<u>mahn</u>·dee *n* **diamon**

**διαμέρισμα** THee·ah·<u>meh</u>·reez·mah **apartment**

**διάβαση πεζών** THee·<u>ah</u>·vah·see peh·<u>zohn</u> **pedestrian crossing**

**διαβατήριο** THiah·vah·<u>tee</u>·ree·oh **passport**

**διαβητικός** THee·ah·vee·tee·<u>kohs</u> **diabetic**

**διαδρομή** THee·ahTH·roh·<u>mee</u> *n* **route**

**διάδρομος** THee·<u>ah</u>·THroh·mohs **aisle seat**

**διαζευγμένος** THee·ah·zehv·<u>ghmeh</u>·nohs **divorced**

**διακοπές** THee·ah·koh·<u>pehs</u> **vacation [holiday BE]**

**διακόπτης** THiah·<u>koh</u>·ptees *n* **switch**

**διαμέρισμα** THee·ah·mehr·ees·mah *n* **flat**

**διάρροια** THee·<u>ah</u>·ree·ah **diarrhea**

**διάσημος** THee·<u>ah</u>·see·mohs **famous**

**διεθνής** THee·eth·<u>nees</u> **international**

**διεθνής φοιτητική κάρτα** THee·ehth·<u>nees</u> fee·tee·tee·<u>kee</u> <u>kahr</u>·tah **International Student Card**

**διερμηνέας** THee·ehr·mee·<u>neh</u>·ahs

**interpreter**

**διεύθυνση** THee·<u>ehf</u>·theen·see *n*
**address**

**διευθυντής** THee·ehf·theen·<u>dees</u>
**manager**

**δικηγόρος** THee·kee·<u>ghoh</u>·rohs
**lawyer**

**δίκλινο δωμάτιο** <u>THeek</u>·lee·noh
THoh·<u>mah</u>·tee·oh **double room**

**δίνω** <u>THee</u>·noh **give**

**διόρθωμα** THee·<u>ohr</u>·thoh·mah *n* **trim**

**δίπλα** <u>THeep</u>·lah **next to**

**διπλό κρεβάτι** THeep·<u>loh</u> kreh·<u>vah</u>·tee
**twin bed**

**δίσκος** <u>THees</u>·kohs **tray**

**διψάω** THee·<u>psah</u>·oh **thirsty**

**δοκιμάζω** THoh·kee·<u>mah</u>·zoh **try on**

**δολάριο** THoh·<u>lah</u>·ree·oh **dollar**

**δόντι** <u>THohn</u>·dee **tooth**

**δοσολογία** THoh·soh·loh·<u>yee</u>·ah
**dosage**

**δουλειά** THoo·<u>liah</u> **job**

**δουλεύω** THoo·<u>leh</u>·voh **work**

**δρομολόγιο** THroh·moh·<u>loh</u>·yee·oh
**time table**

**δρόμος** <u>THroh</u>·mohs **road, street,
way**

**δυνατός** THee·nah·<u>tohs</u> *adj* **loud**

**δυσάρεστος** THee·<u>sah</u>·reh stohs
**unpleasant**

**δύσκολος** <u>THee</u>·skoh·lohs **difficult**

**δυσπεψία** THes·peh·<u>psee</u>·ah
**indigestion**

**δυστυχώς** THees·tee·<u>khohs</u>
**unfortunately**

**δυτικά** THee·tee·<u>kah</u> **west**

**δωμάτιο** THoh·<u>mah</u>·tee·oh *n* **room**

**δώρο** <u>THoh</u>·roh **gift**

## E

**ελιά** eh·liah **olive**

**εμβόλιο** ehm·<u>voh</u>·lee·oh **vaccination**

**εμπορικό κέντρο** ehm·boh·ree·<u>koh</u>
<u>keh</u>·ntroh **shopping mall [centre
BE]**

**εγγύηση** eh·<u>gee</u>·ee·see *n* **guarantee**

**εγγυώμαι** eh·gee·oh·meh *v*
**guarantee**

**έγκαυμα ηλίου** <u>ehn</u>·gahv·mah
ee·<u>lee</u>·oo *n* **sun burn**

**έγκυος** <u>eh</u>·gee·ohs **pregnant**

**έδαφος** <u>eh</u>·THah·fohs **ground (earth)**

**εδώ** eh·<u>THoh</u> **here**

**εδώ κοντά** eh·<u>THoh</u> kohn·<u>dah</u> **nearby**

**εθνική οδός** ehth·nee·<u>kee</u> oh·<u>THohs</u>
**highway, motorway**

**εθνικός** eth·nee·<u>kohs</u> **national**

**εθνικός δρυμός** eth·nee·<u>kohs</u>
THree·<u>mohs</u> **nature reserve**

**είμαι** <u>ee</u>·meh **be**

**είμαι κουφός** koo·<u>fohs</u> **deaf**

**είδη οικιακής χρήσεως** <u>ee</u>·THee
ee·kee·ah·<u>kees</u> <u>khree</u>·seh·ohs
**household articles**

**ειδική ανάγκη** ee·THee·<u>kee</u>
ah·<u>nahn</u>·gkee **special requirement**

**ειδικός** ee·THee·<u>kohs</u> **specialist**

**είδος** <u>ee</u>·THohs **kind (sort)**

**εισιτήριο** ee·see·<u>tee</u>·ree·oh **fare (ticket)**

**εισιτήριο με επιστροφή** ee·see·<u>tee</u>·ree·oh meh eh·pee·stroh·<u>fee</u> **roundtrip [return BE] ticket**

**εκδρομή** ehk·THroh·<u>mee</u> **excursion**

**εκεί** eh·<u>kee</u> **there, over there**

**εκείνα** eh·<u>kee</u>·nah **those**

**έκθεση** <u>ehk</u>·theh·see **exhibition**

**έκπτωση** <u>ehk</u>·ptoh·see **reduction**

**έκτακτη ανάγκη** <u>ehk</u>·tahk·tee ah·<u>nah</u>·gee **emergency**

**ελάχιστος** eh·<u>lah</u>·khees·tohs **minimum**

**ελεύθερο δωμάτιο** eh·<u>lehf</u>·theh·roh THoh·<u>mah</u>·tee·oh **vacancy**

**ελεύθερος** eh·<u>lehf</u>·theh·rohs *adj* **free, single, vacant**

**ελικόπτερο** eh·lee·<u>kohp</u>·teh·roh **helicopter**

**Ελλάδα** eh·<u>lah</u>·THah **Greece**

**Έλληνας** <u>eh</u>·lee·nahs **Greek (nationality)**

**ελληνικός** eh·lee·nee·<u>kohs</u> *adj* **Greek**

**ένα βράδυ** <u>eh</u>·nah vrah·THee **overnight**

**ένα τέταρτο** <u>eh</u>·nah teh·tah·rtoh **quarter (quantity)**

**ενδιαφέρων** en·THee·ah·<u>feh</u>·rohn **interesting**

**ένεση** <u>eh</u>·neh·see **injection**

**ενήλικας** eh·<u>nee</u>·lee·kahs **adult**

**ενοχλώ** eh·noh·<u>khloh</u> **disturb**

**έντομο** <u>ehn</u>·doh·moh **insect**

**εντομοαπωθητικό** ehn·doh·moh·ah·poh·thee·tee·<u>koh</u> **insect repellent**

**έντυπο** <u>ehn</u>·dee·poh *n* **form**

**εντυπωσιακός** ehn·dee·poh·see·ah·<u>kohs</u> **impressive**

**ενυδατική κρέμα** eh·nee·THah·tee·<u>kee</u> <u>kreh</u>·mah **moisturizer (cream)**

**εξάνθημα** eh·<u>ksahn</u>·thee·mah *n* **rash**

**εξαργυρώνω** eh·ksahr·ghee·<u>roh</u>·noh *v* **cash**

**εξόγκωμα** eh·<u>ksoh</u>·goh·mah *n* **lump (medical)**

**έξοδος** <u>eh</u>·ksoh·THohs *n* **gate (airport); exit**

**έξοδος κινδύνου** <u>eh</u>·ksoh·THohs keen·<u>THee</u>·noo **emergency, fire exit**

**εξοχή** eh·ksoh·<u>khee</u> **countryside**

**έξοχος** <u>eh</u>·ksoh·khohs **superb**

**εξπρές** ehk·<u>sprehs</u> **express (mail)**

**εξυπηρέτηση** eh·ksee·pee·<u>reh</u>·tee·see **facility**

**έξω** <u>eh</u>·ksoh *adv* **out**

**έξω** <u>eh</u>·ksoh *adj* **outside**

**εξωλέμβιο** eh·ksoh·<u>lehm</u>·vee·oh **motorboat**

**εξωτερικός** eh·ksoh·teh·ree·<u>kohs</u> **outdoor**

**επαναλαμβάνω** eh·pah·nah·lahm·<u>vah</u>·noh *v* **repeat**

**επάνω** eh·<u>pah</u>·noh **upstairs**

επείγον eh·<u>pee</u>·ghohn **urgent**

επιμένω eh·pee·<u>meh</u>·noh **insist**

επιβάτης eh·pee·<u>vah</u>·tees **passenger**

επιβεβαιώνω eh·pee·veh·veh·<u>oh</u>·noh **confirm**

επίβλεψη eh·<u>peev</u>·leh·psee **supervision**

επίθεση eh·<u>pee</u>·theh·see n **attack**

επίθετο eh·<u>pee</u>·theh·toh **surname**

επικοινωνώ eh·pee·kee·noh·<u>noh</u> v **contact**

επιληπτικός eh·pee·leep·tee·<u>kohs</u> **epileptic**

επίπεδο eh·<u>pee</u>·peh·THoh **level (even)**

επίπεδος eh·<u>pee</u>·peh·THohs adj **flat**

έπιπλα <u>eh</u>·peep·lah **furniture**

επιπλέον eh·peep·<u>leh</u>·ohn **spare (extra)**

επισκευάζω eh·pee·skeh·<u>vah</u>·zoh v **repair**

επισκευή eh·pee·skeh·<u>vee</u> n **repair**

επισκευή παπουτσιών eh·pee·skeh·<u>vee</u> pah·poo·<u>tsiohn</u> **shoe repair**

επίσκεψη eh·<u>pees</u>·keh·psee n **visit**

επιστροφή χρημάτων eh·pees·troh·<u>fee</u> khree·<u>mah</u>·tohn n **refund**

επιταγή eh·pee·tah·<u>yee</u> n **check [cheque BE] (bank)**

επιτίθεμαι eh·pee·<u>tee</u>·theh·meh v **attack**

επιτόκιο eh·pee·<u>toh</u>·kee·oh **interest rate**

επόμενος eh·<u>poh</u>·meh·nohs **next**

έρχομαι <u>ehr</u>·khoh·meh **come**

ερώτηση eh·<u>roh</u>·tee·see n **question**

εστιατόριο ehs·tee·ah·<u>toh</u>·ree·oh **restaurant**

εσωτερική γραμμή eh·soh·theh·ree·<u>kee</u> ghrah·<u>mee</u> **extension (number)**

εσωτερική πισίνα eh·soh·teh·ree·<u>kee</u> pee·<u>see</u>·nah **indoor pool**

εσωτερικός eh·soh·teh·ree·<u>kohs</u> **indoor**

ετικέτα eh·tee·<u>keh</u>·tah n **label**

έτοιμος eh·tee·mohs adj **ready**

ευθεία ehf·<u>thee</u>·ah **straight ahead**

εύκολος <u>ehf</u>·koh·lohs adj **easy**

ευρώ ehv·<u>roh</u> **euro**

Ευρωπαϊκή Ένωση ehv·roh·pah·ee·<u>kee</u> eh·noh·see **European Union**

ευτυχώς ehf·tee·<u>khohs</u> **fortunately**

ευχαριστιέμαι ehf·khah·rees·<u>tieh</u>·meh **enjoy**

ευχάριστος ehf·<u>khah</u>·rees·tohs **pleasant**

εφημερίδα eh·fee·meh·<u>ree</u>·THah **newspaper**

έφηβος <u>eh</u>·fee·vohs **teenager**

έχω <u>eh</u>·khoh **have (possession)**

## Z

ζαχαροπλαστείο zah·khah·rohp·lahs·<u>tee</u>·oh **pastry store**

ζεστός zes·<u>tohs</u> **hot, warm (weather)**

**ζημιά** zee·miah n **damage**
**ζητώ** zee·toh **ask**
**ζωγραφίζω** zohgh·rah·fee·zoh v
**paint**
**ζωγράφος** zohgh·rah·fohs **painter**
**ζώνη** zoh·nee **belt**
**ζώνη για χρήματα** zoh·nee yah
khree·mah·tah **money-belt**

## Η

**ημερομηνία λήξεως**
ee·meh·roh·mee·nee·ah
lee·kseh·ohs **expiration date**
**ημερολόγιο** ee·meh·roh·loh·yee·oh
**calendar**
**ημικρανία** ee·mee·krah·nee·ah
**migraine**
**ηλεκτρικός** ee·lehk·tree·kohs **electric**
**ηλεκτρονικό εισιτήριο** ee·leh·
ktroh·nee·koh ee·see·tee·ree·oh
**e-ticket**
**ηλεκτρονικό ταχυδρομείο**
**(e-mail)** ee·lehk·troh·nee·koh
tah·hee·dro·mee·oh (ee·meh·eel)
**ηλεκτροπληξία**
ee·leh·ktroh·plee·ksee·ah **shock**
**(electric)**
**ηλίαση** ee·lee·ah·see **sun stroke**
**ηλικιωμένος** ee·lee·kee·oh·meh·nohs
**senior citizen**
**Ηνωμένες Πολιτείες**
ee·noh·meh·nehs poh·lee·tee·ehs
**United Sstates**
**Ηνωμένο Βασίλειο** ee·noh·meh·noh

vah·see·lee·oh **United Kingdom**
**ηρεμιστικό** ee·reh·mee·stee·koh
**sedative**
**ήσυχος** ee·see·khohs adj **quiet**

## Θ

**θάλασσα** thah·lah·sah **sea**
**θέατρο** theh·aht·roh **theater**
**θέλω** theh·loh **want**
**θέρμανση** thehr·mahn·see **heating**
**θερμή πηγή** thehr·mee pee·yee **hot**
**spring**
**θερμόμετρο** thehr·moh·meht·roh
**thermometer**
**θερμοκρασία** theh·rmohk·rah·see·ah
**temperature (body)**
**θερμός** thehr·mohs **thermos flask**
**θέρετρο διακοπών** theh·reh·troh
THee·ah·koh·pohn **vacation resort**
**θέση** theh·see n **location (space),**
**seat**
**θέση δίπλα στο παράθυρο** theh·see
THeep·lah stoh pah·rah·thee·roh
**window seat**
**θηλυκός** thee·lee·kohs **female**
**θορυβώδης** thoh·ree·voh·THees
**noisy**
**θρησκεία** three·skee·ah **religion**
**θυμάμαι** thee·mah·meh **remember**
**θυρίδα** thee·ree·THah **luggage**
**locker (lock-up)**

## Ι

**ιατρική εξέταση** ee·ah·tree·kee

eh·**kseh**·tah·see **examination (medical)**

**ίδιος** ee·THee·ohs **same**

**ιδιωτικό μπάνιο** ee·THee·oh·tee·**koh** bah·nioh **private bathroom**

**ιερέας** ee·eh·**reh**·ahs **priest**

**ινσουλίνη** een·soo·**lee**·nee **insulin**

**ίντερνετ** **ee**·nteh·rnet **internet**

**ίντερνετ καφέ** **ee**·nteh·rnet kah·**feh** **internet cafe**

**ιπποδρομία** ee·poh·THroh·**mee**·ah **horse racing**

**ιστιοπλοϊκό** ees·tee·oh·ploh·ee·**koh** **sailing boat**

**ιστορία** ee·stoh·**ree**·ah **history**

**ισχύει** ee·**skhee**·ee **valid**

**ίσως** **ee**·sohs **maybe, perhaps**

**ιώδειο** ee·**oh**·THee·oh **iodine**

### K

**κάδος απορριμμάτων** kah·THohs ah·poh·ree·**mah**·tohn **trash can**

**καθαρισμός προσώπου** kah·thah·reez·**mohs** proh·**soh**·poo **facial**

**καθαρός** kah·thah·**rohs** **clean**

**καθαρτικό** kah·thahr·tee·**koh** **laxative**

**καθεδρικός ναός** kah·theh·THree·**kohs** nah·**ohs** **cathedral**

**καθήκον** kah·**thee**·kohn **duty (obligation)**

**κάθομαι** **kah**·thoh·meh **sit**

**καθρέφτης** kah·**threhf**·tees *n* **mirror**

**καθυστέρηση** kah·thee·**steh**·ree·see *n* **delay**

**καθυστερώ** kah·thee·steh·**roh** *v* **delay**

**καινούργιος** keh·**noor**·yohs **new**

**καιρός** keh·**rohs** **weather**

**καλά** kah·**lah** *adv* **fine (well)**

**καλαμάκι** kah·lah·**mah**·kee **straw (drinking)**

**καλάθι** kah·**lah**·THee **basket**

**καλός** kah·**lohs** **good**

**καλσόν** kahl·**sohn** *n* **tights**

**κάλτσες** **kahl**·tsehs **socks**

**κάλυμμα φακού** **kah**·lee·mah fah·**koo** **lens cap**

**καλώ** kah·**loh** *v* **call**

**κάμπινγκ** **kah**·mpeeng **camping**

**καναπές** kah·nah·**pehs** **sofa**

**κανένας** kah·**neh**·nahs *adj* **none**

**κάνω ανάληψη** **kah**·noh ah·**nah**·lee·psee **withdraw**

**κάνω εμετό** **kah**·noh eh·meh·**toh** *v* **vomit**

**κάνω κράτηση** **kah**·noh krah·tee·see *v* **book**

**κάνω πεζοπορία** **kah**·noh peh·zoh·poh·**ree**·ah *v* **hike**

**καπέλο** kah·**peh**·loh **hat**

**καπνίζω** kahp·**nee**·zoh *v* **smoke**

**καπνοπωλείο** kahp·noh·poh·**lee**·oh **tobacconist**

**καπνός** kahp·**nohs** **tobacco**

**καραντίνα** kah·rahn·**dee**·nah *n* **quarantine**

**καράφα** kah·**rah**·fah **carafe**

**καρδιά** kahr·THee·<u>ah</u> *v* **heart**

**καρδιακό έμφραγμα** kahr·THee·ah·<u>koh</u> ehm·frahgh·mah **heart attack**

**καροτσάκι** kah·roh·<u>tsah</u>·kee **trolley (cart)**

**καροτσάκια αποσκευών** kah·roh·<u>tsah</u>·kiah ah·pohs·keh·<u>vohn</u> **baggage [BE] carts [trolleys]**

**κάρτα-κλειδί** <u>kahr</u>·tah klee·<u>dee</u> **key card**

**καρτποστάλ** kahrt·poh·<u>stahl</u> **post card**

**κασκόλ** kahs·<u>kohl</u> **scarf**

**κασσίτερος** kah·<u>see</u>·teh·rohs **pewter**

**κάστρο** <u>kahs</u>·troh **castle**

**καταδυτικός εξοπλισμός** kah·tah·THee·tee·<u>kohs</u> eh·ksoh·pleez·<u>mohs</u> **diving equipment**

**καταλαβαίνω** kah·tah·lah·<u>veh</u>·noh **understand**

**κατάλληλος** kah·<u>tah</u>·lee·lohs **suitable**

**καταρράχτης** kah·tah·<u>rahkh</u>·tees **waterfall**

**κατάστημα** kah·<u>tah</u>·stee·mah **shop (store)**

**κατάστημα με αντίκες** kah·<u>tah</u>·stee·mah meh ahn·<u>tee</u>·kehs **antiques store**

**κατάστημα με είδη δώρων** kah·<u>tahs</u>·tee·mah meh ee·THee·<u>THoh</u>·rohn **gift store**

**κατάστημα με υγιεινές τροφές** kah·<u>tahs</u>·tee·mah meh ee·yee·ee·<u>nehs</u> troh·<u>fehs</u> **health food store**

**κατάστημα μεταχειρισμένων ειδών** kah·<u>tah</u>·stee·mah meh·tah·khee·reez·<u>meh</u>·nohn ee·<u>THohn</u> **second-hand shop**

**κατάστημα αθλητικών ειδών** kah·<u>tahs</u>·tee·mah ath·lee·tee·<u>kohn</u> ee·<u>THohn</u> **sporting goods store**

**κατάστημα ρούχων** kah·<u>tahs</u>·tee·mah <u>roo</u>·khohn **clothing store**

**κατάστημα σουβενίρ** kah·<u>tahs</u>·tee·mah soo·veh·<u>neer</u> **souvenir store**

**κατάστημα υποδημάτων** kah·<u>tah</u>·stee·mah ee·poh·THee·<u>mah</u>·tohn **shoe store**

**καταστρέφω** kah·tah·<u>streh</u>·foh *v* **damage**

**κατάψυξη** kah·<u>tah</u>·psee·ksee **freezer**

**κατεβαίνω** kah·teh·<u>veh</u>·noh **get off (transport)**

**κατειλημένος** kah·tee·lee·<u>meh</u>·nohs **occupied**

**κάτι** <u>kah</u>·tee **something**

**κάτοχος** <u>kah</u>·toh·khohs **owner**

**κατσαβίδι** kah·tsah·<u>vee</u>·THee **screwdriver**

**κατσαρόλα** kah·tsah·<u>roh</u>·lah **saucepan**

**κάτω** <u>kah</u>·toh *adj* **lower (berth)**

**καύσωνας** kahf·soh·nahs **heat wave**
**καφετέρια** kah·feh·teh·ree·ah **cafe**
**κέντρο της πόλης** kehn·droh tees poh·lees **downtown area**
**κεφάλι** keh·fah·lee n **head**
**κήπος** kee·pohs n **garden**
**κιθάρα** kee·thah·rah **guitar**
**κινηματογράφος** kee·nee·mah·tohgh·rah·fohs **movie theater**
**κίνηση** kee·nee·see **traffic**
**κινητό** kee·nee·toh **cell phone [mobile phone BE]**
**κίτρινος** keet·ree·nohs **yellow**
**κλειδαριά** klee·THahr·yah n **lock (door)**
**κλειδί** klee·THee n **key**
**κλειδώνω** klee·THoh·noh v **lock (door)**
**κλειστός** klees·tohs adj **shut**
**κλεμένος** kleh·meh·nos **stolen**
**κλέφτης** klehf·tees **thief**
**κλήση** klee·see n **call**
**κλιματισμός** klee·mah·teez·mohs **air conditioning**
**κλοπή** kloh·pee **theft**
**κομμωτήριο** koh·moh·tee·ree·oh **hair dresser**
**κόμβος** kohm·vohs **junction (intersection)**
**κοιμάμαι** kee·mah·meh v **sleep**
**κοιλάδα** kee·lah·THah **valley**
**κοιτάω** kee·tah·oh v **look**
**κολύμβηση** koh·leem·vee·see **swimming**

**κοντά** kohn·dah adv **near**
**κοντός** kohn·dohs adj **short**
**κορίτσι** koh·ree·tsee **girl**
**κορυφή** koh·ree·fee n **peak**
**κοσμηματοπωλείο** kohz·mee·mah·toh·poh·lee·oh **jeweler**
**κουβέρτα** koo·veh·rtah **blanket**
**κουζίνα** koo·zee·nah **stove**
**κουνούπι** koo·noo·pee **mosquito**
**κουρασμένος** koo·rahz·meh·nohs **tired**
**κουστούμι** koos·too·mee **men's suit**
**κουταλάκι** koo·tah·lah·kee **teaspoon**
**κουτάλι** koo·tah·lee n **spoon**
**κουτί** koo·tee **carton**
**κουτί πρώτων βοηθειών** koo·tee proh·tohn voh·ee·thee·ohn **first-aid kit**
**κράμπα** krahm·bah n **cramp**
**κραγιόν** krah·yohn **lipstick**
**κρατώ** krah·toh v **keep**
**κρέμα ξυρίσματος** kreh·mah ksee·reez·mah·tohs **shaving cream**
**κρεμάστρα** kreh·mahs·trah **hanger**
**κρεβάτι** kreh·vah·tee **bed**
**κρυολόγημα** kree·oh·loh·yee·mah n **cold (flu)**
**κρύος** kree·ohs adj **cold (temperature)**
**κρύσταλλο** kree·stah·loh n **crystal**
**κύμα** kee·mah n **wave**
**κυλικείο** kee·lee·kee·oh **snack bar**
**κυλιόμενες σκάλες**

kee·lee·<u>oh</u>·meh·nehs skah·lehs
**escalator**
**Κύπρος** <u>kee</u>·prohs **Cyprus**
**κύριος** <u>kee</u>·ree·ohs **main**
**κωδικός περιοχής** koh·THee·<u>kohs</u>
peh·ree·oh·<u>khees</u> **area code**
**κωπηλασία** koh·pee·lah·<u>see</u>·ah
**rowing**

## Λ

**λάμπα** <u>lahm</u>·bah **lamp, light bulb**
**λάθος** <u>lah</u>·thohs **error, wrong**
**λαιμόκοψη** leh·<u>moh</u>·koh·psee **neck**
(shirt)
**λαιμός** leh·<u>mohs</u> **throat**
**λάστιχο** <u>lahs</u>·tee·khoh **tire [tyre BE]**
**λειτουργία** lee·toor·<u>yee</u>·ah n **mass**
(church)
**λεκές** leh·<u>kehs</u> n **stain**
**λεξικό** leh·ksee·<u>koh</u> **dictionary**
**λεπτό** lehp·<u>toh</u> n **minute (time)**
**λεπτός** lehp·<u>tohs</u> adj **thin**
**λέω** <u>leh</u>·oh **tell**
**λεωφορείο** leh·oh·foh·<u>ree</u>·oh **bus**
**ληστεία** lees·<u>tee</u>·ah **robbery**
**λιμάνι** lee·<u>mah</u>·nee n **harbor**
**λίμνη** <u>leem</u>·nee **lake**
**λιμνούλα** leem·<u>noo</u>·lah n **pond**
**λιγότερο** lee·<u>ghoh</u>·teh·roh **less**
**λιπαντικό** lee·pahn·dee·<u>koh</u>
**lubricant**
**λιπαρός** lee·pah·<u>rohs</u> **greasy (hair,**
skin)
**λιποθυμώ** lee·poh·thee·<u>moh</u> **faint**

**λίρα** <u>lee</u>·rah **pound (sterling)**
**λίτρο** <u>lee</u>·troh **liter**
**λογαριασμός** loh·ghahr·yahz·<u>mohs</u>
**check (bill), account**
**λοσιόν** loh·<u>siohn</u> **lotion**
**λοσιόν μαυρίσματος** loh·<u>siohn</u>
mahv·<u>rees</u>·mah·tohs **sun tan lotion**
**λουκέτο** loo·<u>keh</u>·toh **padlock**
**λουλούδι** loo·<u>loo</u>·THee **flower**
**λουρί ρολογιού** loo·<u>ree</u> roh·loh·<u>yioo</u>
**watch strap**
**λόφος** <u>loh</u>·fohs **hill**

## Μ

**μαγιό** mah·<u>yoh</u> **swimming trunks,**
**swimsuit**
**μαθαίνω** mah·<u>theh</u>·noh **learn**
**μάθημα ξένης γλώσσας** <u>mah</u>·thee
mah kseh·nees ghloh·sahs **language**
**course**
**μακιγιάζ** mah·kee·<u>yahz</u> **make-up**
**μακριά** mahk·ree·<u>ah</u> adv **far**
**μακρύς** mak·<u>rees</u> adj **long**
**μαλλιά** mah·<u>liah</u> **hair**
**μανικιούρ** mah·nee·<u>kioor</u> **manicure**
**μαξιλαροθήκη**
mah·ksee·lah·roh·<u>thee</u>·kee **pillow**
**case**
**μαργαριτάρι** mahr·ghah·ree·<u>tah</u>·ree
**pearl**
**μάρτυρας** <u>mahr</u>·tee·rahs **witness**
**μας** mahs **our**
**μασάζ** mah·<u>sahz</u> n **massage**
**μάσκα** <u>mahs</u>·kah n **mask (diving)**

μάτι <u>mah</u>·tee *n* **eye**

μαχαίρι mah·<u>kheh</u>·ree **knife**

με meh **with**

με άμμο meh <u>ah</u>·moh **sandy (beach)**

με υπότιτλους meh ee·<u>poh</u>·teet·loos **subtitled**

με χαλίκια meh khah·<u>lee</u>·kiah **pebbly (beach)**

μεγαλοπρεπής meh·ghah·lohp·reh·<u>pees</u> **magnificent**

μεγάλος meh·<u>ghah</u>·lohs *adj* **big, large**

μέγεθος <u>meh</u>·yeh·thohs *n* **size**

μέδουσα <u>meh</u>·THoo·sah **jellyfish**

μένω <u>meh</u>·noh *v* **stay**

μεριά mehr·<u>yah</u> **side (of road)**

μερίδα meh·<u>ree</u>·THah *n* **portion**

μερικές φορές meh·ree·<u>kehs</u> foh·<u>rehs</u> **sometimes**

μέσα <u>meh</u>·sah **inside**

μεσημεριανό meh·see·mehr·yah·<u>noh</u> *n* **lunch**

μετά meh·<u>tah</u> **after**

μετακομίζω meh·tah·koh·<u>mee</u>·zoh *v* **move (room)**

μέταλλο <u>meh</u>·tah·loh *n* **metal**

μετάξι meh·<u>tah</u>·ksee **silk**

μεταφέρω meh·tah·<u>feh</u>·roh **transfer**

μεταφορά meh·tah·foh·<u>rah</u> *n* **transit**

μεταφράζω meh·tah·<u>frah</u>·zoh **translate**

μετάφραση meh·<u>tah</u>·frah·see **translation**

μεταφραστής meh·tah·frah·<u>stees</u> **translator**

μέτρηση <u>meh</u>·tree·see **measurement**

μετρητά meht·ree·<u>tah</u> *n* **cash**

μετρό meh·<u>troh</u> **subway**

μετρώ meht·<u>roh</u> *v* **measure**

μη καπνίζοντες mee kap·<u>nee</u>·zon·des **non-smoking**

μήκος <u>mee</u>·kohs **length**

μήνας του μέλιτος <u>mee</u>·nahs too <u>meh</u>·lee·tohs **honeymoon**

μήνυμα <u>mee</u>·nee·mah *n* **message**

μηχανή mee·khah·<u>nee</u> **engine**

μια φορά miah foh·<u>rah</u> **once**

μικρός meek·<u>rohs</u> **little, small**

μιλώ mee·<u>loh</u> **speak**

μινι-μπαρ <u>mee</u>·nee bahr **mini-bar**

μισός mee·<u>sohs</u> **half**

μνημείο mnee·<u>mee</u>·oh **memorial, monument**

μολυσμένος moh·leez·<u>meh</u>·nohs **infected**

μονάδα moh·<u>nah</u>·THah **unit**

μοναδικός moh·nah·THee·<u>kohs</u> **unique**

μονόκλινο δωμάτιο moh·<u>noh</u>·klee·noh THoh·<u>mah</u>·tee·oh **single room**

μονοπάτι moh·noh·<u>pah</u>·tee **path, trail**

μοντέρνος moh·<u>deh</u>·rnohs **modern**

μοτοποδήλατο moh·toh·poh·<u>THee</u>·lah·toh **moped**

μουσείο moo·<u>see</u>·oh **museum**

**μουσική** moo·see·<u>kee</u> **music**
**μουσικός** moo·see·<u>kohs</u> **musician**
**μουστάκι** moos·<u>tah</u>·kee **moustache**
**μπαγιάτικος** bah·<u>yah</u>·tee·kohs **stale**
**μπάνιο** <u>bah</u>·nioh **bathroom,
   lavatory**
**μπαρ** bahr **bar**
**μπάσκετ** <u>bah</u>·skeht **basketball**
**μπαστούνια του σκι** bahs·<u>too</u>·niah
   too skee **ski poles**
**μπαταρία** bah·tah·<u>ree</u>·ah **battery**
**μπέιμπι σίτερ** <u>beh</u>·ee·bee <u>see</u>·tehr
   **babysitter**
**μπικίνι** bee·<u>kee</u>·nee **bikini**
**μπλούζα** <u>bloo</u>·zah **blouse**
**μπλουζάκι** bloo·<u>zah</u>·kee **T-shirt**
**μπλου-τζην** bloo·<u>jeen</u> **jeans**
**μποξ** bohks **n boxing**
**μπότα** <u>boh</u>·tah **boot**
**μπότες πεζοπορίας** <u>boh</u>·tehs
   peh·zoh·poh·<u>ree</u>·ahs **walking boots**
**μπότες του σκι** <u>boh</u>·tehs too skee **ski
   boots**
**μπουκάλι** boo·<u>kah</u>·lee **bottle**
**μπρελόκ** breh·<u>lohk</u> **key ring**
**μύγα** <u>mee</u>·ghah **n fly (insect)**
**μυρίζω** mee·<u>ree</u>·zoh **v smell**
**μυς** mees **n muscle**
**μύτη** <u>mee</u>·tee **n nose**
**μύωπας** <u>mee</u>·oh·pahs **short-sighted
   [BE]**
**μωρό** moh·<u>roh</u> **baby**

**N**

**ναός** nah·<u>ohs</u> **temple**
**ναυαγοσώστης**
   nah·vah·ghoh·<u>sohs</u>·tees **lifeguard**
**ναυαγοσωστική λέμβος**
   nah·vah·ghoh·sohs·tee·<u>kee</u>
   lehm·vohs **lifeboat**
**ναυτία** nahf·<u>tee</u>·ah **nausea, travel
   sickness**
**νέος** <u>neh</u>·ohs **young**
**νερό** neh·<u>roh</u> **n water**
**νεύρο** <u>nehv</u>·roh **nerve**
**νεφρό** nehf·<u>roh</u> **kidney**
**νιπτήρας** nee·<u>ptee</u>·rahs **sink
   (bathroom)**
**νόμιμος** <u>noh</u>·mee·mohs **legal**
**νομίζω** noh·<u>mee</u>·zoh **think**
**νόμισμα** <u>noh</u>·meez·mah **currency**
**νοικιάζω** nee·<u>kiah</u>·zoh **v hire, rent**
**νοσοκόμα** noh·soh·<u>koh</u>·mah **n nurse**
**νοσοκομείο** noh·soh·koh·<u>mee</u>·oh
   **hospital**
**νόστιμος** <u>nohs</u>·tee·mohs **delicious**
**Νοτιοαφρικανός**
   noh·tee·oh·ahf·ree·kah·<u>nohs</u> **South
   African (nationality)**
**νότιος** <u>noh</u>·tee·ohs **adj south**
**ντεμοντέ** deh·mohn·<u>deh</u> **old-
   fashioned**
**ντήζελ** <u>dee</u>·zehl **diesel**
**ντουζ** dooz **n shower**
**ντουζίνα** doo·<u>zee</u>·nah **dozen**
**νύχι** <u>nee</u>·khee **n nail**
**νύχτα** <u>neekh</u>·tah **night**

**νυχτερινό κέντρο** neekh·teh·ree·noh kehn·droh **night club**
**νωρίς** noh·rees **early**

## Ξ

**ξαπλώνω** ksah·ploh·noh **lie down**
**ξενάγηση** kseh·nah·yee·see **guided tour**
**ξενάγηση στα αξιοθέατα** kseh·nah·yee·see stah ah·ksee·oh·theh·ah·tah **sightseeing tour**
**ξεναγός** kseh·nah·ghohs **tour guide**
**ξένο συνάλλαγμα** kseh·noh see·nah·lahgh·mah **foreign currency**
**ξενοδοχείο** kseh·noh·THoh·khee·oh **hotel**
**ξένος** kseh·nohs **foreign**
**ξενώνας νεότητας** kseh·noh·nahs neh·oh·tee·tahs **youth hostel**
**ξεχνώ** ksehkh·noh **forget**
**ξεχωριστά** kseh·khoh·ree·stah **separately**
**ξινός** ksee·nohs **sour**
**ξοδεύω** ksoh·THeh·voh **spend**
**ξύλο** ksee·loh **wood (material)**
**ξυπνώ** kseep·noh v **wake**
**ξυραφάκι** ksee·rah·fah·kee **razor, razor blade**

## O

**ομάδα** oh·mah·THah n **team**
**όμορφος** oh·mohr·fohs adj **beautiful, pretty**
**ομπρέλλα** ohm·breh·lah **sun shade**
**οβάλ** oh·vahl **oval**
**οδηγία** oh·THee·yee·ah **instruction**
**οδηγός καταστήματος** oh·THee·ghohs kah·tahs·tee·mah·tohs **store guide**
**οδηγός ψυχαγωγίας** oh·THee·ghohs psee·khah·ghoh·yee·ahs **entertainment guide**
**οδηγώ** oh·THee·ghoh v **drive**
**οδική βόηθεια** oh·THee·kee voh·ee·thee·ah **road assistance**
**οδοντίατρος** oh·THohn·dee·ah·trohs **dentist**
**οδοντόβουρτσα** oh·THohn·doh·voor·tsah **tooth brush**
**οδοντόπαστα** oh·THohn·doh·pahs·tah **tooth paste**
**οικογένεια** ee·koh·yeh·nee·ah **family**
**οινοποιείο** ee·noh·pee·ee·oh **winery**
**όνομα** oh·noh·mah n **name**
**όπερα** oh·peh·rah **opera**
**οπωροπωλείο** oh·poh·roh·poh·lee·oh **greengrocer [BE]**
**οργανωμένος** ohr·ghah·noh·meh·nohs **organized**
**ορχήστρα** ohr·khees·trah **orchestra**
**οτιδήποτε** oh·tee·THee·poh·teh **anything**
**οτοστόπ** oh·toh·stohp **hitchhiking**

**οφείλω** oh·<u>fee</u>·loh **have to (obligation)**

**οφθαλμίατρος** ohf·thahl·<u>mee</u>·aht·rohs **optician**

## Π

**παγοπέδιλα** pah·ghoh·<u>peh</u>·THee·lah **skates**

**πάγος** <u>pah</u>·ghohs *n* **ice**

**παιδική χαρά** peh·THee·<u>kee</u> khah·<u>rah</u> **playground**

**παιδικό κρεβάτι** peh·THee·<u>koh</u> kreh·<u>vah</u>·tee **crib [cot BE]**

**παίζω** <u>peh</u>·zoh *v* **play (games, music)**

**παιχνίδι** pehkh·<u>nee</u>·THee *n* **game (toy), round**

**παιχνίδι βίντεο** pehkh·<u>nee</u>·THee <u>vee</u>·deh·oh **video game**

**πακέτο** pah·<u>keh</u>·toh **parcel**

**πακέτο για το σπίτι** pah·<u>keh</u>·toh yah toh <u>spee</u>·tee **take away**

**παλιά πόλη** pah·<u>liah</u> <u>poh</u>·lee **old town**

**παλιός** pah·<u>liohs</u> **old (thing)**

**πάνα μωρού** <u>pah</u>·nah moh·<u>roo</u> **diaper**

**Πανεπιστήμιο** pah·neh·pees·<u>tee</u>·mee·oh **university**

**πάνες μωρού** <u>pah</u>·nehs moh·<u>roo</u> **nappies**

**πανόραμα** pah·<u>noh</u>·rah·mah **panorama**

**παντελόνι** pahn·deh·<u>loh</u>·nee **pants [trousers BE]**

**παντοπωλείο** pahn·doh·poh·<u>lee</u>·oh **minimart**

**παντόφλες** pahn·<u>dohf</u>·lehs **slippers**

**παντρεμένος** pahn·dreh·<u>meh</u>·nohs **married**

**πάνω** <u>pah</u>·noh *adj* **top, upper (berth**

**παπούτσι** pah·<u>poo</u>·tsee **shoe**

**πάρα πολύ** <u>pah</u>·rah poh·<u>lee</u> **too (extreme)**

**παραγγέλνω** pah·rah·<u>gehl</u>·noh *v* **order**

**παράδειγμα** pah·<u>rah</u>·THeegh·mah **example**

**παραδοσιακός** pah·rah·THoh·see·ah·<u>kohs</u> **traditional**

**παράθυρο** pah·<u>rah</u>·thee·roh **window**

**παραλαβή αποσκευών** pah·rah·lah·<u>vee</u> ah·poh·skeh·<u>vohn</u> **baggage [BE] claim**

**παραλία** pah·rah·<u>lee</u>·ah **beach**

**παραλία γυμνιστών** pah·rah·<u>lee</u>·ah yeem·nees·<u>tohn</u> **nudist beach**

**παραλυσία** pah·rah·lee·<u>see</u>·ah **paralysis**

**παράνομος** pah·<u>rah</u>·noh·mohs **illegal**

**παράξενος** pah·<u>rah</u>·kseh·nohs **strange**

**παραπάνω** pah·rah·<u>pah</u>·noh **more**

**παρεξήγηση** pah·reh·<u>ksee</u>·yee·see **misunderstanding**

**πάρκο** <u>pahr</u>·koh *n* **park**

**παρκόμετρο** pahr·<u>koh</u>·meht·roh **parking meter**

**πάρτυ** <u>pah</u>·rtee *n* **party (social gathering)**

παυσίπονο pahf·<u>see</u>·poh·noh **painkiller**

παχύς pah·<u>khees</u> adj **fat (person)**

πέδιλα <u>peh</u>·THee·lah **sandals**

πεζόδρομος peh·<u>zohTH</u>·roh·mohs **pedestrian zone**

περιμένω peh·ree·<u>meh</u>·noh v **hold on, wait**

περιμένω στην ουρά peh·ree·<u>meh</u>·noh steen oo·<u>rah</u> v **queue [BE]**

περιέχω peh·ree·<u>eh</u>·khoh **contain**

περιοδικό peh·ree·oh·THee·<u>koh</u> **magazine**

περίοδος peh·<u>ree</u>·oh·THohs **period (menstrual)**

περιοχή peh·ree·oh·<u>khee</u> **region**

περιοχή για καπνίζοντες peh·ree·oh·<u>khee</u> yah kahp·<u>nee</u>·zohn·dehs **smoking area**

περιοχή για πικνίκ peh·ree·oh·<u>khee</u> yah peek neek **picnic area**

περίπτερο peh·<u>ree</u>·pteh·roh **newsstand, kiosk**

περνώ pehr·<u>noh</u> v **pass**

περπατώ pehr·pah·<u>toh</u> v **walk**

περσίδες peh·<u>rsee</u>·THehs **blinds**

πετάω peh·<u>tah</u>·oh v **fly**

πετσέτα peh·<u>tseh</u>·tah **napkin**

πέφτω <u>pehf</u>·toh v **fall**

πηγαίνω pee·<u>yeh</u>·noh **go**

πιάτσα ταξί piah·tsah tah·<u>ksee</u> **taxi rank [BE]**

πίεση <u>pee</u>·eh·see **blood pressure**

πιθανός pee·thah·<u>nohs</u> **possible**

πινακίδα pee·nah·kee·<u>THah</u> **road sign**

πίνω <u>pee</u>·noh v **drink**

πίπα <u>pee</u>·pah **pipe (smoking)**

πιπίλα pee·<u>pee</u>·lah **pacifier [soother BE]**

πισίνα pee·<u>see</u>·nah **swimming pool**

πιστοποιητικό ασφάλειας pees·toh·pee·ee·tee·<u>koh</u> ahs·<u>fah</u>·lee·ahs **insurance certificate**

πιστωτική κάρτα pees·toh·tee·<u>kee</u> <u>kahr</u>·tah **credit card**

πιτσαρία pee·tsah·<u>ree</u>·ah **pizzeria**

πλαγιά plah·<u>yah</u> **slope (ski)**

πλαστική σακούλα plahs·tee·<u>kee</u> sah·<u>koo</u>·lah **plastic bag**

πλατίνα plah·<u>tee</u>·nah **platinum**

πλευρό plehv·<u>roh</u> **rib**

πλημμύρα plee·<u>mee</u>·rah n **flood**

πληγή plee·<u>yee</u> **wound (cut)**

πληροφορίες plee·roh·foh·<u>ree</u>·ehs **information**

πληρωμή plee·roh·<u>mee</u> **payment**

πληρώνω plee·<u>roh</u>·noh v **pay**

πλοίο <u>plee</u>·oh n **ship**

πλυντήριο pleen·<u>deer</u>·ee·oh **washing machine**

πνεύμονας <u>pnehv</u>·moh·nahs **lung**

πόμολο <u>poh</u>·moh·loh n **handle**

ποδήλατο poh·<u>THee</u>·lah·toh **bicycle**

πόδι <u>poh</u>·THee **foot, leg**

ποδόσφαιρο poh·<u>THohs</u>·feh·roh **soccer [football BE]**

**ποιότητα** pee·oh·tee·tah **quality**

**πόλη** poh·lee **town**

**πολυκατάστημα**
poh·lee·kah·<u>tahs</u>·tee·mah
**department store**

**πολυτέλεια** poh·lee·<u>teh</u>·lee·ah **luxury**

**πολύτιμος** poh·<u>lee</u>·tee·mohs
**valuable**

**πονόδοντος** poh·<u>noh</u>·THohn·dohs
**toothache**

**πονοκέφαλος** poh·noh·<u>keh</u>·fah·lohs
**headache**

**πονόλαιμος** poh·<u>noh</u>·leh·mohs **sore
throat**

**πόνος** <u>poh</u>·nohs n **pain**

**πόνος στο αυτί** <u>poh</u>·nohs stoh ahf·<u>tee</u>
**earache**

**πόρτα** <u>pohr</u>·tah **door**

**πορτοφόλι** pohr·toh·<u>foh</u>·lee **wallet**

**ποσό** poh·<u>soh</u> n **amount**

**ποσότητα** poh·<u>soh</u>·tee·tah **quantity**

**ποταμός** poh·tah·<u>mohs</u> **river**

**ποτέ** poh·<u>teh</u> **never**

**ποτήρι** poh·<u>tee</u>·ree **glass (container)**

**ποτό** poh·<u>toh</u> n **drink**

**πουκάμισο** poo·<u>kah</u>·mee·soh **shirt**

**πράσινος** <u>prah</u>·see·nohs **green**

**πρέπει** <u>preh</u>·pee v **must**

**πρεσβεία** prehz·<u>vee</u>·ah **embassy**

**πρεσβύωπας** prehz·<u>vee</u>·oh·pahs
**long-sighted [BE]**

**πρήξιμο** <u>pree</u>·ksee·moh **swelling**

**πρησμένος** preez·<u>meh</u>·nohs **swollen**

**πρίζα** <u>pree</u>·zah n **plug, socket**

**πριν** preen **before**

**πρόβλεψη** <u>prohv</u>·leh·psee n **forecast**

**πρόβλεψη καιρού** <u>prohv</u>·leh·psee
keh·<u>roo</u> **weather forecast**

**πρόβλημα** <u>prohv</u>·lee·mah **problem**

**πρόγραμμα** <u>prohgh</u>·rah·mah n
**program**

**πρόγραμμα θεαμάτων** proh·<u>ghrah</u>·
mah theh·ah·<u>mah</u>·tohn **program
of events**

**προς** prohs **towards**

**προσαρμοστής** proh·sahr·moh·<u>stees</u>
**adaptor**

**πρόσβαση** <u>prohz</u>·vah·see n **access**

**προσγειώνομαι**
prohz·yee·<u>oh</u>·noh·meh v **land**

**προσκαλώ** prohs·kah·<u>loh</u> v **invite**

**πρόσκληση** <u>prohs</u>·klee·see **invitation**

**πρόστιμο** <u>prohs</u>·tee·moh n **fine
(penalty)**

**πρόσωπο** <u>proh</u>·soh·poh n **face**

**προσωρινός** proh·soh·ree·<u>nohs</u>
**temporary**

**προτείνω** proh·<u>tee</u>·noh **suggest**

**προφέρω** proh·<u>feh</u>·roh **pronounce**

**προφυλακτικό** proh·fee·lah·
ktee·<u>koh</u> **condom**

**προωθώ** proh·oh·<u>thoh</u> **forward**

**πρωί** proh·<u>ee</u> **morning**

**πρωινό** proh·ee·<u>noh</u> **breakfast**

**πρώτη θέση** <u>proh</u>·tee <u>theh</u>·see **first
class**

**πτήση** <u>ptee</u>·see **flight**

**πυρετός** pee·reh·<u>tohs</u> **fever**

**πυροσβεστήρας** pee·rohz·vehs·**tee**·rahs **fire extinguisher**

**πυροσβεστική** pee·rohz·vehs·tee·**kee** **fire brigade [BE]**

**πυτζάμες** pee·**jah**·mehs **pajamas**

## Ρ

**ραδιόφωνο** rah·THee·**oh**·foh·noh n **radio**

**ρακέτα** rah·**keh**·tah **racket (tennis, squash)**

**ραντεβού** rahn·deh·**voo** **appointment**

**ράφι** **rah**·fee n **shelf**

**ρεματιά** reh·mah·**tiah** **ravine**

**ρεσεψιόν** reh·seh·**psiohn** **reception (hotel)**

**ρεύμα ποταμού** **rehv**·mah poh·tah·**moo** **rapids**

**ρηχή πισίνα** ree·**khee** pee·**see**·nah **paddling pool**

**ρομαντικός** roh·mahn·dee·**kohs** **romantic**

**ρολόι** roh·**loh**·ee n **watch**

**ρυάκι** ree·**ah**·kee n **stream**

## Σ

**σμαράγδι** zmah·**rahgh**·THee **emerald**

**σαμπουάν** sahm·poo·**ahn** n **shampoo**

**σαγιονάρες** sah·yoh·nah·**rehs** **flip-flops**

**σαγόνι** sah·**ghoh**·nee **jaw**

**σάκκος** **sah**·kohs **knapsack**

**σαλόνι** sah·**loh**·nee **living room**

**σάουνα** **sah**·oo·nah **sauna**

**σαπούνι** sah·**poo**·nee n **soap**

**σατέν** sah·**tehn** **satin**

**σβήνω** **svee**·noh v **turn off**

**σβώλος** **svoh**·lohs n **lump**

**σεζ-λονγκ** sehz lohng **deck chair**

**σενιάν** seh·**niahn** **rare (steak)**

**σερβιέτες** sehr·vee·**eh**·tehs **sanitary towels**

**σεσουάρ** seh·soo·**ahr** **hair dryer**

**σήμα** **see**·mah **sign (road)**

**σημαία** see·**meh**·ah n **flag**

**σημαίνω** see·**meh**·noh v **mean**

**σημείο** see·**mee**·oh n **point**

**σίδερο** **see**·THeh·roh n **iron**

**σιδερώνω** see·THeh·**roh**·noh v **iron, press**

**σιδηροδρομικός σταθμός** see·THee·rohTH·roh·mee·**kohs** stahth·**mohs** **rail station**

**σκάλα** **skah**·lah **ladder**

**σκάλες** **skah**·lehs **stairs**

**σκηνή** skee·**nee** **tent**

**σκι** skee **skiing**

**σκιά** skee·**ah** **shade (darkness)**

**σκοπός** skoh·**pohs** **purpose**

**σκούπα** **skoo**·pah n **broom**

**σκουπίδια** skoo·**peeTH**·yah **trash [rubbish BE]**

**σκούρος** **skoo**·rohs adj **dark (color)**

**σλιπ** sleep **briefs**

**σόλα** **soh**·lah **sole (shoes)**

**σορτς** sohrts n **shorts**

**σουβενίρ** soo·veh·**neer** **souvenir**

**σουπερμάρκετ** soo-pehr-<u>mahr</u>-keht **supermarket**

**σουτιέν** soo-<u>tiehn</u> **bra**

**σπα** spah **spa**

**σπάγγος** <u>spah</u>-gohs *n* **string (cord)**

**σπάνιος** <u>spah</u>-nee-ohs **rare (unusual)**

**σπασμένος** spahz-<u>meh</u>-nohs **broken**

**σπάω** <u>spah</u>-oh *v* **break**

**σπήλαιο** <u>spee</u>-leh-oh *n* **cave**

**σπίρτο** <u>speer</u>-toh *n* **match (to start fire)**

**σπονδυλική στήλη** spohn-THee-lee-<u>kee</u> <u>stee</u>-lee **spine**

**σπουδάζω** spoo-<u>THah</u>-zoh *v* **study**

**σταματώ** stah-mah-<u>toh</u> *v* **stop**

**στάδιο** <u>stah</u>-THee-oh **stadium**

**σταθμός μετρό** stahth-<u>mohs</u> meh-<u>troh</u> **subway [underground BE] station**

**σταθμός λεωφορείων** stahTH-<u>mohs</u> leh-oh-foh-<u>ree</u>-ohn **bus station**

**στάση** <u>stah</u>-see **exposure (photos), stop (bus)**

**στάση λεωφορείου** <u>stah</u>-see leh-oh-foh-<u>ree</u>-oo **bus stop**

**στέγη** <u>steh</u>-yee *n* **roof**

**στέλνω** <u>stehl</u>-noh **send**

**στενός** steh-<u>nohs</u> *adj* **narrow, tight**

**στήθος** <u>stee</u>-THohs **breast**

**στόμα** <u>stoh</u>-mah *n* **mouth**

**στομάχι** stoh-<u>mah</u>-khee *n* **stomach**

**στομαχόπονος** stoh-mah-<u>khoh</u>-poh-nohs **stomach ache**

**στολή** stoh-<u>lee</u> *n* **uniform**

**στολή δύτη** stoh-<u>lee</u> <u>THee</u>-tee **wetsuit**

**στρογγυλός** strohn-gkee-<u>lohs</u> *adj* **round**

**στυλ** steel *n* **style**

**στυλό** stee-<u>loh</u> *n* **pen**

**συμπεριλαμβάνεται** seem-beh-ree-lahm-<u>vah</u>-neh-teh **included**

**σύζυγος** <u>see</u>-zee-ghohs **husband, wife**

**συκώτι** see-<u>koh</u>-tee **liver**

**σύμπτωμα** <u>seem</u>-ptoh-mah **symptom**

**συναγερμός πυρκαγιάς** see-nah-yehr-<u>mohs</u> peer-kah-<u>yahs</u> **fire alarm**

**συναντώ** see-nahn-<u>doh</u> **meet**

**συνέδριο** see-<u>neh</u>-THree-oh **conference**

**συνταγή γιατρού** seen-dah-<u>yee</u> yaht-<u>roo</u> **prescription**

**συνταγογραφώ** seen-dah-ghoh-ghrah-<u>foh</u> **prescribe**

**συνταξιούχος** seen-dah-ksee-<u>oo</u>-khohs **retired**

**σύντομα** <u>seen</u>-doh-mah **soon**

**συντριβάνι** seen-dree-<u>vah</u>-nee **fountain**

**συστάσεις** see-<u>stah</u>-sees **introductions**

**συστήνω** see-<u>stee</u>-noh **introduce, recommend**

**συχνός** seekh-<u>nohs</u> *adj* **frequent**

**σφηνωμένος** sfee-noh-<u>meh</u>-nohs **jammed**

**σφράγισμα** sfrah·yeez·mah **filling (dental)**

**σφυρί** sfee·<u>ree</u> **hammer**

**σχέδιο** skheh·THee·oh *n* **plan**

**σχήμα** skhee·mah *n* **shape**

**σχισμένος** skheez·<u>meh</u>·nohs **torn**

**σχοινί** skhee·<u>nee</u> *n* **rope**

**σχολή σκι** skhoh·<u>lee</u> skee **ski school**

**σωσίβιο** soh·<u>see</u>·vee·oh **lifejacket**

**σωστός** sohs·<u>stohs</u> *adj* **right (correct)**

**T**

**ταμπόν** tahm·<u>bohn</u> **tampon**

**τάβλι** <u>tah</u>·vlee **backgammon**

**ταγιέρ** tah·<u>yehr</u> **women's suit**

**ταΐζω** tah·<u>ee</u>·zoh *v* **feed**

**ταινία** teh·<u>nee</u>·ah **movie**

**ταξί** tah·<u>ksee</u> **taxi**

**ταξίδι** tah·<u>ksee</u>·THee **journey**

**ταξίδι με πλοίο** tah·<u>ksee</u>·THee meh <u>plee</u>·oh **boat trip**

**ταξιδιωτική επιταγή** tah·ksee·THee·oh·tee·<u>kee</u> eh·pee·tah·<u>yee</u> **traveler's check [traveller's cheque BE]**

**ταξιδιωτικό γραφείο** tah·ksee·THyoh·tee·<u>koh</u> ghrah·<u>fee</u>·oh **travel agency**

**ταξιτζής** tah·ksee·<u>jees</u> **taxi driver**

**ταυτότητα** tahf·<u>toh</u>·tee·tah **identification**

**ταχυδρομείο** tah·kheeTH·roh·<u>mee</u>·oh **post office**

**ταχυδρομική επιταγή** tah·kheeTH·roh· mee·<u>kee</u> eh·pee·tah·<u>yee</u> **money order**

**ταχυδρομικό κουτί** tah·kheeTH·roh·mee·<u>koh</u> koo·<u>tee</u> **mailbox [postbox BE]**

**τεμάχιο** teh·<u>mah</u>·khee·oh **piece**

**τελειώνω** teh·lee·<u>oh</u>·noh *v* **end**

**τελευταί ος** teh·lehf·<u>teh</u>·ohs **last**

**τελεφερίκ** teh·leh·feh·<u>reek</u> **cablecar**

**τέλος** <u>teh</u>·lohs *n* **end**

**τελωνειακή δήλωση** teh·loh·nee·ah·<u>kee</u> THee·loh·see **customs declaration (tolls)**

**τελωνείο** teh·loh·<u>nee</u>·oh **customs (tolls)**

**τέννις** <u>teh</u>·nees **tennis**

**τετράγωνος** teht·<u>rah</u>·ghoh·nohs **square**

**τζετ-σκι** jeht skee **jet-ski**

**τζόγκιγκ** joh·geeng **jogging**

**τζόγος** <u>joh</u>·ghohs **gambling**

**τηλεκάρτα** tee·leh·<u>kahr</u>·tah **phone card**

**τηλεόραση** tee·leh·<u>oh</u>·rah·see **TV**

**τηλεφώνημα** tee·leh·<u>foh</u>·nee·mah **phone call**

**τηλεφωνικός θάλαμος** tee·leh·foh·nee·<u>kohs</u> <u>thah</u>·lah·mohs **telephone booth**

**τηλεφωνικός κατάλογος** tee·leh·foh·nee·<u>kohs</u> kah·<u>tah</u>·loh·ghohs **telephone directory**

**τηλέφωνο** tee·<u>leh</u>·foh·noh *n* **phone**

**την** teen **per**

**τιμή συναλλάγματος** tee·mee see·nah·<u>lahgh</u>·mah·tohs **exchange rate**

**τιμή εισόδου** tee·<u>mee</u> ee·<u>soh</u>·ΤΗoo **entrance fee**

**τιρμπουσόν** teer·boo·<u>sohn</u> **corkscrew**

**τοίχος** tee·khohs **wall**

**τοπικός** toh·pee·<u>kohs</u> **local**

**τοστιέρα** toh·<u>stieh</u>·rah **toaster**

**τουαλέτα** too·ah·<u>leh</u>·tah **restroom [toilet BE]**

**τούνελ** <u>too</u>·nehl **tunnel**

**τουρίστας** too·<u>rees</u>·tahs **tourist**

**τουριστική θέση** too·ree·stee·<u>kee</u> <u>theh</u>·see **economy class**

**τουριστικός οδηγός** too·ree·stee·<u>kohs</u> oh·ΤΗee·<u>ghohs</u> **guide book**

**τραβώ το καζανάκι** trah·<u>voh</u> toh kah·zah·<u>nah</u>·kee **flush**

**τραμ** trahm **tram**

**τράπεζα** <u>trah</u>·peh·zah **bank**

**τραπέζι** trah·<u>peh</u>·zee **table**

**τραπεζομάντηλο** trah·peh·zoh·<u>mahn</u>·dee·loh **tablecloth**

**τραυματισμένος** trahv·mah·teez·<u>meh</u>·nohs **injured**

**τρένο** <u>treh</u>·noh **train**

**τρέχω** <u>treh</u>·khoh *v* **run, speed**

**τρόμπα** <u>troh</u>·mbah *n* **pump**

**τρόλλεϋ** <u>troh</u>·leh·ee **trolley-bus**

**τρύπα** <u>tree</u>·pah **hole (in clothes)**

**τρώω** <u>troh</u>·oh **eat**

**τσάντα** <u>tsahn</u>·dah **handbag**

**τσίμπημα** <u>tsee</u>·bee·mah *n* **bite, sting (insect)**

**τσίμπημα κουνουπιού** <u>tseem</u>·bee·mah koo·noo·<u>piooh</u> **mosquito bite**

**τυπικός** tee·pee·<u>kohs</u> **typical**

**τύχη** <u>tee</u>·khee **luck**

## Υ

**υγρό πιάτων** eegh·<u>roh</u> <u>piah</u>·tohn **dishwashing detergent**

**υπεραστικό λεωφορείο** ee·peh·rahs·tee·<u>koh</u> leh·oh·foh·<u>ree</u>·oh **long-distance bus**

**υπεραστικό τηλεφώνημα** ee·pehr·ahs·tee·<u>koh</u> tee·leh·<u>foh</u>·nee·mah **long-distance call**

**υπέρβαρο** ee·<u>pehr</u>·vah·roh **excess baggage [BE]**

**υπηκοότητα** ee·pee·koh·<u>oh</u>·tee·tah **nationality**

**υπηρεσία** ee·pee·reh·<u>see</u>·ah *n* **service (administration, business)**

**υπηρεσία δωματίου** ee·pee·reh·<u>see</u>·ah ΤΗoh·mah·<u>tee</u>·oo **room service**

**υπηρεσία πλυντηρίου** ee·pee·reh·<u>see</u>·ah pleen·dee·<u>ree</u>·oo **laundry service**

**υπνόσακκος** ee·pnoh·sah·kohs **sleeping bag**

**υπνωτικό χάπι** eep·noh·tee·koh khah·pee **sleeping pill**

**υπόγειος** ee·poh·ghee·ohs **underground [BE]**

**υπολογιστής** ee·poh·loh·yee·stees **computer**

**υπόνομος** ee·poh·noh·mohs **sewer**

**ύφασμα** ee·fahs·mah **fabric (cloth)**

**ύψος** ee·psohs **height**

## Φ

**φακός** fah·kohs **flashlight, lens**

**φακός επαφής** fah·kohs eh·pah·fees **contact lens**

**υπηρεσία φαξ** ee·pee·reh·see·ah fahks **fax facility**

**φάρμα** fahr·mah n **farm**

**φάρμακα** fahr·mah·kah **medication**

**φαρδύς** fahr·THees **loose (fitting), wide**

**φάρος** fah·rohs **lighthouse**

**φέρνω** fehr·noh **bring**

**φέρυ-μπωτ** feh·ree boht **ferry**

**φεστιβάλ** fehs·tee·vahl **festival**

**φεύγω** fehv·ghoh v **leave (depart)**

**φιλμ** feelm n **film (camera)**

**φίλη** fee·lee **girlfriend**

**φιλί** fee·lee n **kiss**

**φιλοδώρημα** fee·loh·THoh·ree·mah **gratuity**

**φίλος** fee·lohs **friend, boyfriend**

**φίλτρο** feel·troh n **filter**

**φιλώ** fee·loh v **kiss**

**φλέβα** fleh·vah **vein**

**φλεγμονή** flegh·moh·nee **inflammation**

**φλυτζάνι** flee·jah·nee **cup**

**φοβερός** foh·veh·rohs **terrible**

**φοβισμένος** foh·veez·meh·nohs **frightened**

**φοιτητής** fee·tee·tees **student**

**φόρεμα** foh·reh·mah n **dress**

**φόρος** foh·rohs **duty (customs), tax**

**φορώ** foh·roh v **wear**

**φούρνος** foor·nohs **oven**

**φούρνος μικροκυμάτων** foor·nohs mee·kroh·kee·mah·tohn **microwave (oven)**

**φούστα** foo·stah **skirt**

**φούτερ** foo·tehr **sweatshirt**

**ΦΠΑ** fee·pee·ah **sales tax**

**φράγμα** frahgh·mah n **lock (river, canal)**

**φράση** frah·see n **phrase**

**φράχτης** frahkh·tees n **fence**

**φρέσκος** frehs·kohs adj **fresh**

**φτάνω** ftah·noh **arrive**

**φτηνός** ftee·nohs **cheap, inexpensive**

**φτιάχνω τις βαλίτσες** ftee·ahkh·noh tees vah·lee·tsehs v **pack (baggage)**

**φυλακή** fee·lah·kee n **prison**

**φύση** fee·see **nature**

**φυτό** fee·toh n **plant**

**φως** fohs n **light (electric)**

**φώτα** foh·tah **lights (car)**

**φωτογραφία** foh·tohgh·rah·fee·ah
v **photo**

**φωτογραφική μηχανή**
foh·tohgh·rah·fee·kee mee·khah·nee
**camera**

**φωτοτυπικό** foh·toh·tee·pee·koh
**photocopier**

## Χ

**χαμηλώνω** khah·mee·loh·noh v **turn
down (volume, heat)**

**χαλί** khah·lee **rug**

**χαλκός** khahl·kohs **copper**

**χάπι** khah·pee **tablet**

**χάρτης** khahr·tees n **map**

**χαρτί** khar·tee **paper**

**χαρτί κουζίνας** khah·rtee
koo·zee·nahs **kitchen**

**χαρτί υγείας** khahr·tee ee·yee·ahs
**toilet paper**

**χαρτομάντηλο**
khahr·toh·mahn·dee·loh **tissue**

**χαρτομάντηλο**
khah·rtoh·mahn·dee·loh
**handkerchief**

**χείλη** khee·lee **lips**

**χειροκίνητος** khee·roh·kee·nee·tohs
**manual (car)**

**χειρότερος** khee·roh·teh·rohs **worse**

**χιλιόμετρα** khee·lioh·meh·trah
**mileage**

**χιονίζει** khioh·nee·zee v **snow**

**χλιαρός** khlee·ah·rohs **lukewarm**

**χόμπυ** khoh·bee **hobby (pastime)**

**χοντρός** khohn·drohs **thick**

**χορεύω** khoh·reh·voh v **dance**

**χορτοφάγος** khohr·toh·fah·ghohs
**vegetarian**

**χρειάζομαι** khree·ah·zoh·meh v **need**

**χρέωση υπηρεσίας** khreh·oh·see
ee·pee·reh·see·ahs **service charge**

**χρήματα** khree·mah·tah **money**

**χρησιμοποιώ** khree·see·moh·pee·oh
v **use**

**χρήσιμος** khree·see·mohs **useful**

**χρονική περίοδος** khroh·nee·kee
peh·ree·oh·THohs **period (time)**

**χρυσός** khree·sohs n **gold**

**χρώμα** khroh·mah n **color**

**χρωστώ** khroh·stoh **owe**

**χτένα** khteh·nah n **comb**

**χτενίζω** khteh·nee·zoh v **comb**

**χτες** khtehs **yesterday**

**χώρα** khoh·rah **country (nation)**

**χωριό** khohr·yoh **village**

**χωρίς** khoh·rees **without**

**χώρος** khoh·rohs n **space (area)**

**χώρος κάμπινγκ** kah·mpeeng
khoh·rohs **campsite**

**χώρος στάθμευσης** khoh·rohs
stahth·mehf·sees **car park [BE]**

**χώρος στάθμευσης** khoh·rohs
stahth·mehf·sees **parking lot**

## Ψ

**ψαλίδι** psah·lee·THee **scissors**

**ψάρεμα** psah·reh·mah **fishing**

**ψάχνω** psahkh·noh **look for**

**ψηλός** psee•<u>lohs</u> **tall**
**ψύλλος** <u>psee</u>•lohs **flea**

## Ω

**ώμος** <u>oh</u>•mohs *n* **shoulder (anatomy)**
**ώρα αιχμής** <u>oh</u>•rah ehkh•<u>mees</u> **rush hour**
**ώρες λειτουργίας** <u>oh</u>•rehs lee•toor•<u>yee</u>•ahs **opening hours**

# Berlitz®

## speaking your language

**phrase book & dictionary**
**phrase book & CD**

**Available in:** Arabic, Cantonese Chinese, Croatian, Czech, Danish, Dutch, English*, Finnish*, French, German, Greek, Hebrew*, Hindi, Hungarian*, Indonesian, Italian, Japanese, Korean, Latin American Spanish, Mandarin Chinese, Mexican Spanish, Norwegian, Polish, Portuguese, Romanian*, Russian, Spanish, Swedish, Thai, Turkish, Vietnamese

*Book only